Rogue Planet /rohg plan-it/ n. A celestial body not not bound to a star.
Expelled from the planetary system in which they formed.
Abandoned.

ROGUE PLANET

D1495931

ONI PRESS

AN ONI PRESS PUBLICATION.

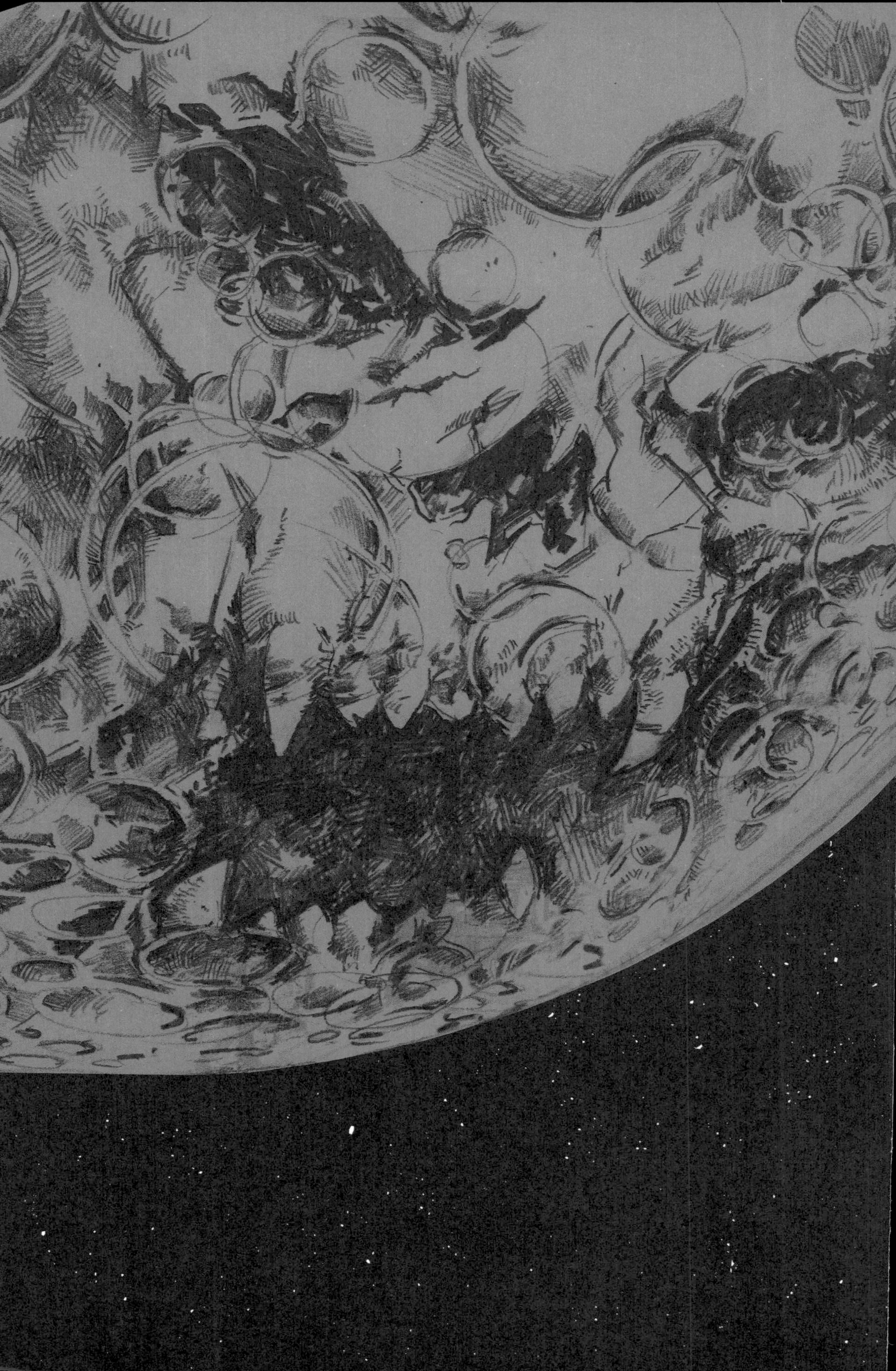

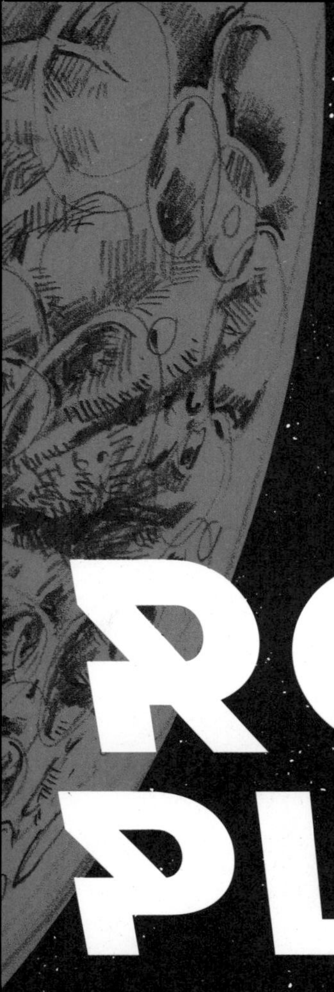

ROGUE PLANET

Written by
CULLEN BUNN

Illustrated by
ANDY MACDONALD

Colored by
NICK FILARDI

Lettered by
CRANK!

Published by Oni-Lion Forge Publishing Group, LLC

James Lucas Jones, president & publisher

Sarah Gaydos, editor in chief

Charlie Chu, e.v.p. of creative & business development

Brad Rooks, director of operations

Amber O'Neill, special projects manager

Margot Wood, director of marketing & sales

Devin Funches, sales & marketing manager

Katie Sainz, marketing manager

Tara Lehmann, publicist

Troy Look, director of design & production

Kate Z. Stone, senior graphic designer

Sonja Synak, graphic designer

Hilary Thompson, graphic designer

Sarah Rockwell, graphic designer

Angie Knowles, digital prepress lead

Vincent Kukua, digital prepress technician

Jasmine Amiri, senior editor

Shawna Gore, senior editor

Amanda Meadows, senior editor

Robert Meyers, senior editor, licensing

Desiree Rodriguez, editor

Grace Scheipeter, editor

Zack Soto, editor

Chris Cerasi, editorial coordinator

Steve Ellis, vice president of games

Ben Eisner, game developer

Michelle Nguyen, executive assistant

Jung Lee, logistics coordinator

Joe Nozemack, publisher emeritus

Edited by
CHARLIE CHU & **ZACK SOTO**
with **DESIREE WILSON**

Designed by
JARED K. FLETCHER

@cullenbunn / @andymacdeez / @nickfil / @ccrank

onipress.com 🅕 | 🅣 | 🅘 lionforge.com

ROGUE PLANET, March 2021. Published by Oni-Lion Forge Publishing Group, LLC, 1319 SE Martin Luther King Jr Blvd., Suite 240, Portland, OR 97214. Rogue Planet is ™ & © Cullen Bunn, Andy MacDonald. All rights reserved. Oni Press logo and icon ™ & © 2021 Oni-Lion Forge Publishing Group, LLC. All rights reserved. Oni Press logo and icon artwork created by Keith A. Wood. The events, institutions, and characters presented in this book are fictional. Any resemblance to actual persons, living or dead, is purely coincidental. No portion of this publication may be reproduced, by any means, without the express written permission of the copyright holders.

Printed in China

Library of Congress Control Number 2020939163

1 2 3 4 5 6 7 8 9 10

ISBN 978-1-62010-708-9
EISBN 978-1-62010-709-6

CHAPTER 01

PLANETFALL

CHAPTER 01 cover colored by NIC KLEIN

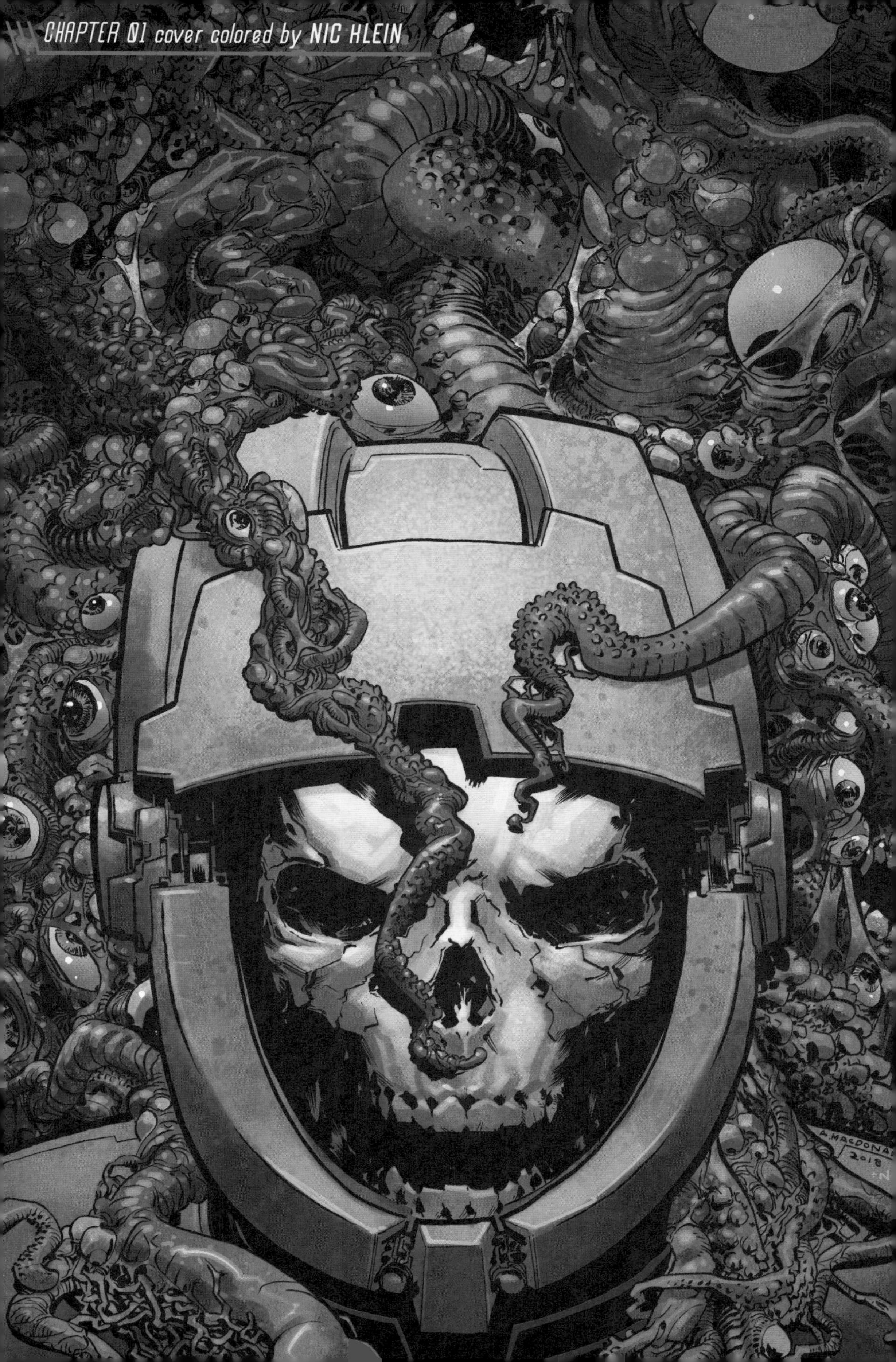
A.MACDONA
2018

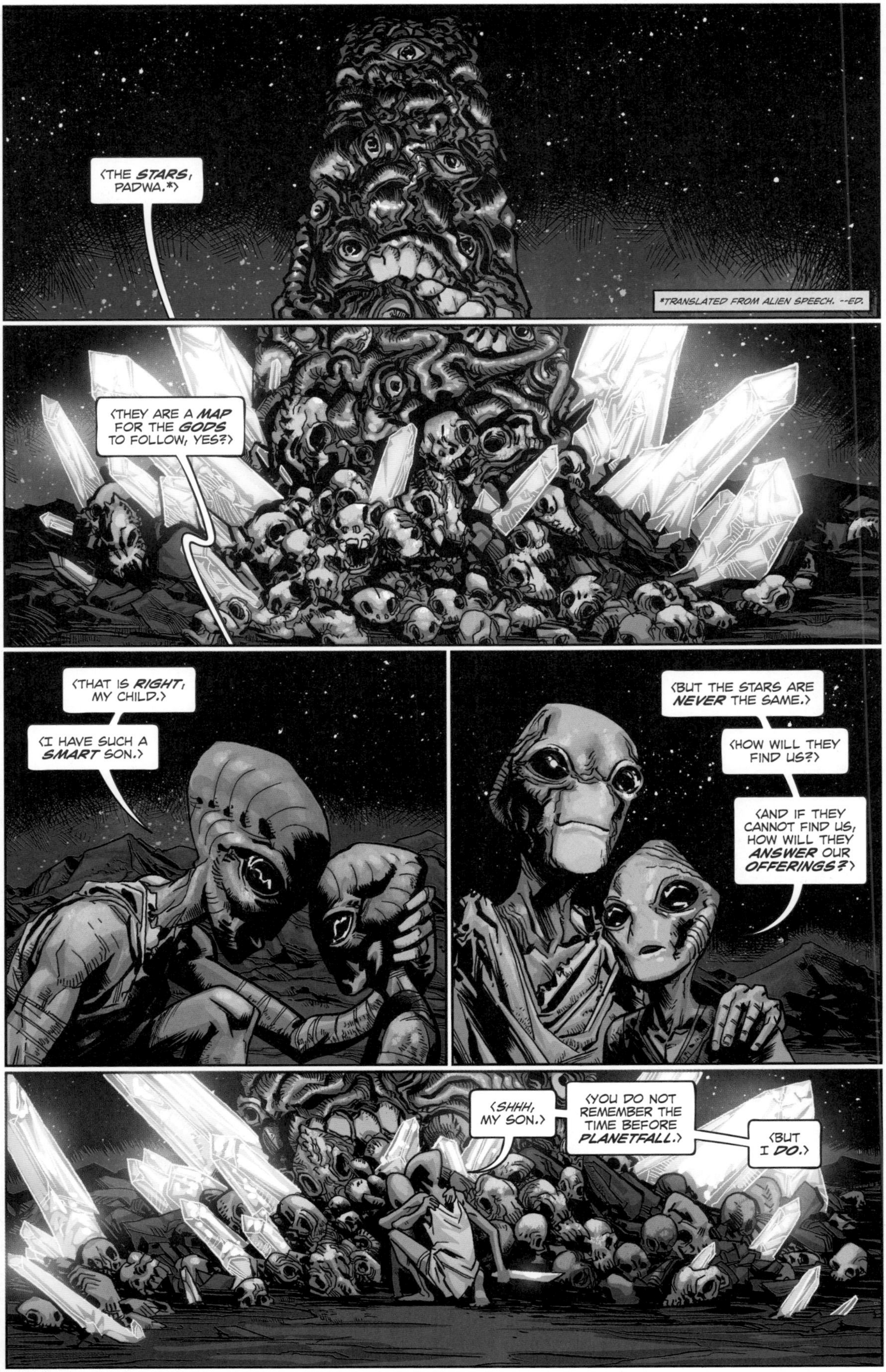
‹THE *STARS*, PADWA.*›
*TRANSLATED FROM ALIEN SPEECH. --ED.
‹THEY ARE A *MAP* FOR THE *GODS* TO FOLLOW, YES?›
‹THAT IS *RIGHT*, MY CHILD.›
‹I HAVE SUCH A *SMART* SON.›
‹BUT THE STARS ARE *NEVER* THE SAME.›
‹HOW WILL THEY FIND US?›
‹AND IF THEY CANNOT FIND US, HOW WILL THEY *ANSWER* OUR *OFFERINGS?*›
‹*SHHH*, MY SON.›
‹YOU DO NOT REMEMBER THE TIME BEFORE *PLANETFALL*.›
‹BUT I *DO*.›

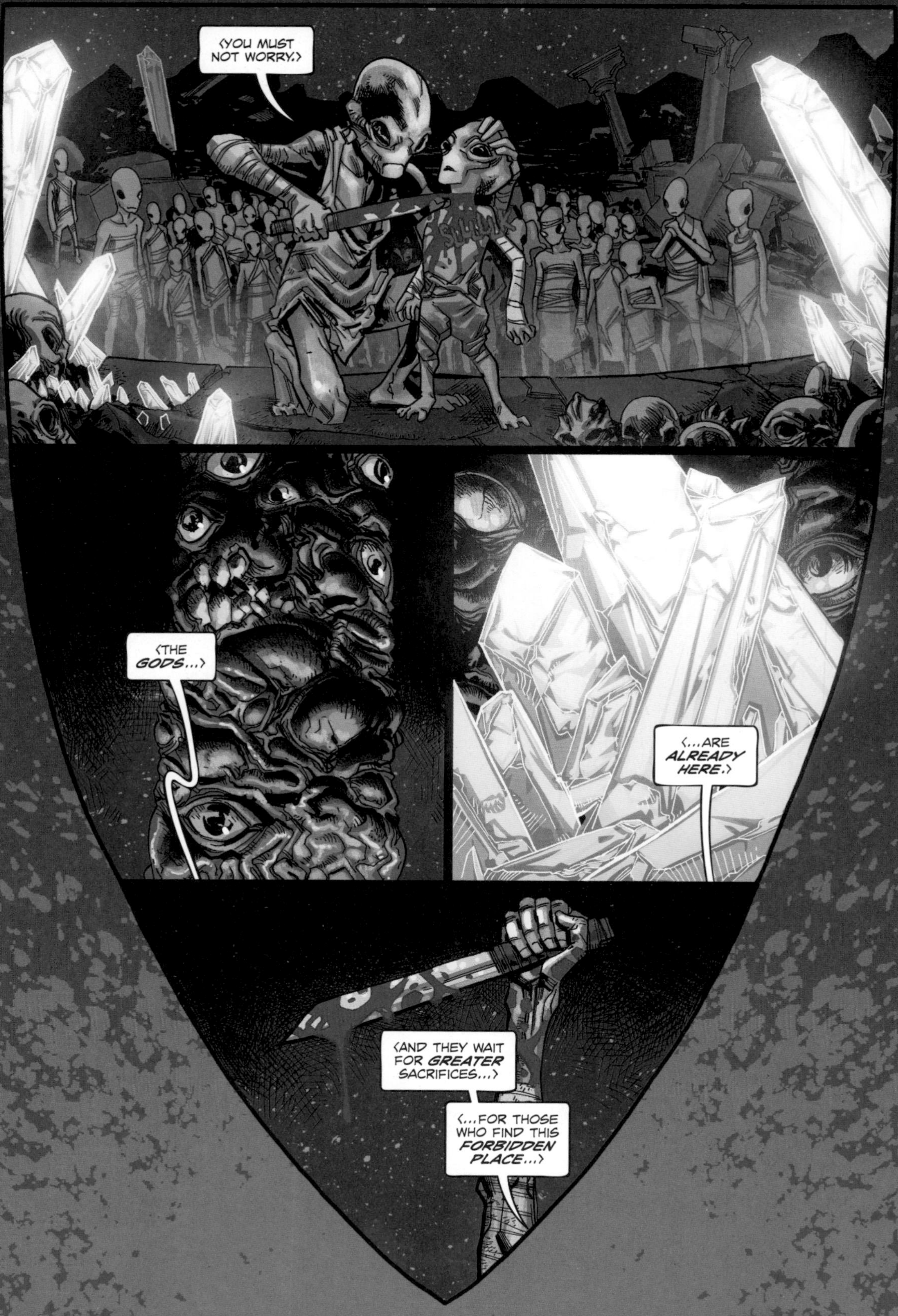
‹YOU MUST NOT WORRY.›
‹THE *GODS*...›
‹...ARE *ALREADY HERE*.›
‹AND THEY WAIT FOR *GREATER* SACRIFICES...›
‹...FOR THOSE WHO FIND THIS *FORBIDDEN PLACE*...›

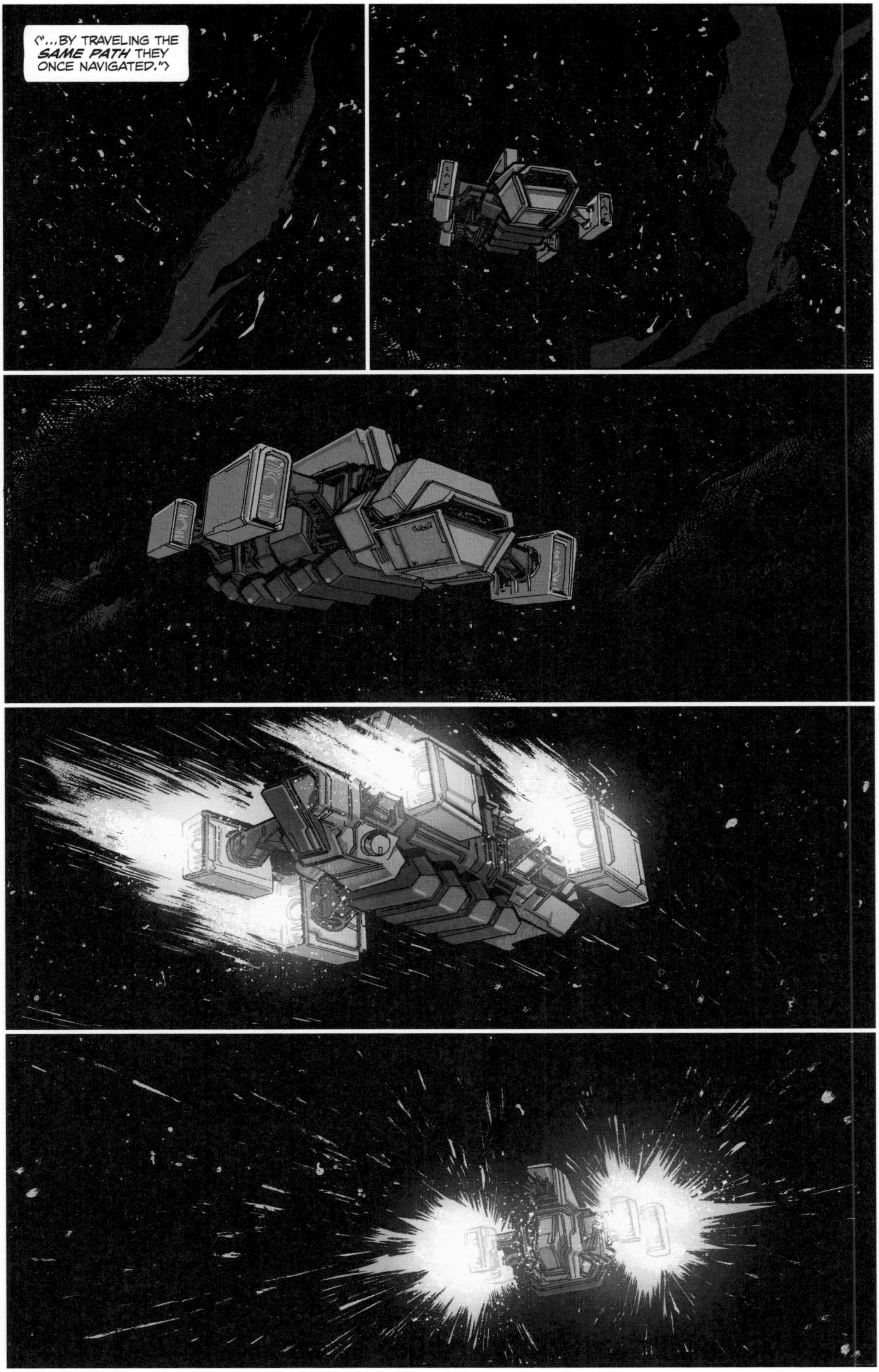

<"...BY TRAVELING THE SAME PATH THEY ONCE NAVIGATED.">

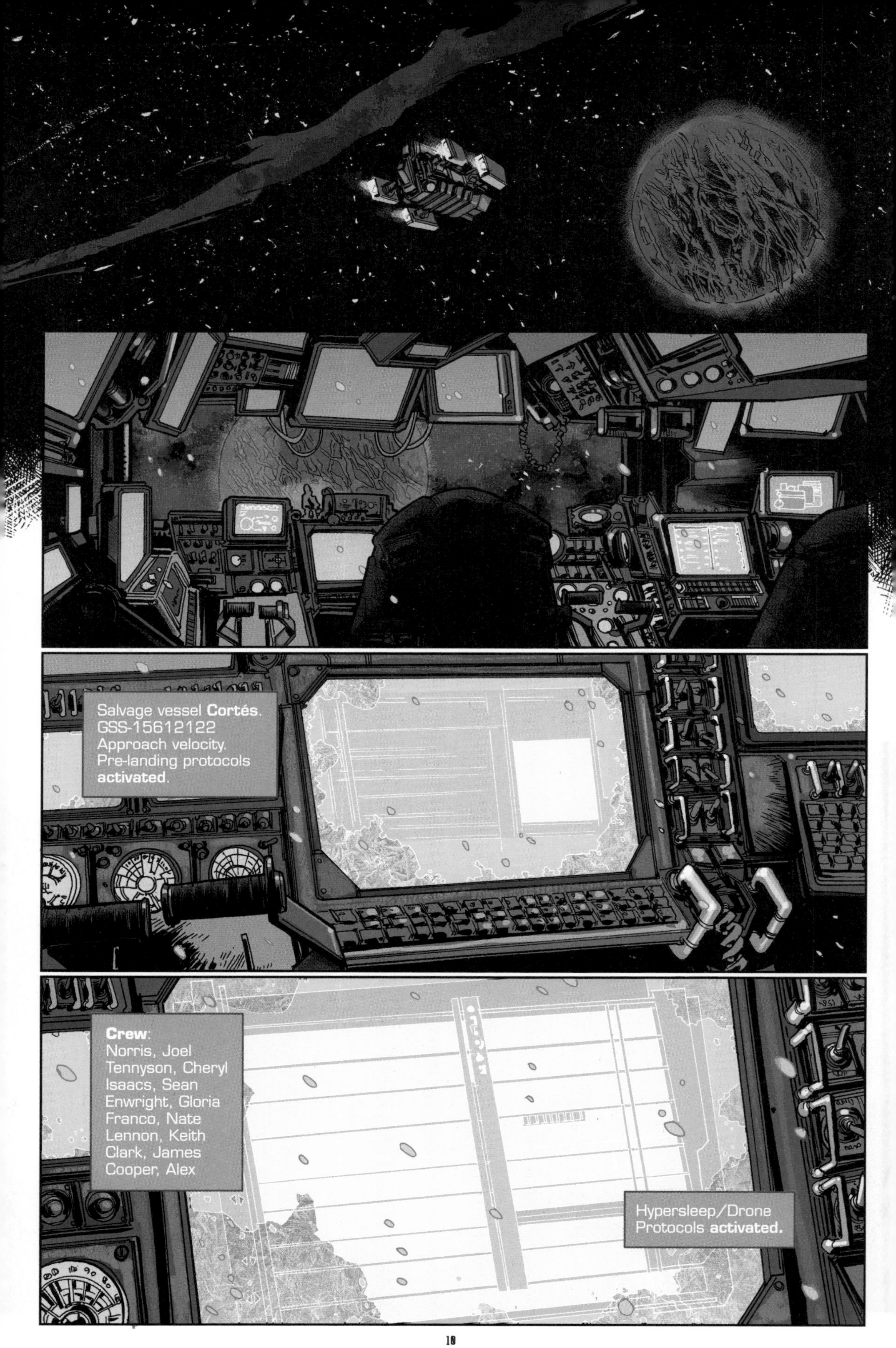
Salvage vessel **Cortés**.
GSS-15612122
Approach velocity.
Pre-landing protocols **activated**.
Crew:
Norris, Joel
Tennyson, Cheryl
Isaacs, Sean
Enwright, Gloria
Franco, Nate
Lennon, Keith
Clark, James
Cooper, Alex
Hypersleep/Drone
Protocols **activated.**

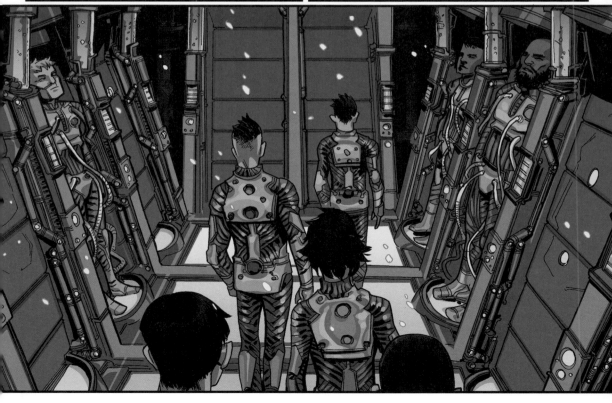

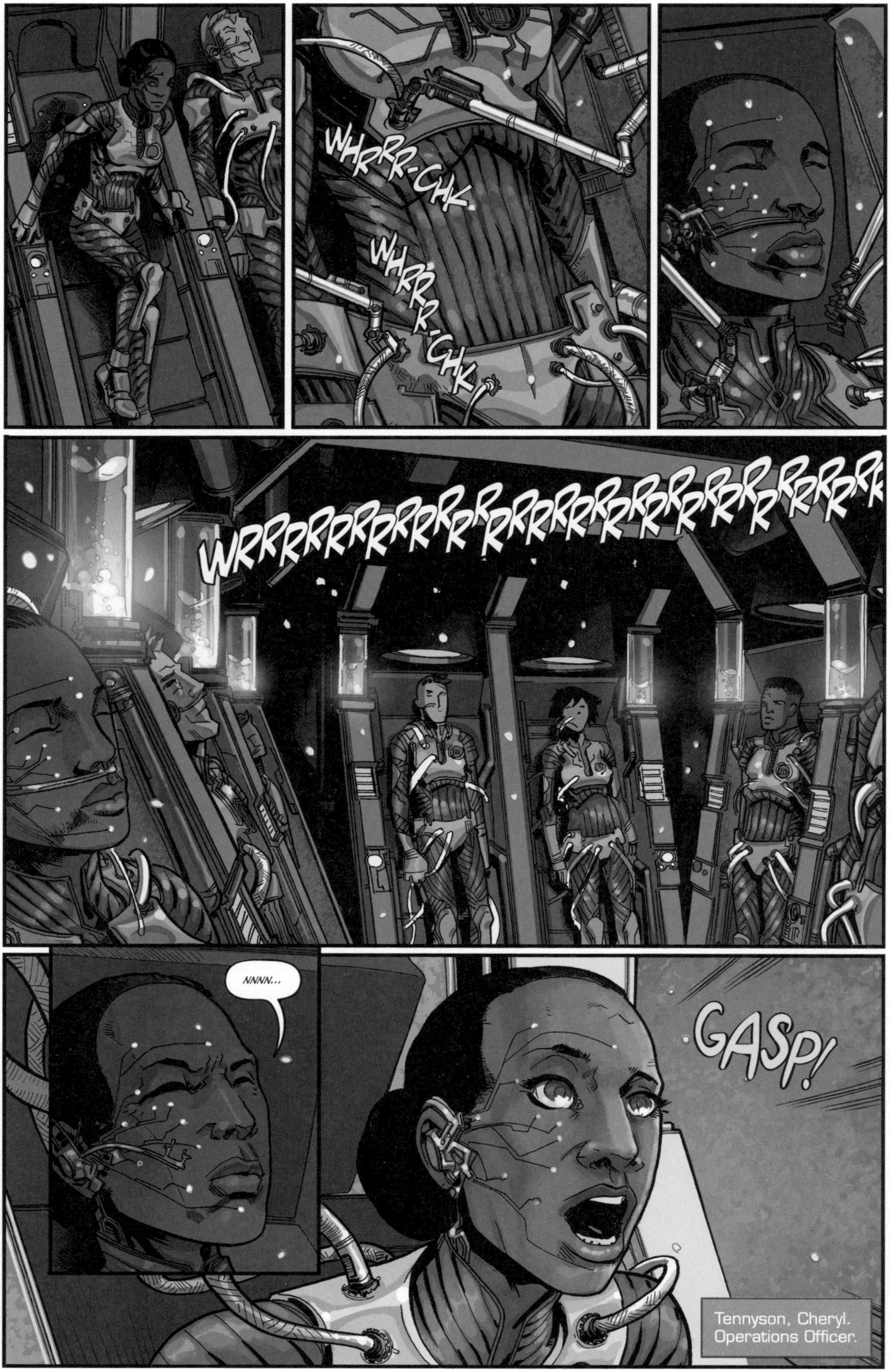
WHRRR-CHK
WHRRR-CHK
WRRRRRRRRRRRRRRRRRRRRRRRRRRRRRRRR
NNNN...
GASP!
Tennyson, Cheryl.
Operations Officer.

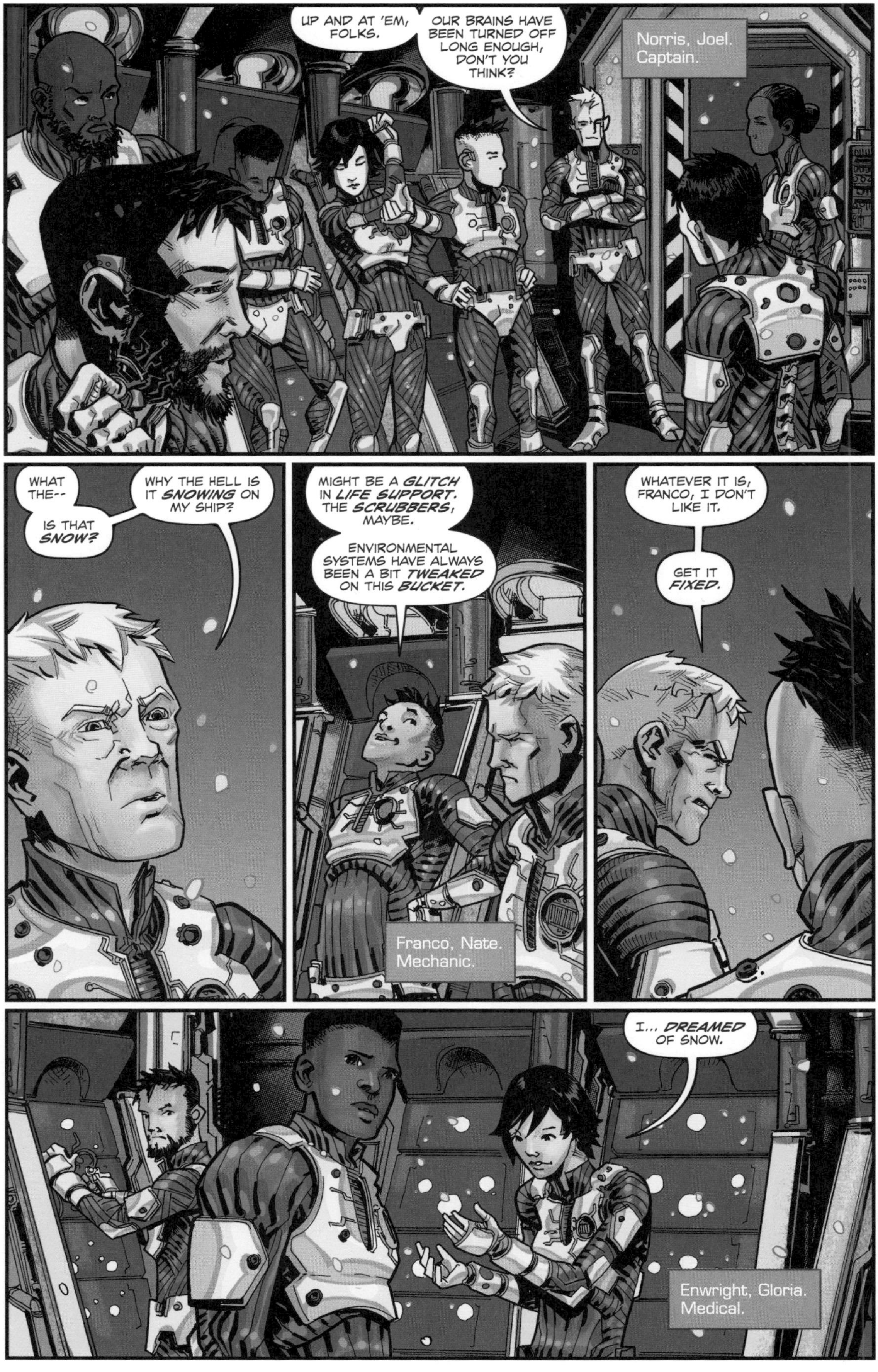
UP AND AT 'EM, FOLKS.
OUR BRAINS HAVE BEEN TURNED OFF LONG ENOUGH, DON'T YOU THINK?
Norris, Joel. Captain.
WHAT THE--
IS THAT *SNOW?*
WHY THE HELL IS IT *SNOWING* ON MY SHIP?
MIGHT BE A *GLITCH* IN *LIFE SUPPORT.* THE *SCRUBBERS*, MAYBE.
ENVIRONMENTAL SYSTEMS HAVE ALWAYS BEEN A BIT *TWEAKED* ON THIS *BUCKET.*
Franco, Nate. Mechanic.
WHATEVER IT IS, FRANCO, I DON'T LIKE IT.
GET IT *FIXED.*
I... *DREAMED* OF SNOW.
Enwright, Gloria. Medical.

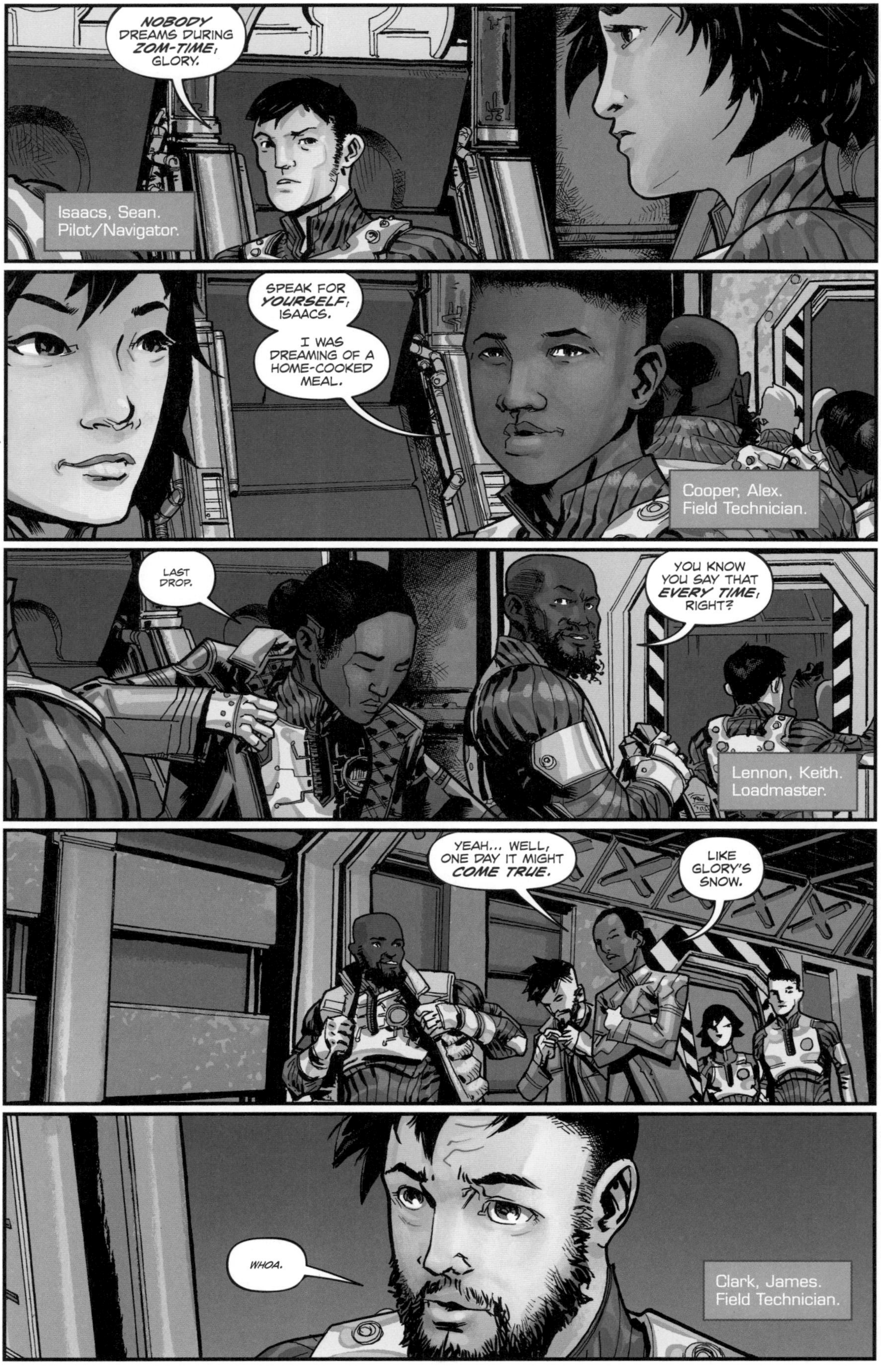
NOBODY DREAMS DURING ZOM-TIME, GLORY.
Isaacs, Sean. Pilot/Navigator.
SPEAK FOR YOURSELF, ISAACS.
I WAS DREAMING OF A HOME-COOKED MEAL.
Cooper, Alex. Field Technician.
LAST DROP.
YOU KNOW YOU SAY THAT EVERY TIME, RIGHT?
Lennon, Keith. Loadmaster.
YEAH... WELL, ONE DAY IT MIGHT COME TRUE.
LIKE GLORY'S SNOW.
WHOA.
Clark, James. Field Technician.

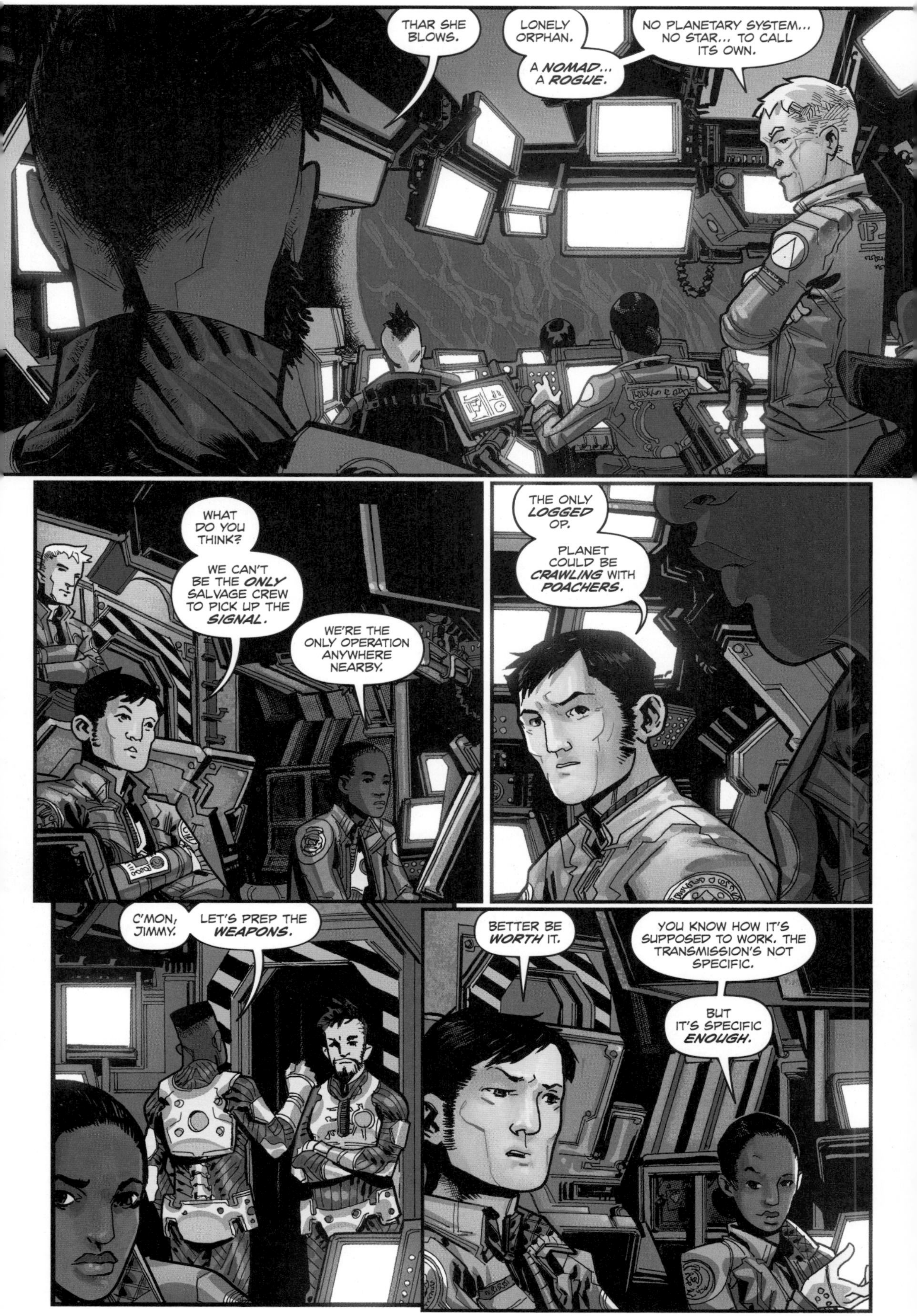

THAR SHE BLOWS.
LONELY ORPHAN.
A NOMAD... A ROGUE.
NO PLANETARY SYSTEM... NO STAR... TO CALL ITS OWN.
WHAT DO YOU THINK?
WE CAN'T BE THE ONLY SALVAGE CREW TO PICK UP THE SIGNAL.
WE'RE THE ONLY OPERATION ANYWHERE NEARBY.
THE ONLY LOGGED OP.
PLANET COULD BE CRAWLING WITH POACHERS.
C'MON, JIMMY.
LET'S PREP THE WEAPONS.
BETTER BE WORTH IT.
YOU KNOW HOW IT'S SUPPOSED TO WORK. THE TRANSMISSION'S NOT SPECIFIC.
BUT IT'S SPECIFIC ENOUGH.

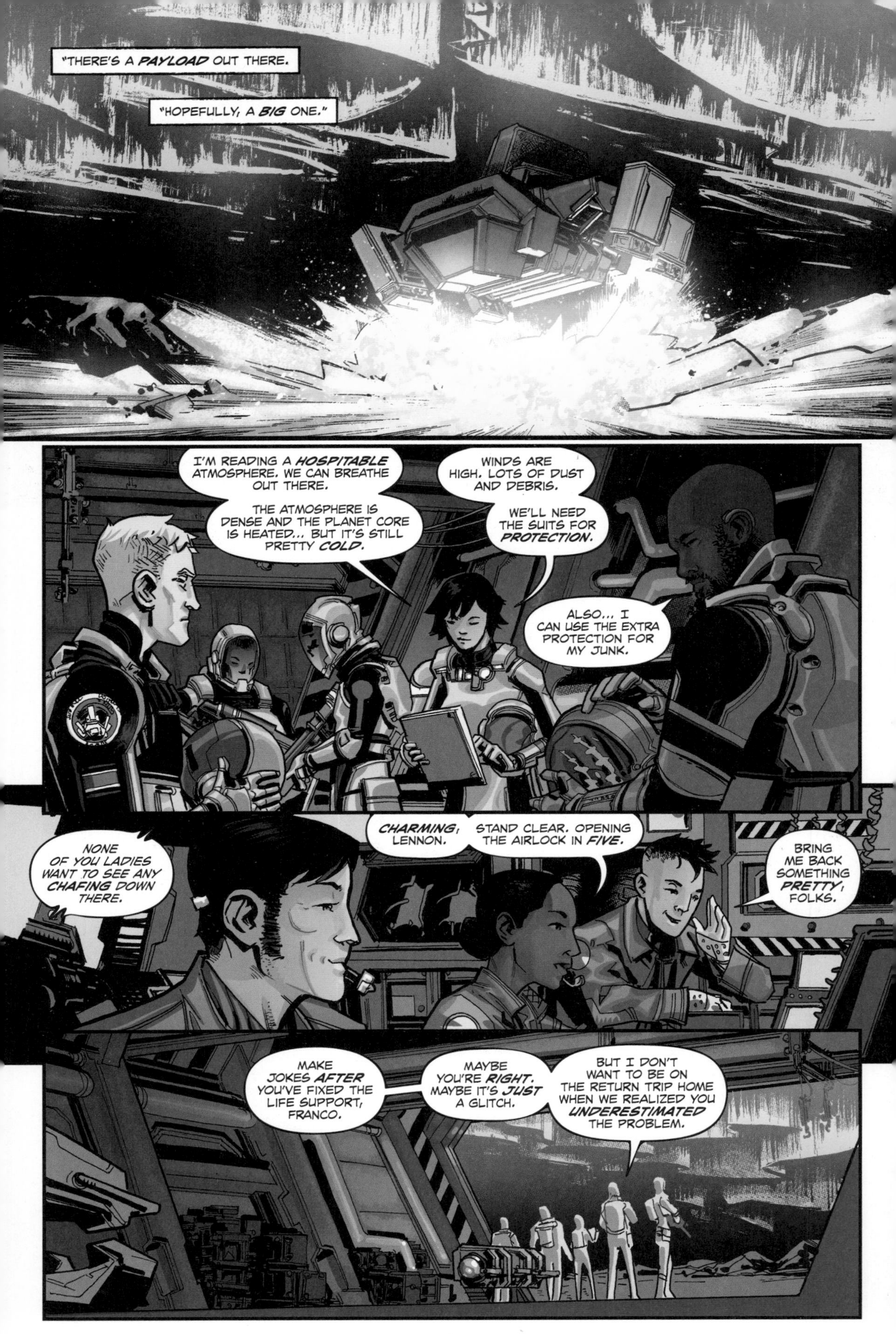
"THERE'S A PAYLOAD OUT THERE.
"HOPEFULLY, A BIG ONE."
I'M READING A HOSPITABLE ATMOSPHERE. WE CAN BREATHE OUT THERE.
THE ATMOSPHERE IS DENSE AND THE PLANET CORE IS HEATED... BUT IT'S STILL PRETTY COLD.
WINDS ARE HIGH. LOTS OF DUST AND DEBRIS.
WE'LL NEED THE SUITS FOR PROTECTION.
ALSO... I CAN USE THE EXTRA PROTECTION FOR MY JUNK.
NONE OF YOU LADIES WANT TO SEE ANY CHAFING DOWN THERE.
CHARMING, LENNON.
STAND CLEAR. OPENING THE AIRLOCK IN FIVE.
BRING ME BACK SOMETHING PRETTY, FOLKS.
MAKE JOKES AFTER YOU'VE FIXED THE LIFE SUPPORT, FRANCO.
MAYBE YOU'RE RIGHT. MAYBE IT'S JUST A GLITCH.
BUT I DON'T WANT TO BE ON THE RETURN TRIP HOME WHEN WE REALIZED YOU UNDERESTIMATED THE PROBLEM.

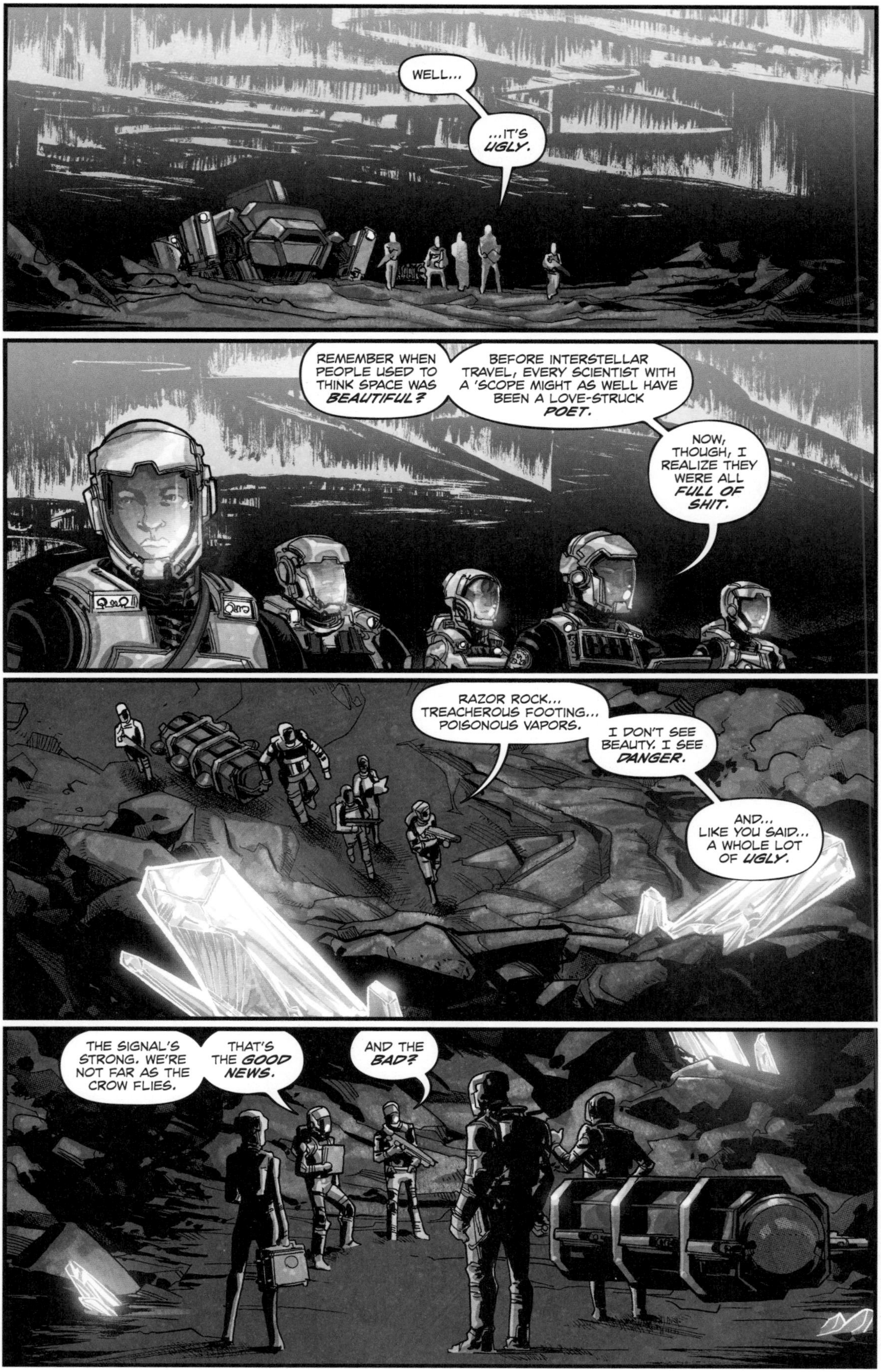

WELL...
...IT'S UGLY.
REMEMBER WHEN PEOPLE USED TO THINK SPACE WAS BEAUTIFUL?
BEFORE INTERSTELLAR TRAVEL, EVERY SCIENTIST WITH A 'SCOPE MIGHT AS WELL HAVE BEEN A LOVE-STRUCK POET.
NOW, THOUGH, I REALIZE THEY WERE ALL FULL OF SHIT.
RAZOR ROCK... TREACHEROUS FOOTING... POISONOUS VAPORS.
I DON'T SEE BEAUTY. I SEE DANGER.
AND... LIKE YOU SAID... A WHOLE LOT OF UGLY.
THE SIGNAL'S STRONG. WE'RE NOT FAR AS THE CROW FLIES.
THAT'S THE GOOD NEWS.
AND THE BAD?

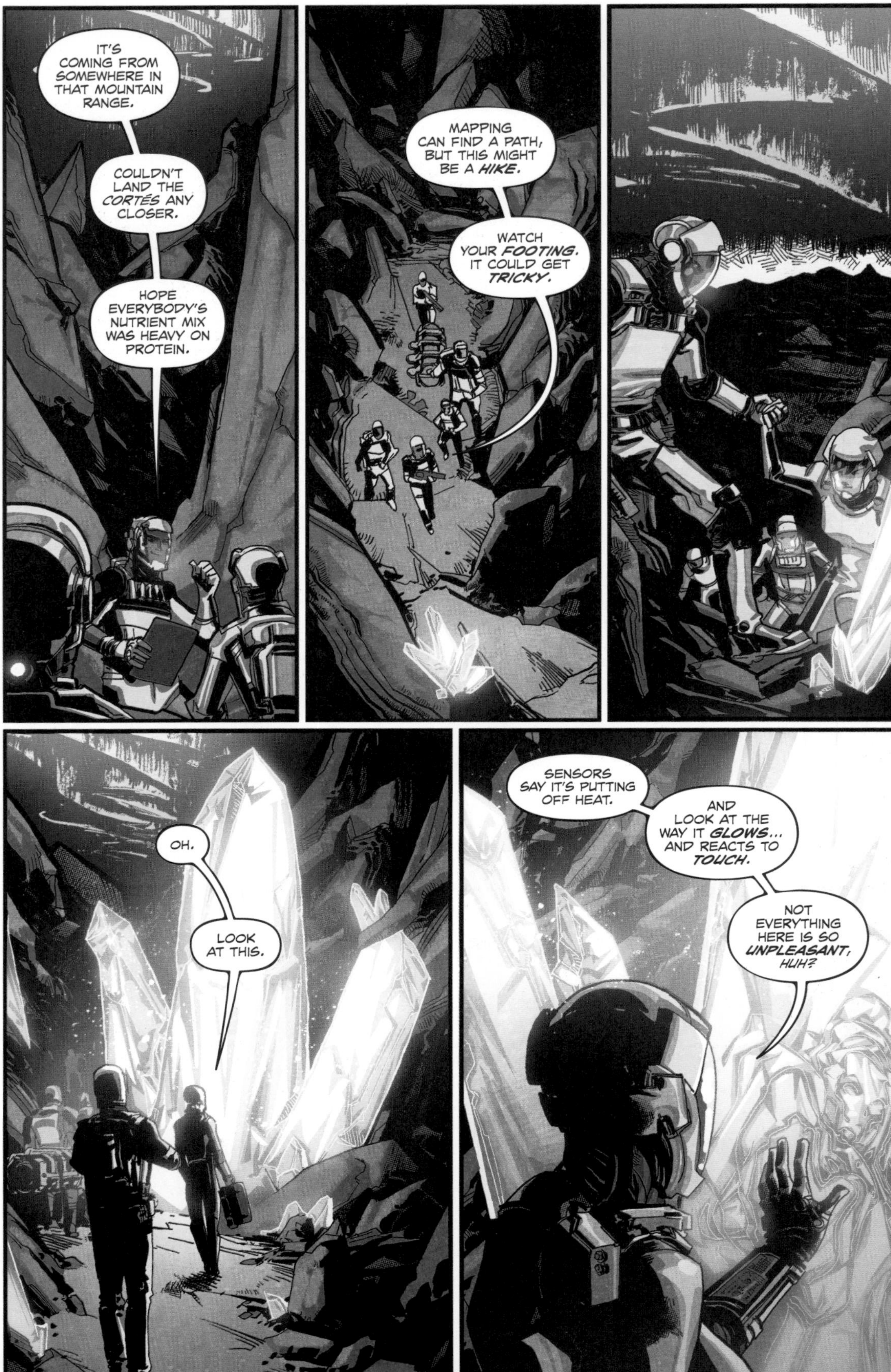
IT'S COMING FROM SOMEWHERE IN THAT MOUNTAIN RANGE.
COULDN'T LAND THE *CORTÉS* ANY CLOSER.
HOPE EVERYBODY'S NUTRIENT MIX WAS HEAVY ON PROTEIN.
MAPPING CAN FIND A PATH, BUT THIS MIGHT BE A *HIKE*.
WATCH YOUR *FOOTING*. IT COULD GET *TRICKY*.
OH.
LOOK AT THIS.
SENSORS SAY IT'S PUTTING OFF HEAT.
AND LOOK AT THE WAY IT *GLOWS*... AND REACTS TO *TOUCH*.
NOT EVERYTHING HERE IS SO *UNPLEASANT*, HUH?

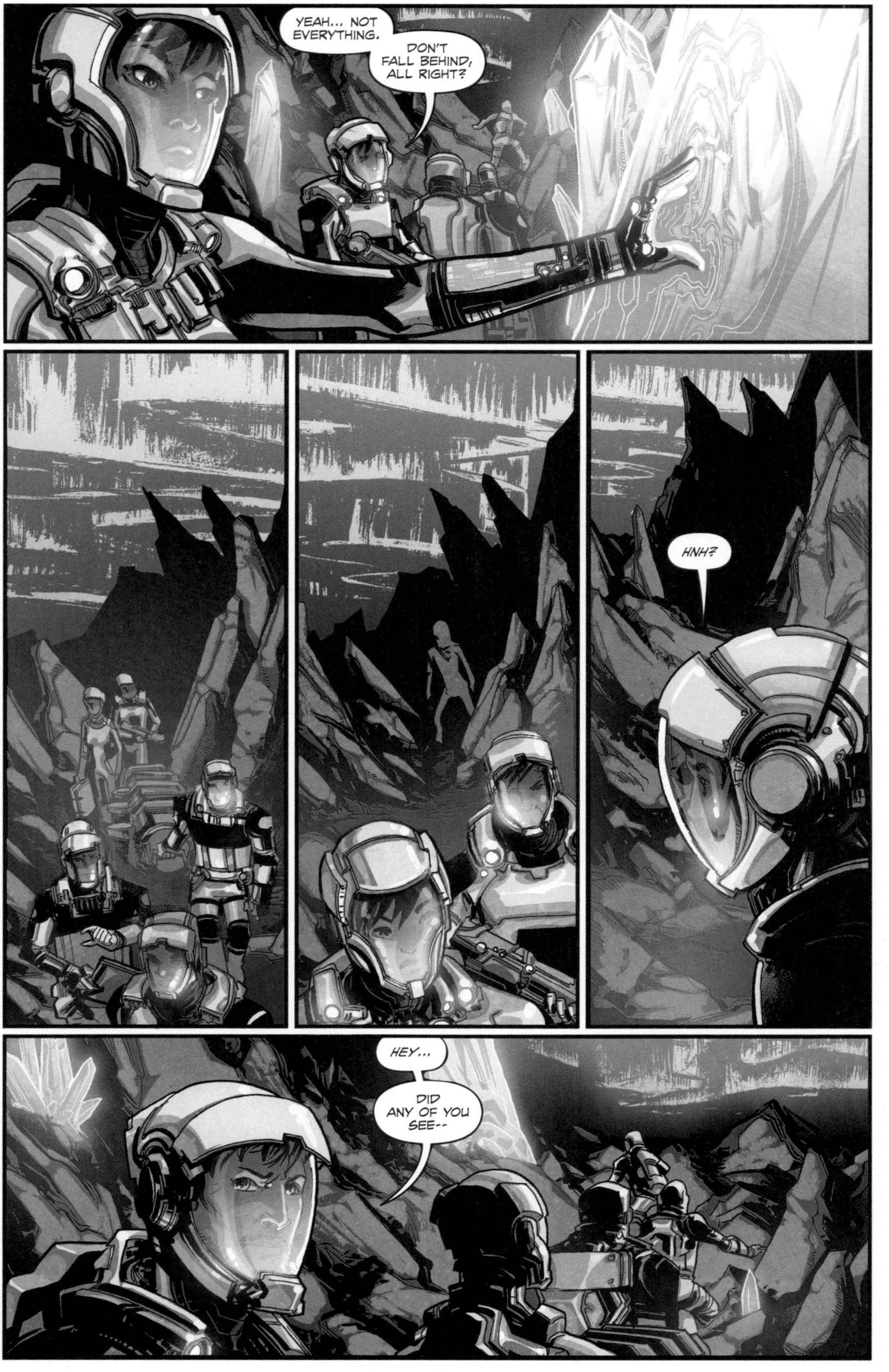
YEAH... NOT EVERYTHING.
DON'T FALL BEHIND, ALL RIGHT?
HNH?
HEY...
DID ANY OF YOU SEE--

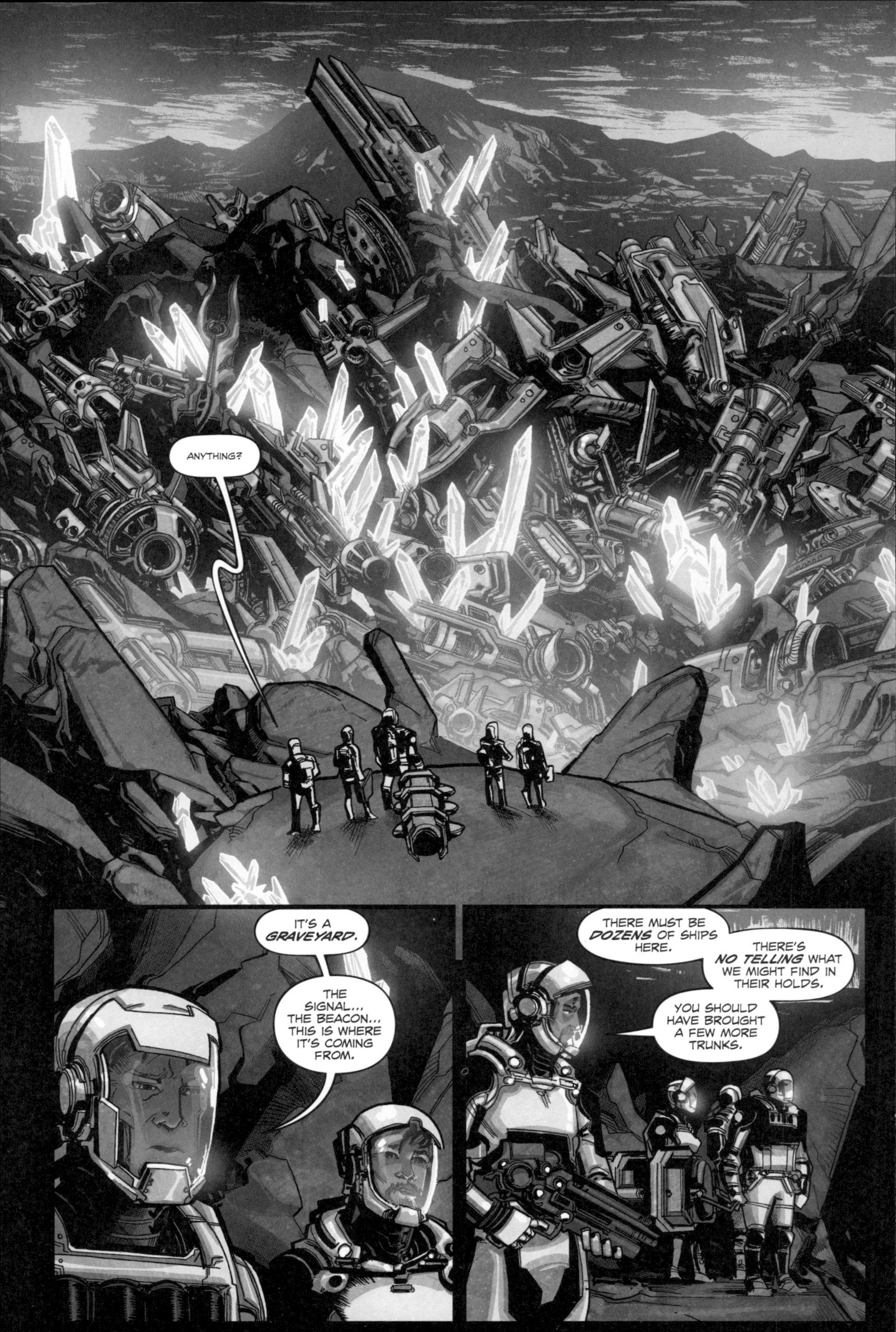
ANYTHING?
IT'S A GRAVEYARD.
THE SIGNAL... THE BEACON... THIS IS WHERE IT'S COMING FROM.
THERE MUST BE DOZENS OF SHIPS HERE.
THERE'S NO TELLING WHAT WE MIGHT FIND IN THEIR HOLDS.
YOU SHOULD HAVE BROUGHT A FEW MORE TRUNKS.

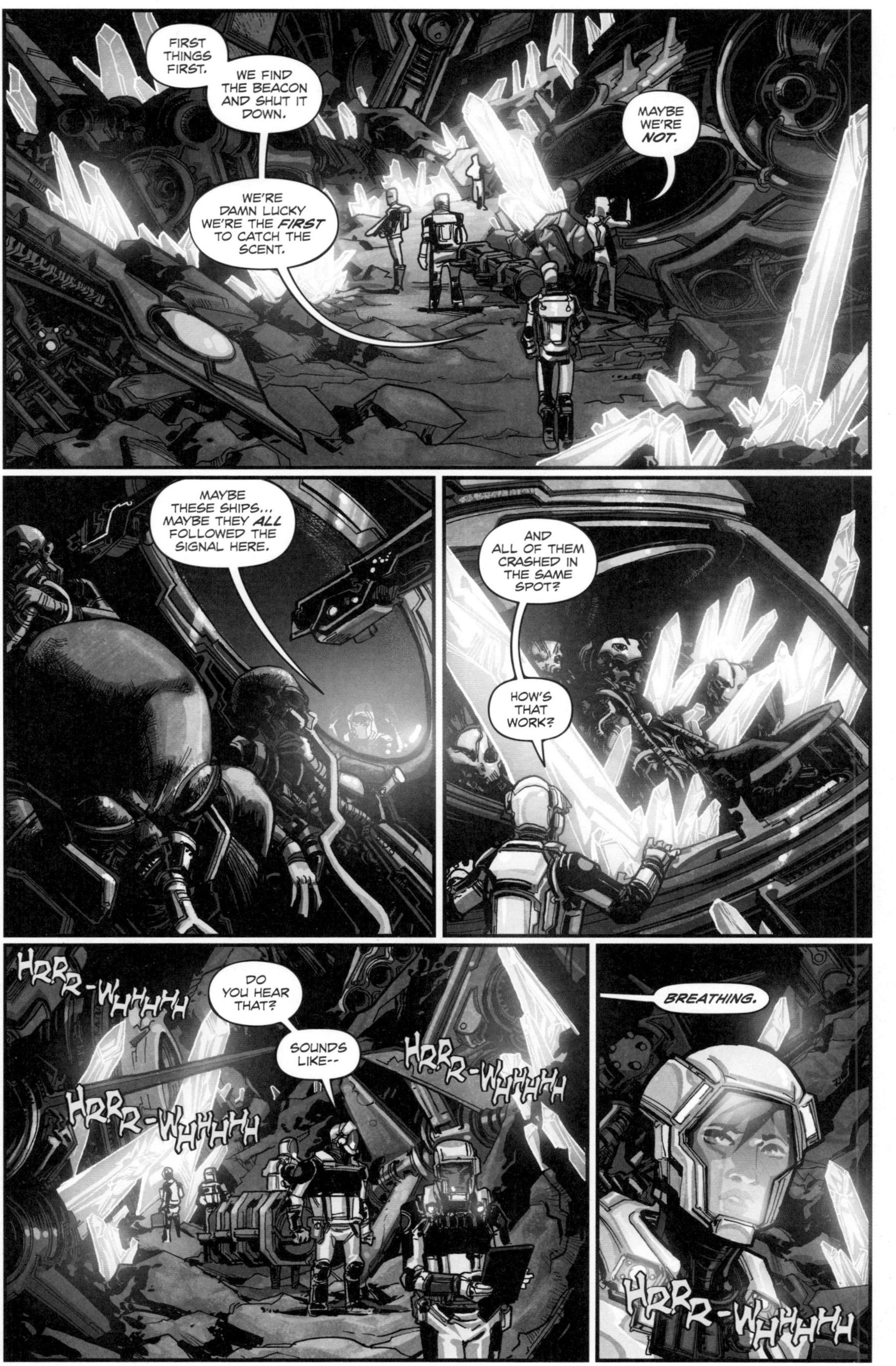
FIRST THINGS FIRST.
WE FIND THE BEACON AND SHUT IT DOWN.
WE'RE DAMN LUCKY WE'RE THE *FIRST* TO CATCH THE SCENT.
MAYBE WE'RE *NOT*.
MAYBE THESE SHIPS... MAYBE THEY *ALL* FOLLOWED THE SIGNAL HERE.
AND ALL OF THEM CRASHED IN THE SAME SPOT?
HOW'S THAT WORK?
HRRR-WHHHHH
DO YOU HEAR THAT?
SOUNDS LIKE--
HRRR-WHHHHH
HRRR-WHHHHH
BREATHING.
HRRR-WHHHHH

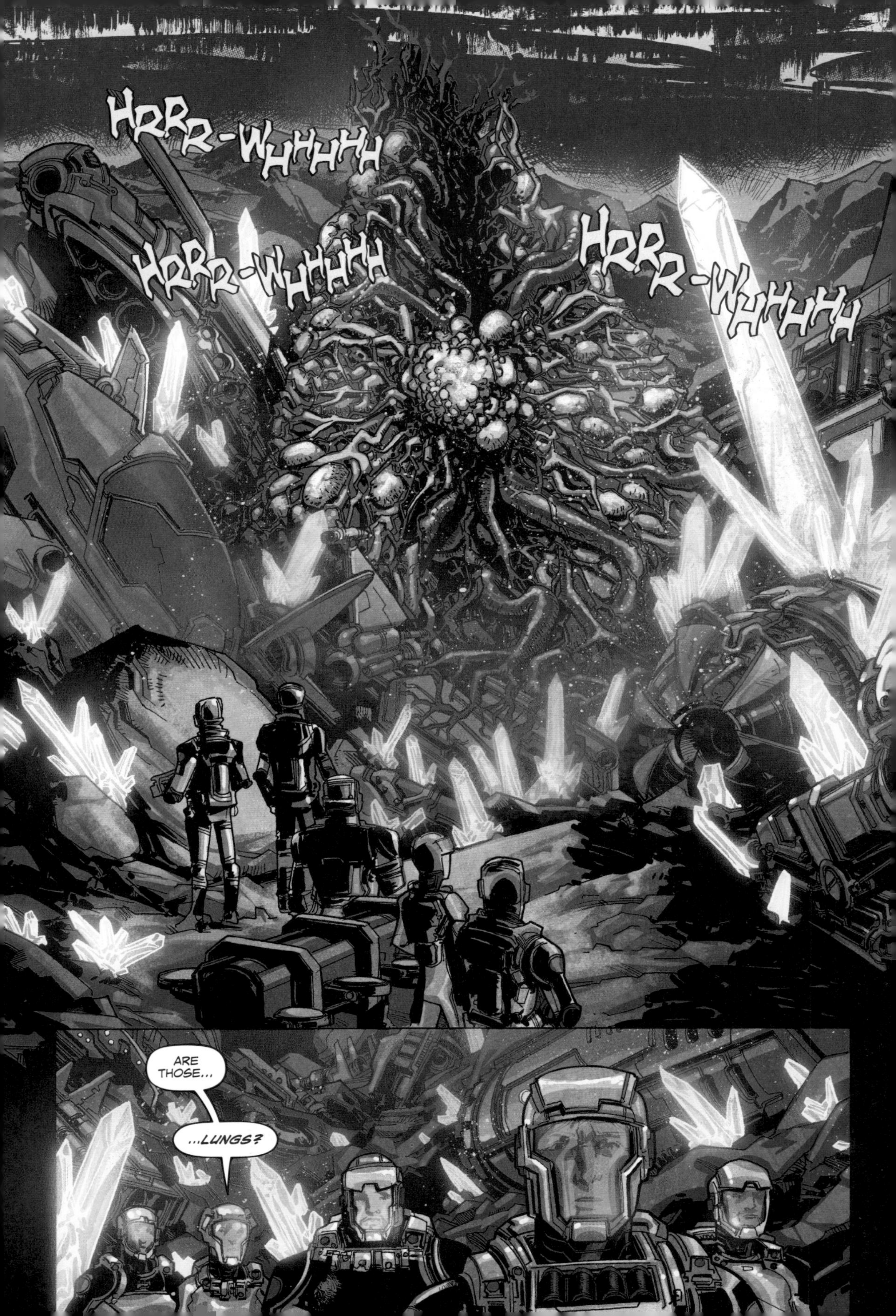
HRRR-WHHHHH
HRRR-WHHHHH
HRRR-WHHHHH
ARE THOSE...
...LUNGS?

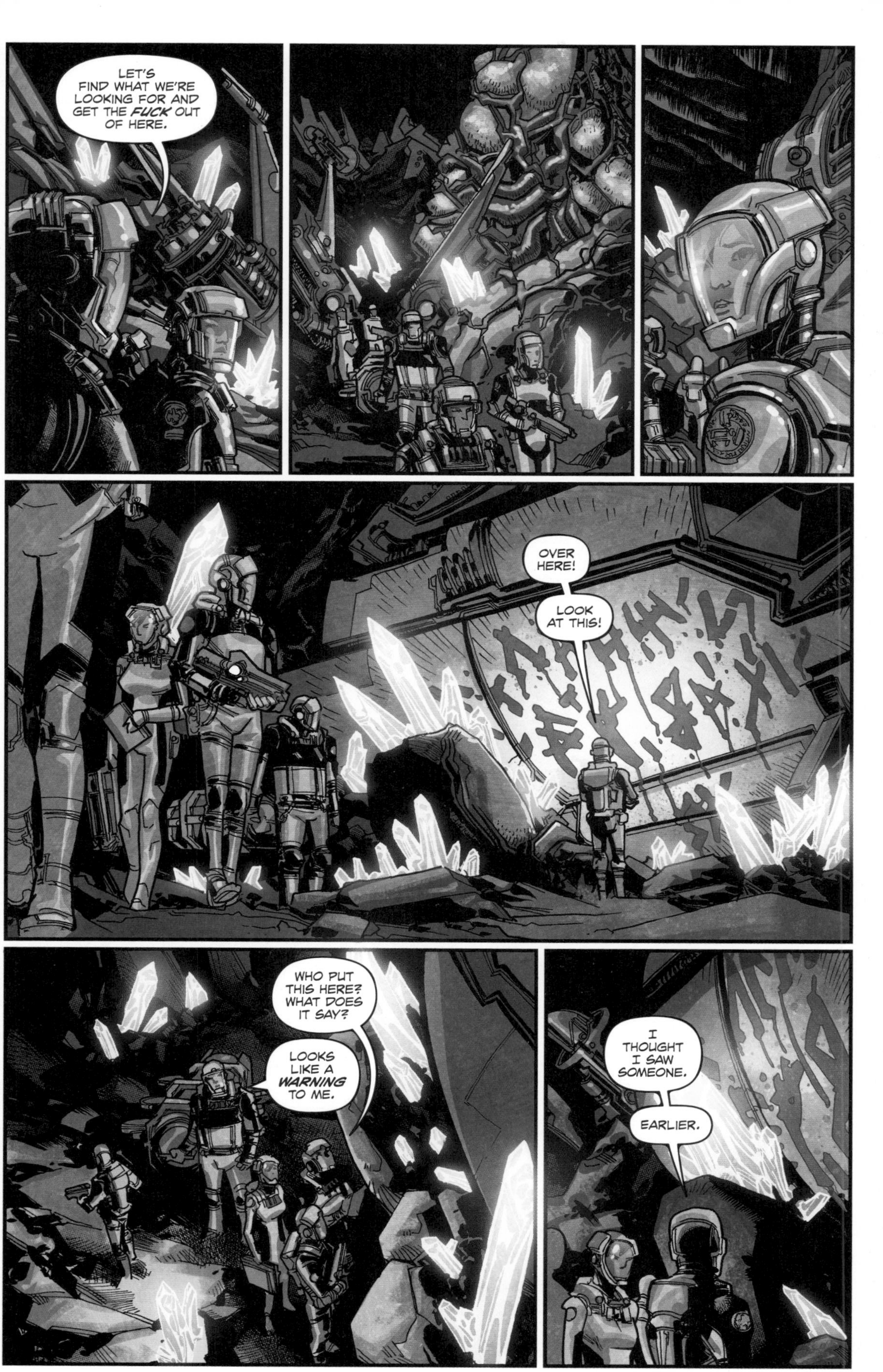
LET'S FIND WHAT WE'RE LOOKING FOR AND GET THE *FUCK* OUT OF HERE.
OVER HERE!
LOOK AT THIS!
WHO PUT THIS HERE? WHAT DOES IT SAY?
LOOKS LIKE A *WARNING* TO ME.
I THOUGHT I SAW SOMEONE.
EARLIER.

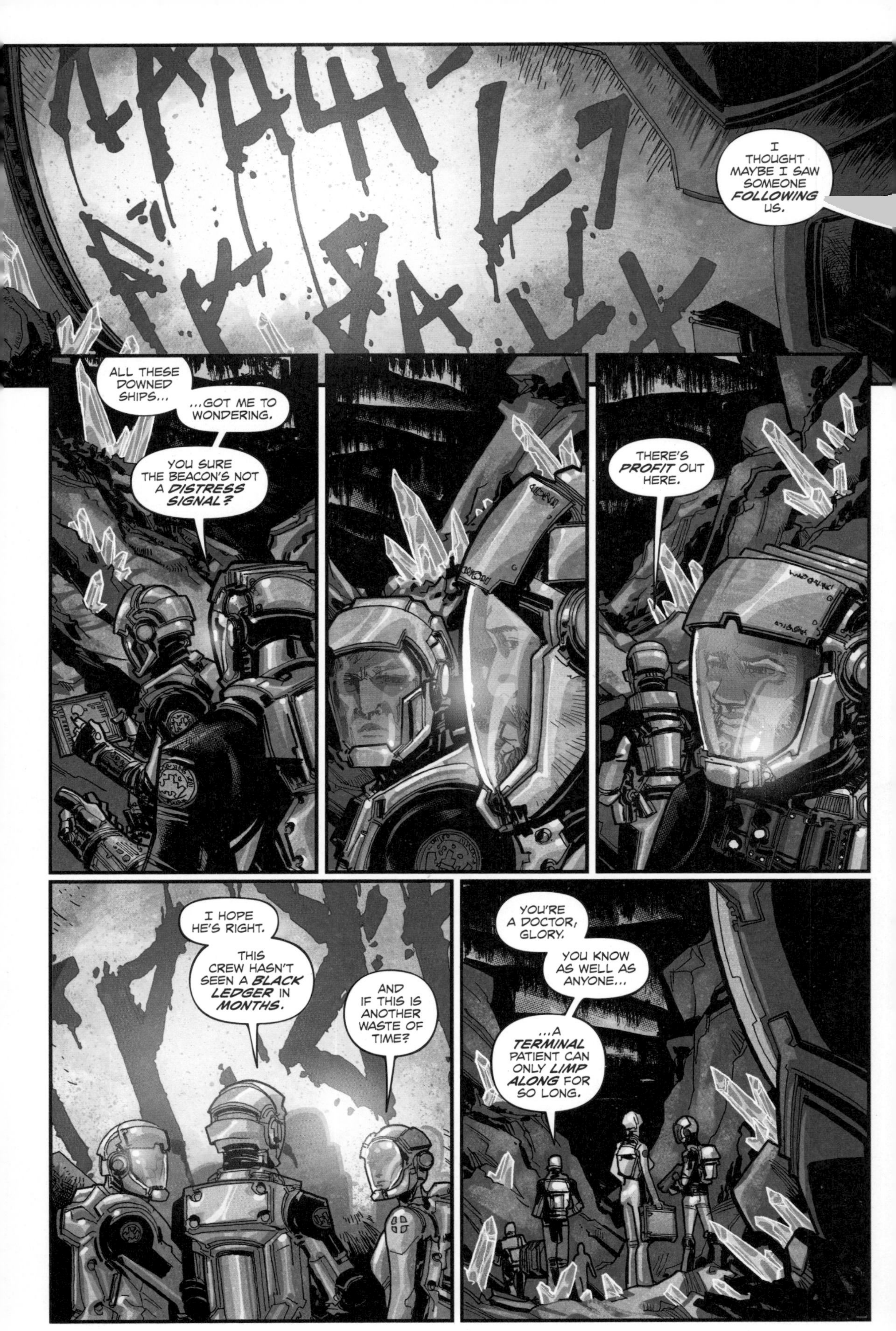
I THOUGHT MAYBE I SAW SOMEONE FOLLOWING US.
ALL THESE DOWNED SHIPS...
...GOT ME TO WONDERING.
YOU SURE THE BEACON'S NOT A DISTRESS SIGNAL?
THERE'S PROFIT OUT HERE.
I HOPE HE'S RIGHT.
THIS CREW HASN'T SEEN A BLACK LEDGER IN MONTHS.
AND IF THIS IS ANOTHER WASTE OF TIME?
YOU'RE A DOCTOR, GLORY.
YOU KNOW AS WELL AS ANYONE...
...A TERMINAL PATIENT CAN ONLY LIMP ALONG FOR SO LONG.

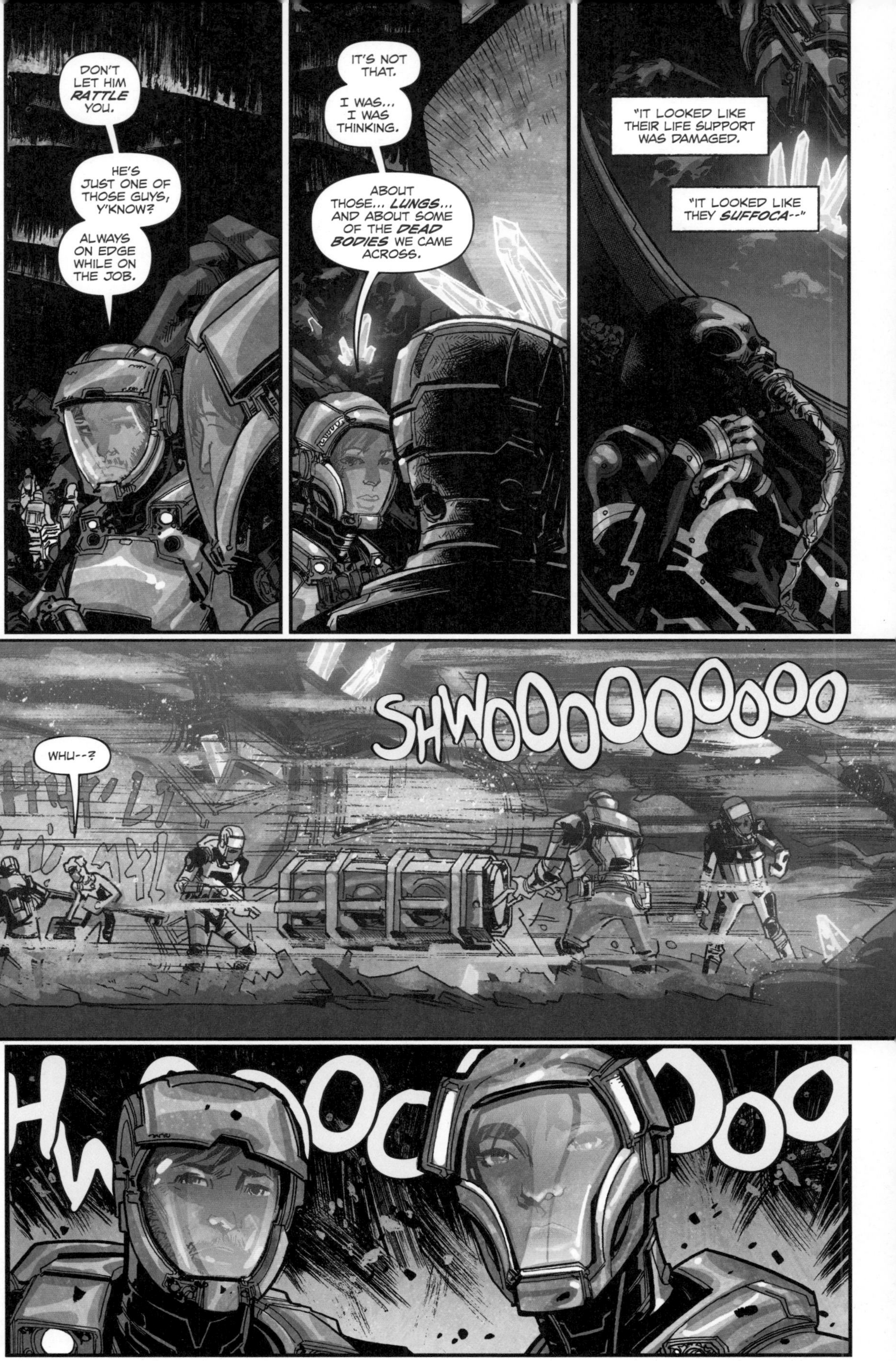
DON'T LET HIM RATTLE YOU.
HE'S JUST ONE OF THOSE GUYS, Y'KNOW?
ALWAYS ON EDGE WHILE ON THE JOB.
IT'S NOT THAT.
I WAS... I WAS THINKING.
ABOUT THOSE... LUNGS... AND ABOUT SOME OF THE DEAD BODIES WE CAME ACROSS.
"IT LOOKED LIKE THEIR LIFE SUPPORT WAS DAMAGED.
"IT LOOKED LIKE THEY SUFFOCA--"
SHWOOOOOOOOOO
WHU--?

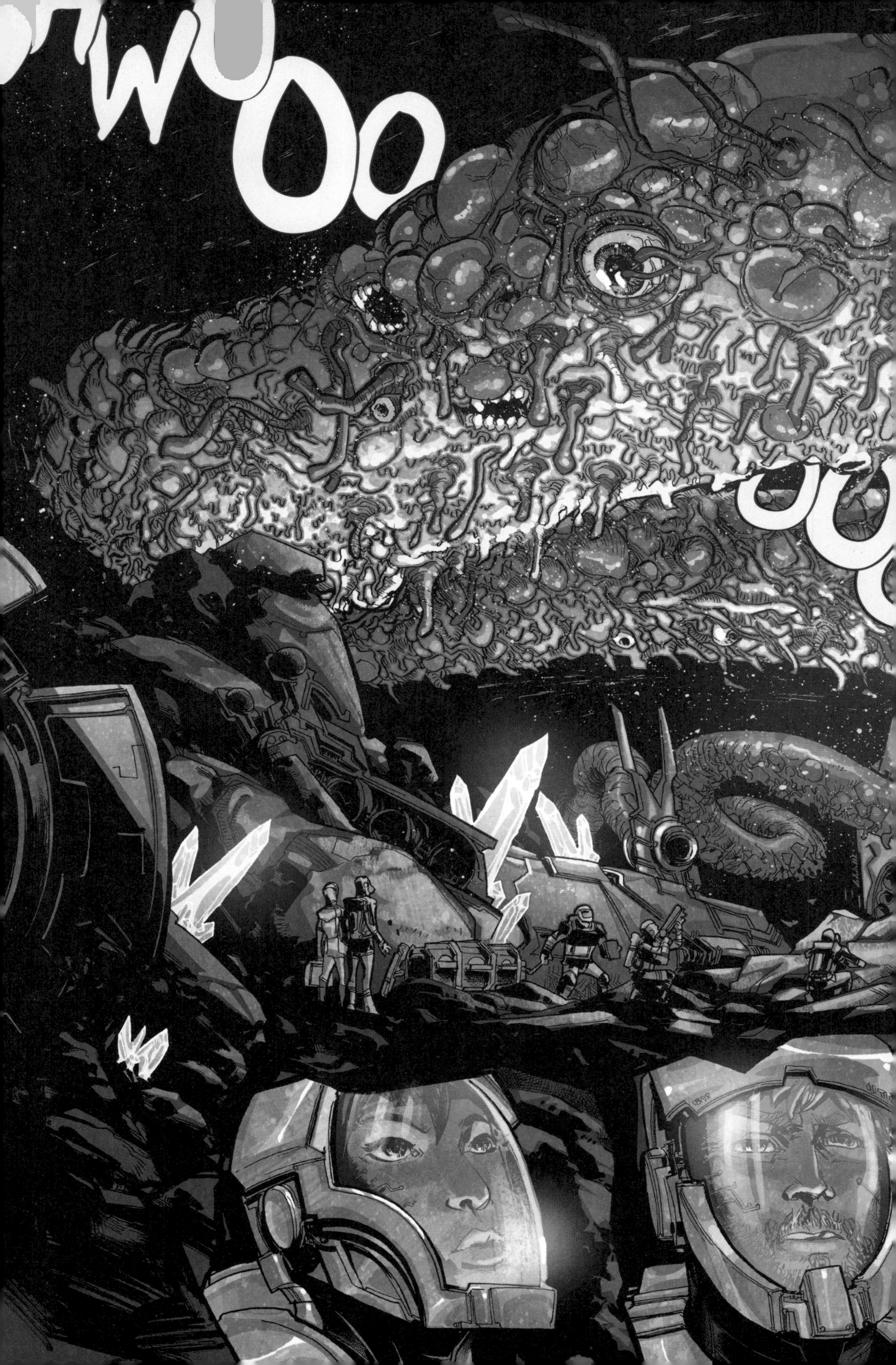
WUOO
OOO

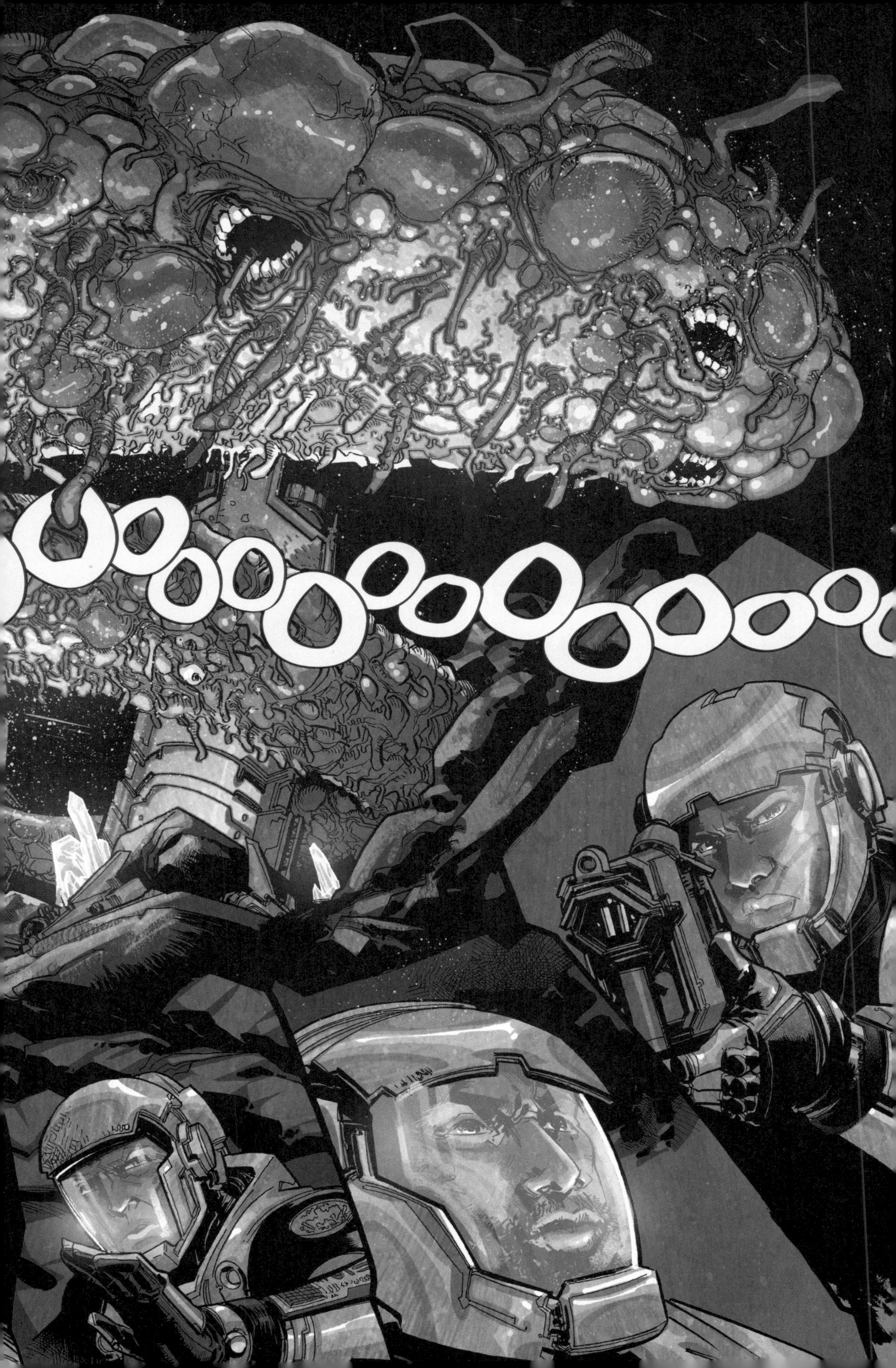
OOOOOOOOOOOOOO

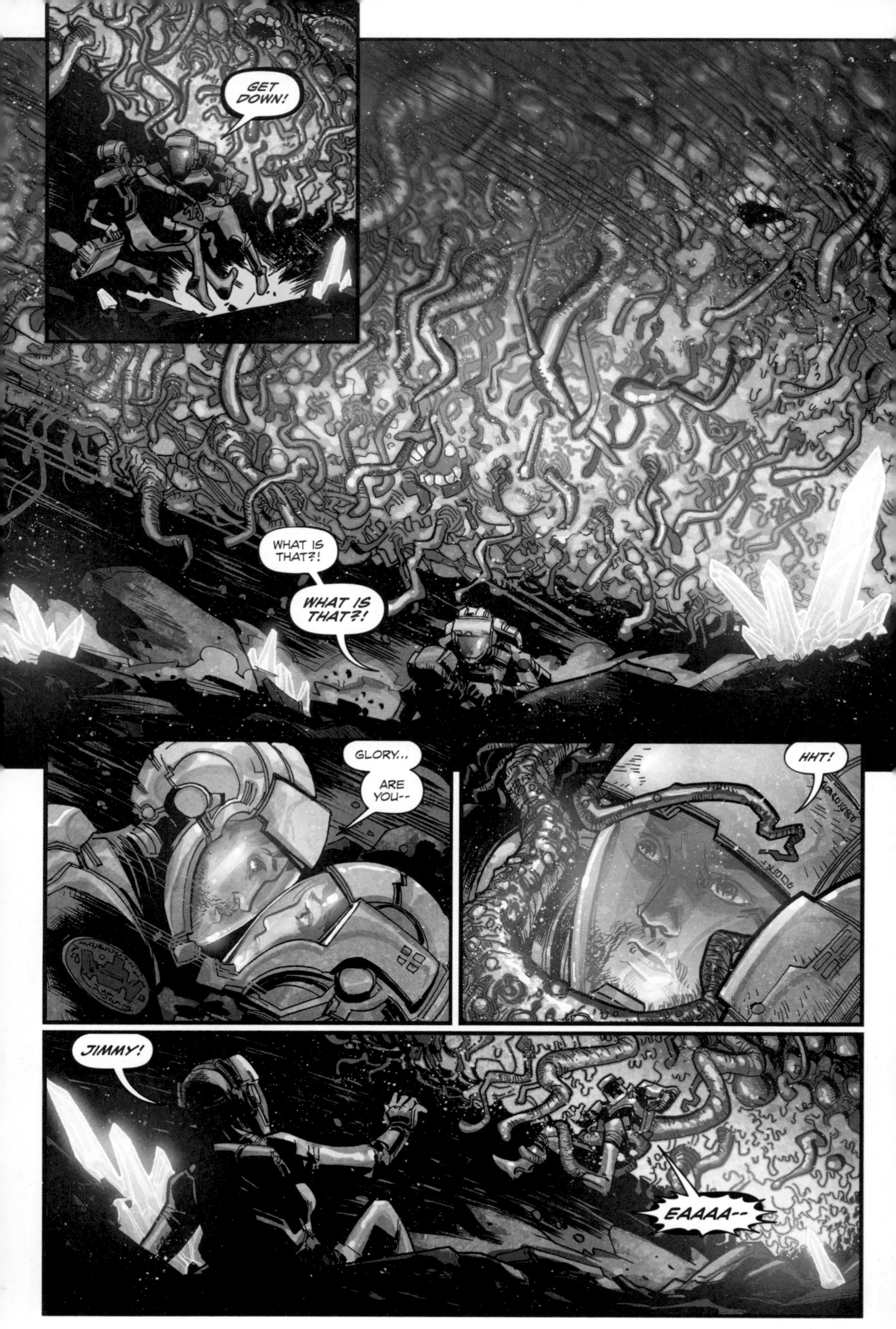
GET DOWN!
WHAT IS THAT?!
WHAT IS THAT?!
GLORY...
ARE YOU--
HHT!
JIMMY!
EAAAA--

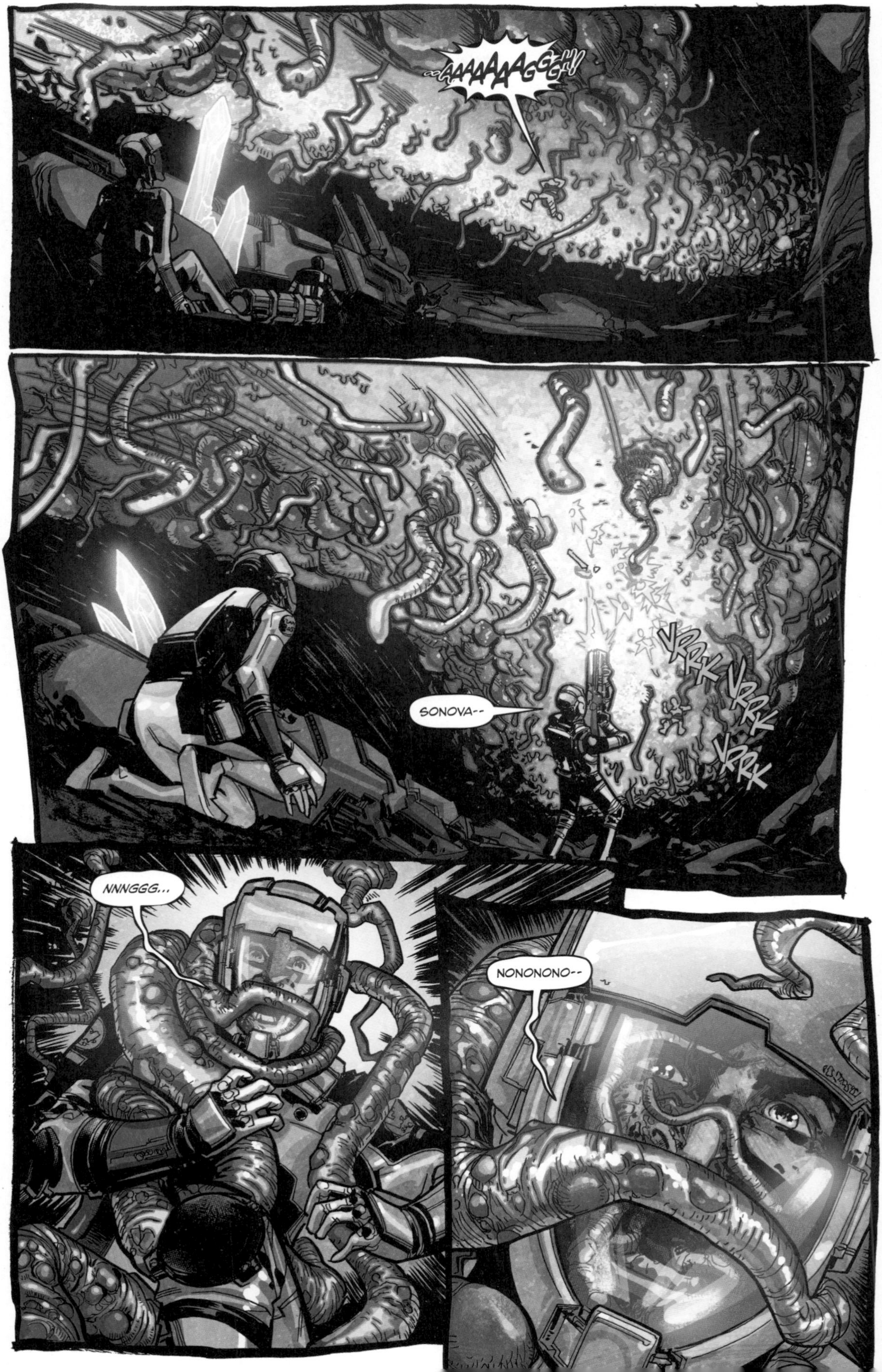

--AAAAAAAGGGH!
SONOVA--
VRRK
VRRK
VRRK
NNNGGG...
NONONONO--

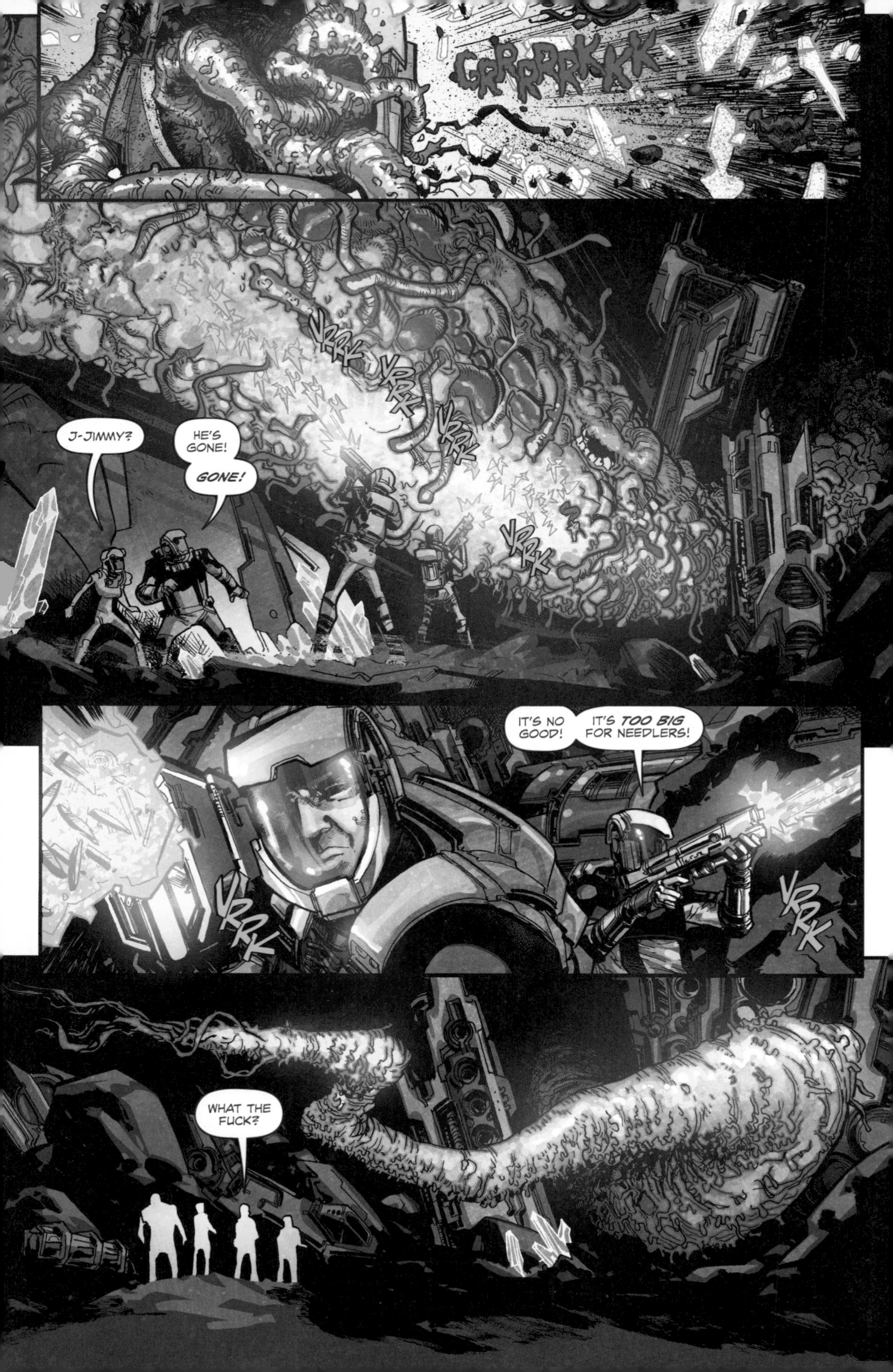
GRRRRRKKK
VRRK
VRRK
VRRK
VRRK
J-JIMMY?
HE'S GONE!
GONE!
IT'S NO GOOD!
IT'S TOO BIG FOR NEEDLERS!
VRRK
VRRK
WHAT THE FUCK?

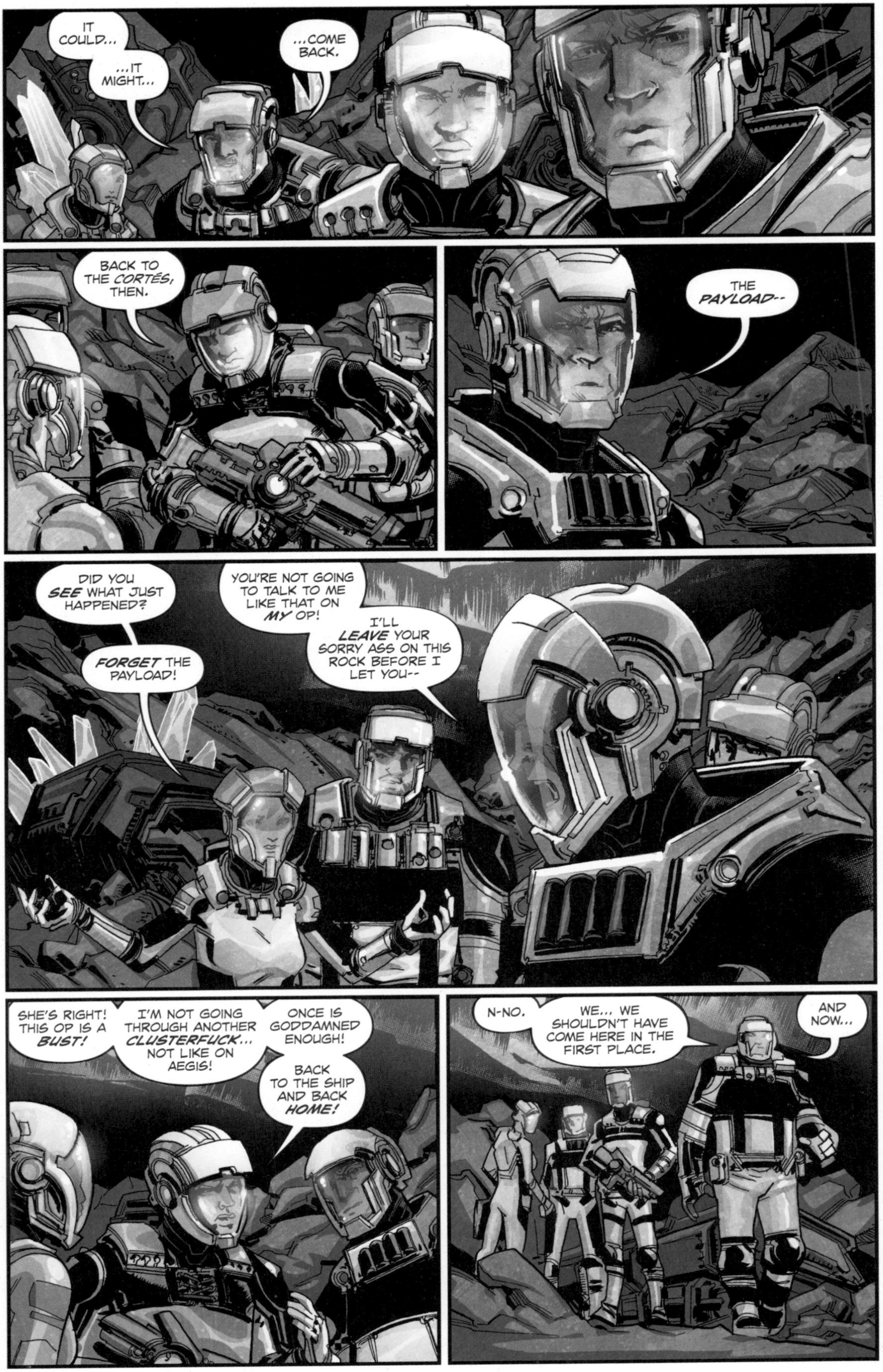
IT COULD...
...IT MIGHT...
...COME BACK.
BACK TO THE CORTÉS, THEN.
THE PAYLOAD--
DID YOU SEE WHAT JUST HAPPENED?
FORGET THE PAYLOAD!
YOU'RE NOT GOING TO TALK TO ME LIKE THAT ON MY OP!
I'LL LEAVE YOUR SORRY ASS ON THIS ROCK BEFORE I LET YOU--
SHE'S RIGHT! THIS OP IS A BUST!
I'M NOT GOING THROUGH ANOTHER CLUSTERFUCK... NOT LIKE ON AEGIS!
ONCE IS GODDAMNED ENOUGH!
BACK TO THE SHIP AND BACK HOME!
N-NO.
WE... WE SHOULDN'T HAVE COME HERE IN THE FIRST PLACE.
AND NOW...

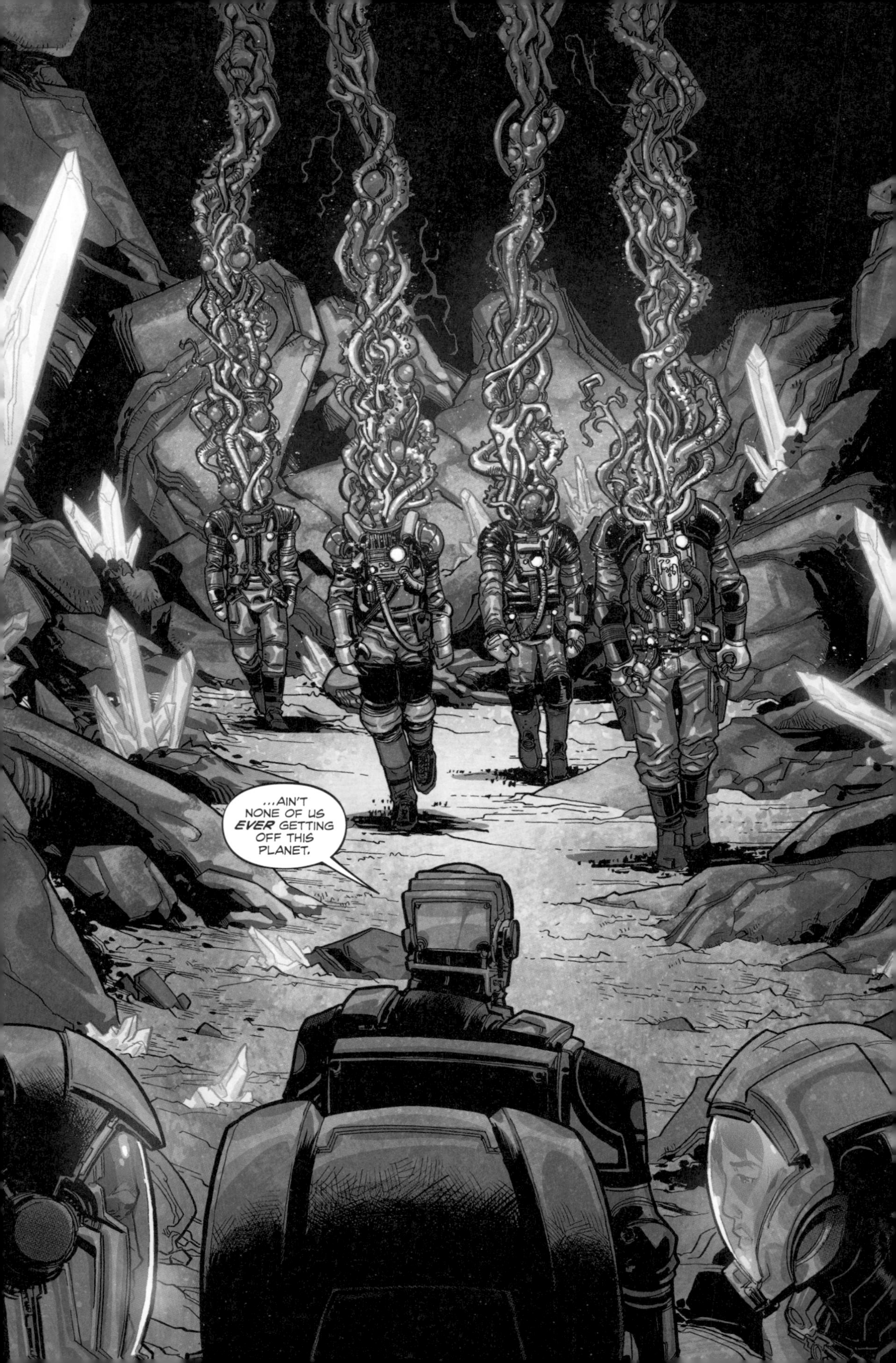
...AIN'T NONE OF US *EVER* GETTING OFF THIS PLANET.

CHAPTER 02

SCARECROWS

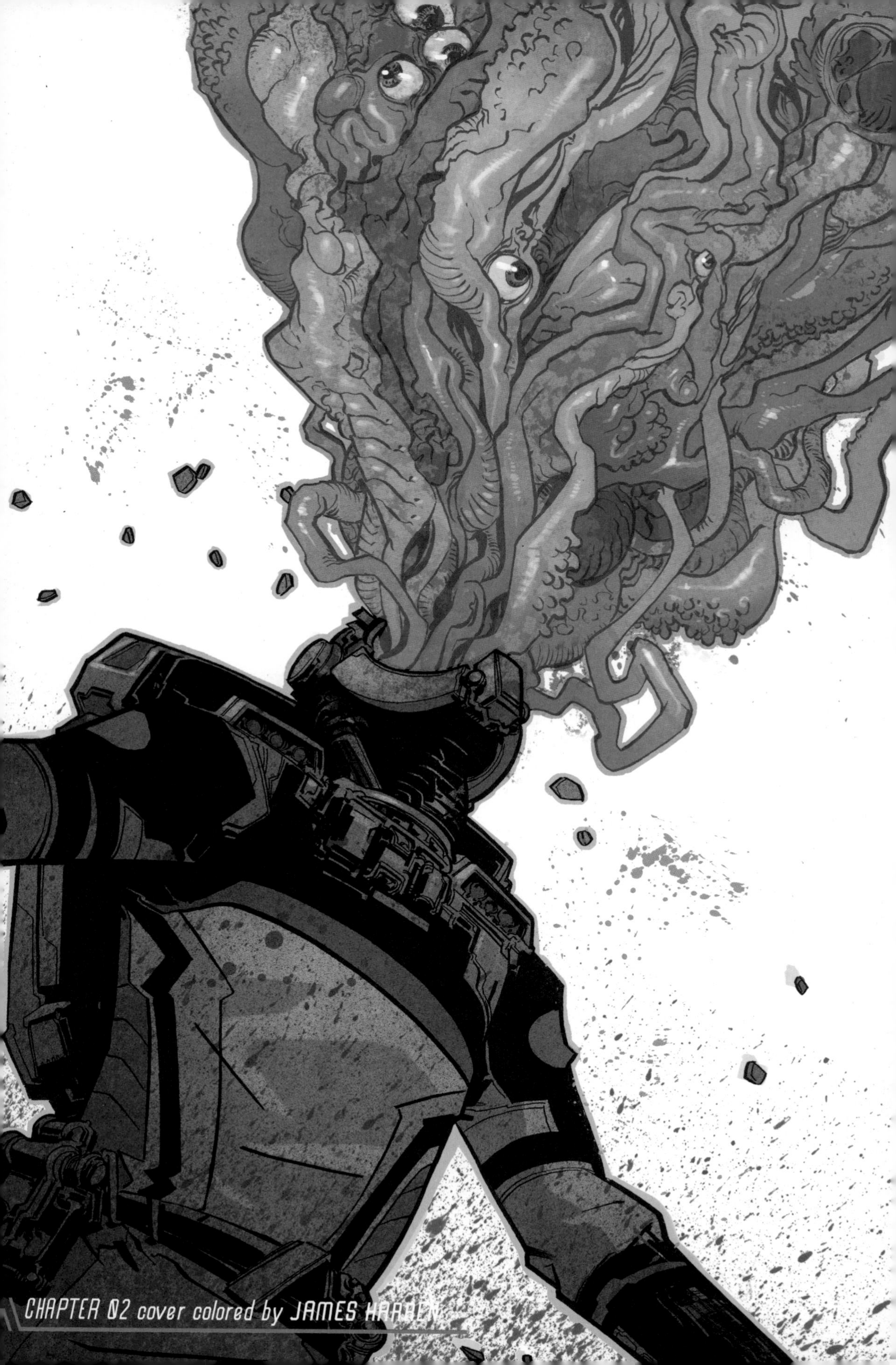

CHAPTER 02 cover colored by JAMES HARREN

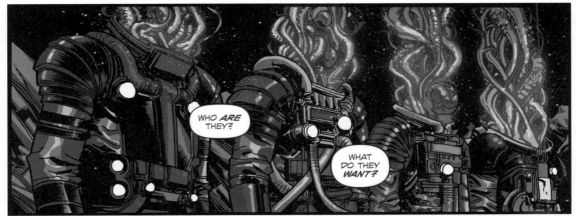

WHO **ARE** THEY?

WHAT DO THEY **WANT?**

DO... DO WE **TALK** TO THEM?

TALK? LOOK AT THEM!

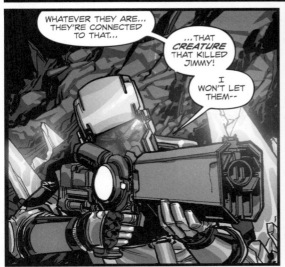

WHATEVER THEY ARE... THEY'RE CONNECTED TO THAT...

...THAT **CREATURE** THAT KILLED JIMMY!

I WON'T LET THEM--

NORRIS-- WAIT. THEY AREN'T ATTACKING US.

NOT **YET**, THEY'RE NOT! WHY WOULD WE GIVE THEM THE CHANCE?

TAKE YOUR HAND OFF MY WEAPON.

I'M STILL IN CHARGE HERE, COOPER!

I'M NOT SAYING OTHERWISE.

YOU START FIRING, THOUGH, AND THEY **WILL** ATTACK.

YOU SAW HOW **INEFFECTUAL** OUR GUNS WERE BEFORE...

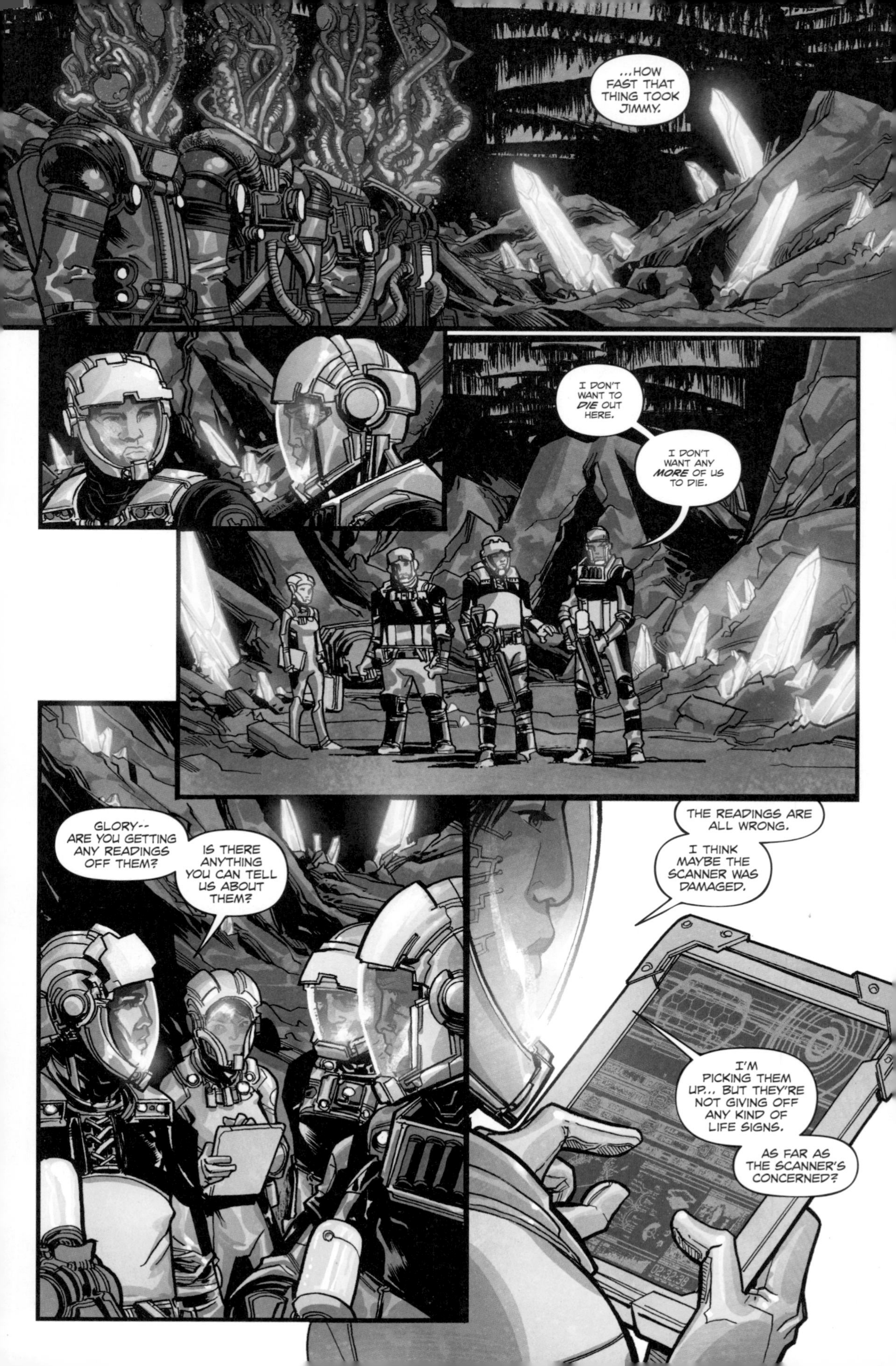
...HOW FAST THAT THING TOOK JIMMY.
I DON'T WANT TO *DIE* OUT HERE.
I DON'T WANT ANY *MORE* OF US TO DIE.
GLORY-- ARE YOU GETTING ANY READINGS OFF THEM?
IS THERE ANYTHING YOU CAN TELL US ABOUT THEM?
THE READINGS ARE ALL WRONG.
I THINK MAYBE THE SCANNER WAS DAMAGED.
I'M PICKING THEM UP... BUT THEY'RE NOT GIVING OFF ANY KIND OF LIFE SIGNS.
AS FAR AS THE SCANNER'S CONCERNED?

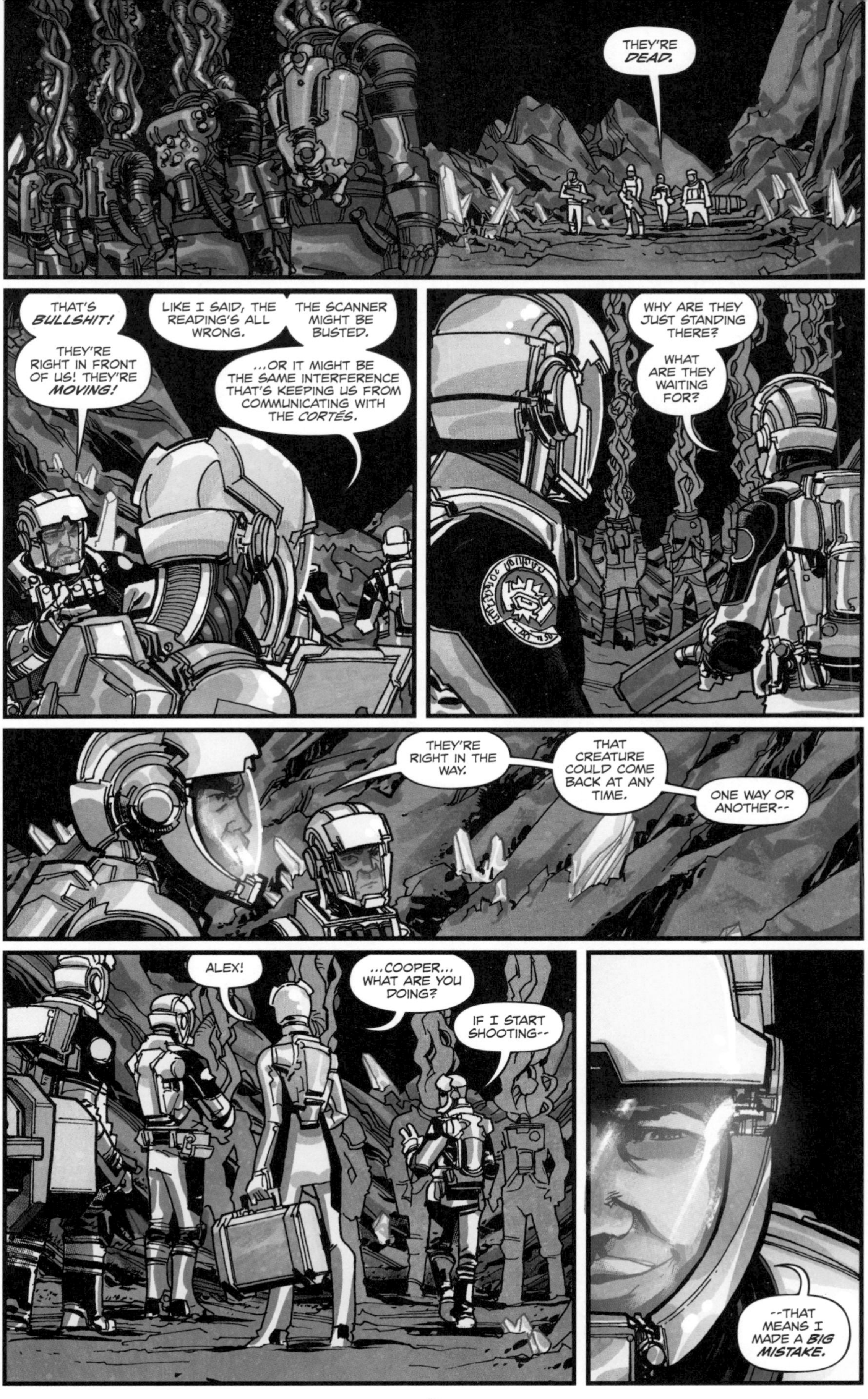
THEY'RE *DEAD.*
THAT'S *BULLSHIT!*
THEY'RE RIGHT IN FRONT OF US! THEY'RE *MOVING!*
LIKE I SAID, THE READING'S ALL WRONG.
THE SCANNER MIGHT BE BUSTED.
...OR IT MIGHT BE THE SAME INTERFERENCE THAT'S KEEPING US FROM COMMUNICATING WITH THE *CORTÉS.*
WHY ARE THEY JUST STANDING THERE?
WHAT ARE THEY WAITING FOR?
THEY'RE RIGHT IN THE WAY.
THAT CREATURE COULD COME BACK AT ANY TIME.
ONE WAY OR ANOTHER--
ALEX!
...COOPER... WHAT ARE YOU DOING?
IF I START SHOOTING--
--THAT MEANS I MADE A *BIG MISTAKE.*

OH, LORD...

...DON'T LET THIS BE A MISTAKE.

I'VE GOT TOO MUCH TO LIVE FOR.

TULIP BACK HOME.

ANNA MARIE ON SIRYN.

DARA ON PREZZON STATION.

SADIE ON TRINOSIS.

WHAT'S-HER-NAME ON KRAVIK.

CONSTANCE ON VADISLAV.

THANK YOU, YOU BEAUTIFUL, BEAUTIFUL LADIES.

GOD BLESS YOUR *LOOSE MORALS.*

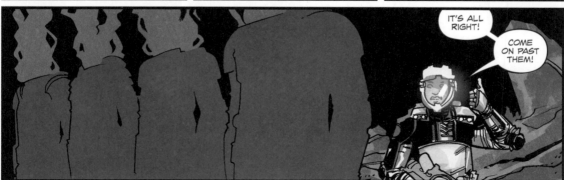

IT'S ALL RIGHT!

COME ON PAST THEM!

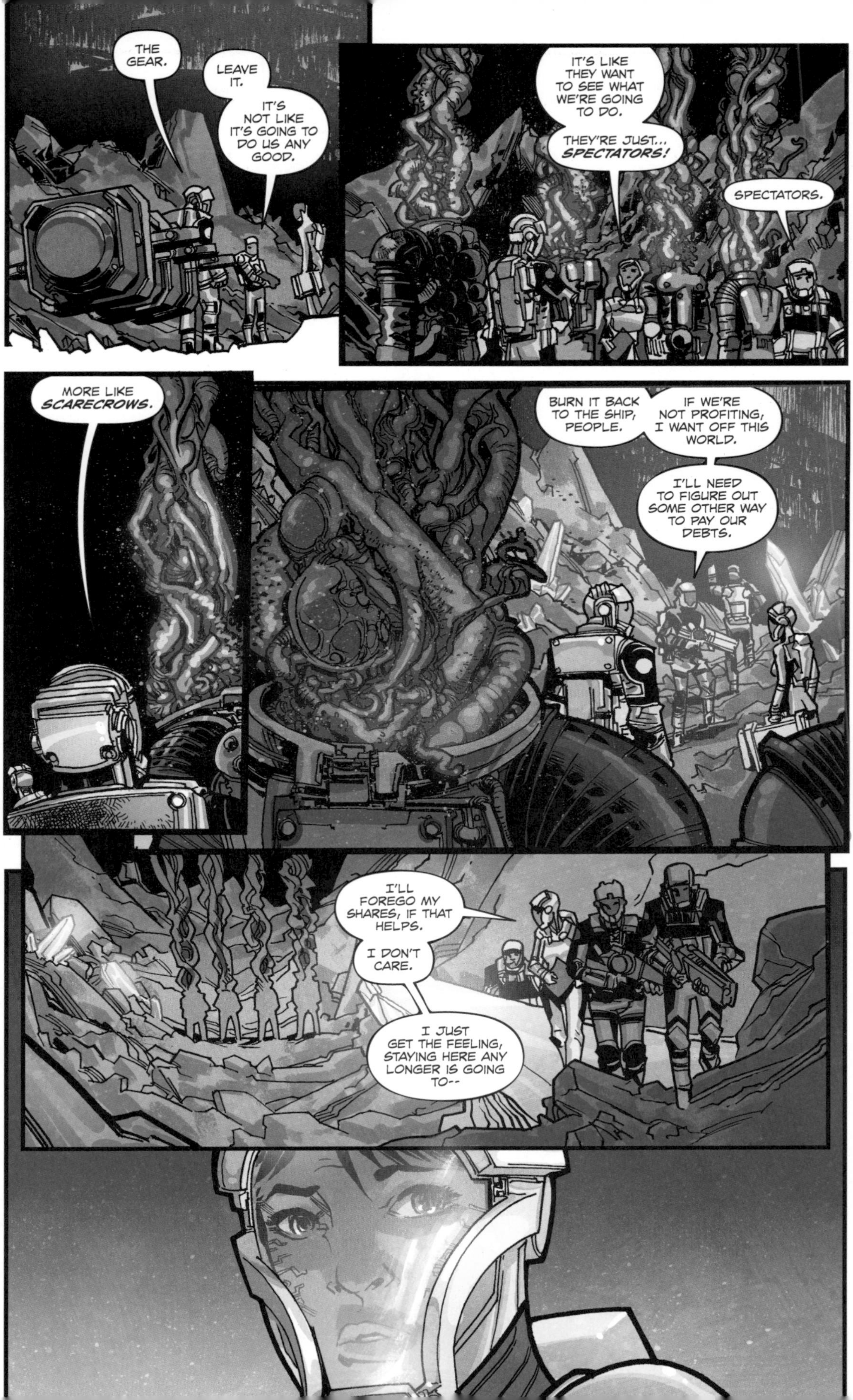
THE GEAR.
LEAVE IT.
IT'S NOT LIKE IT'S GOING TO DO US ANY GOOD.
IT'S LIKE THEY WANT TO SEE WHAT WE'RE GOING TO DO.
THEY'RE JUST... SPECTATORS!
SPECTATORS.
MORE LIKE SCARECROWS.
BURN IT BACK TO THE SHIP, PEOPLE.
IF WE'RE NOT PROFITING, I WANT OFF THIS WORLD.
I'LL NEED TO FIGURE OUT SOME OTHER WAY TO PAY OUR DEBTS.
I'LL FOREGO MY SHARES, IF THAT HELPS.
I DON'T CARE.
I JUST GET THE FEELING, STAYING HERE ANY LONGER IS GOING TO--

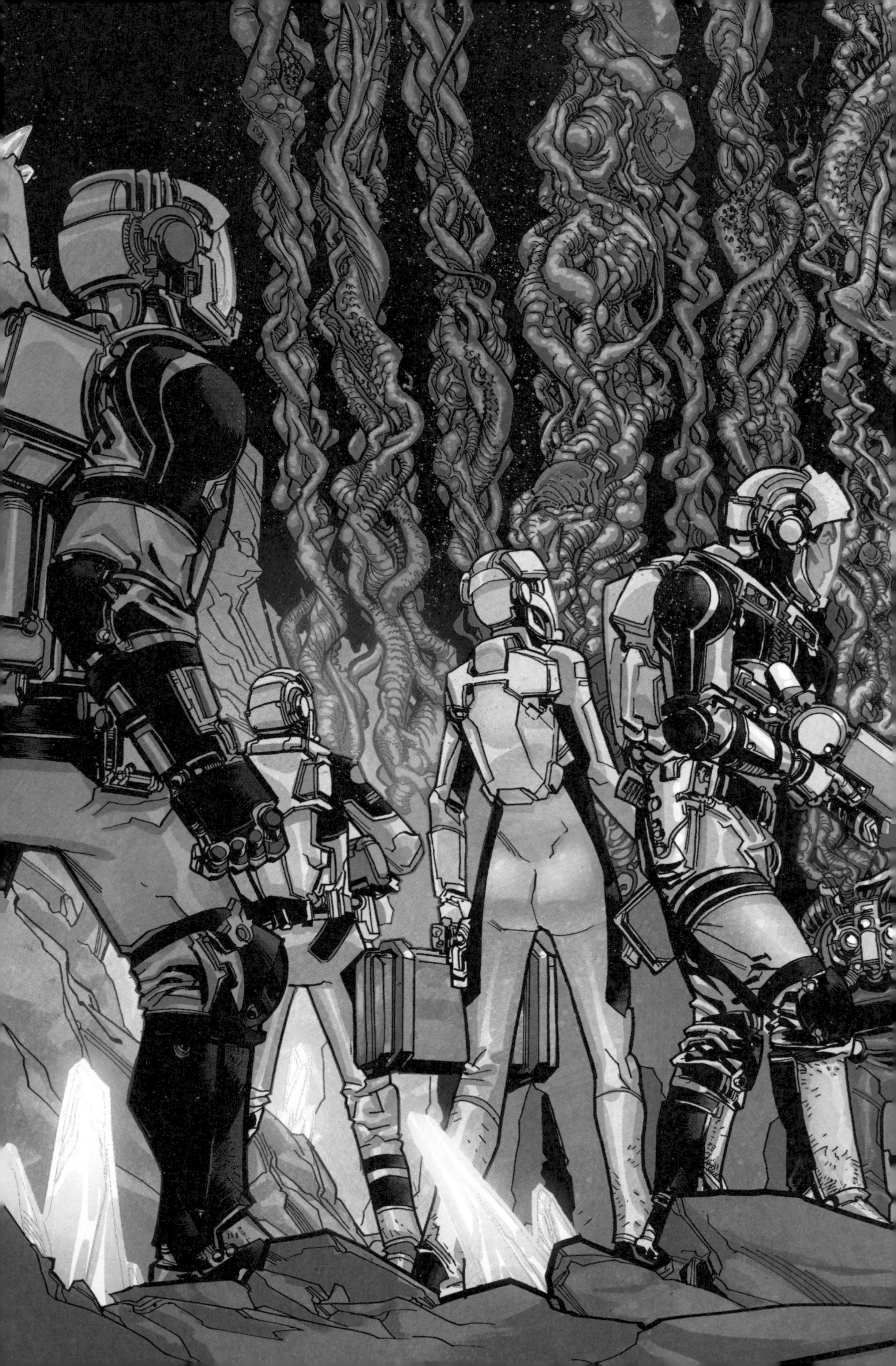

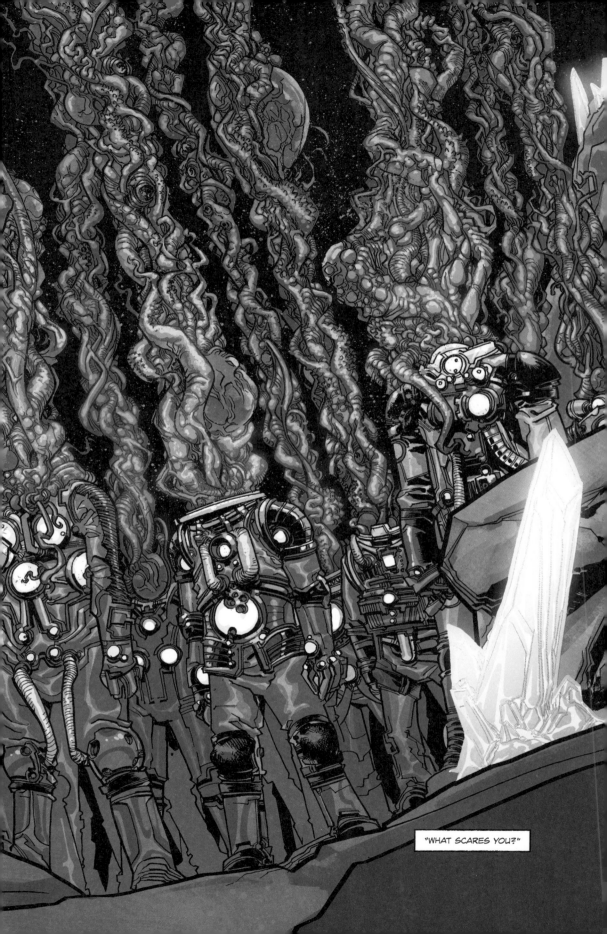

"WHAT SCARES YOU?"

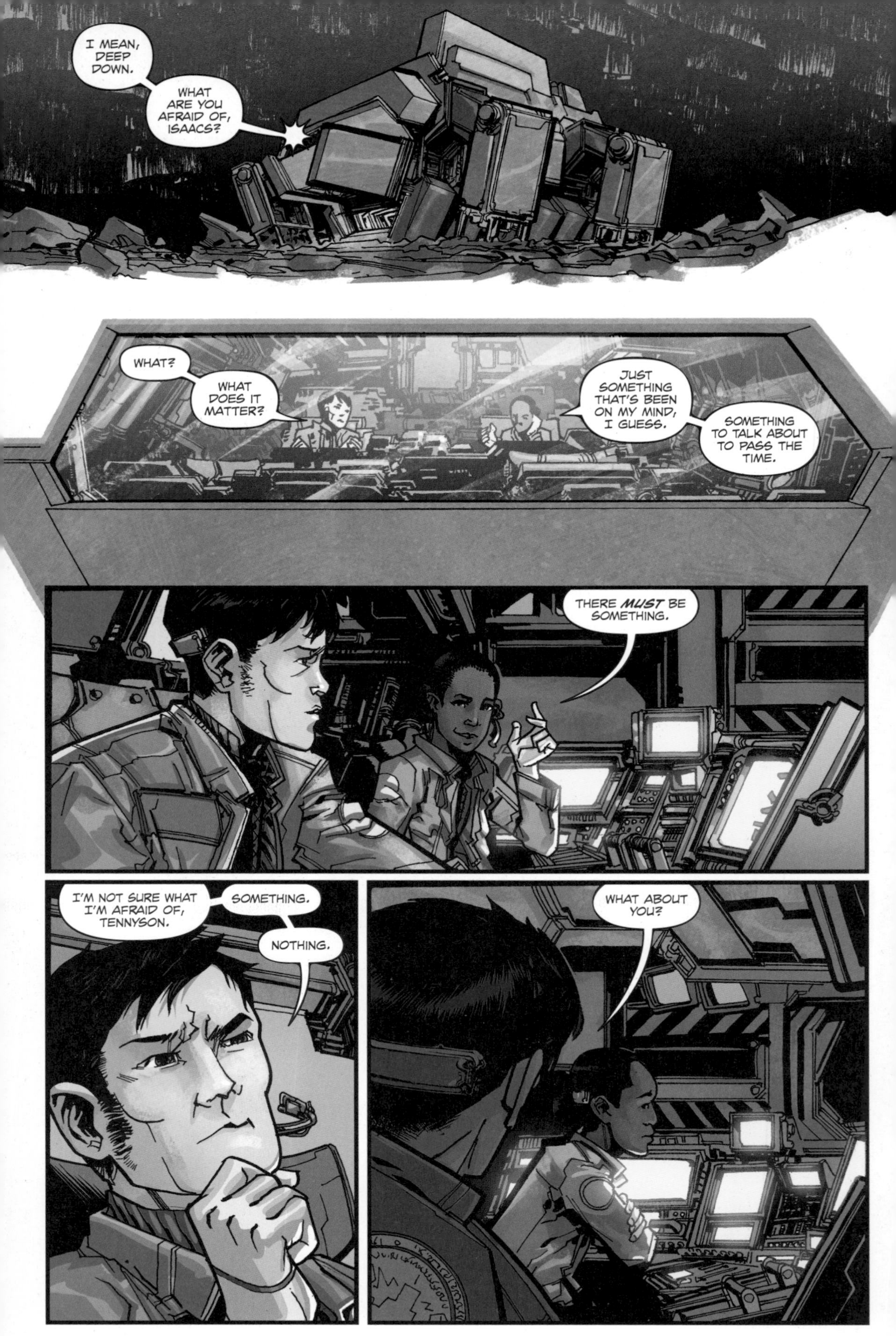
I MEAN, DEEP DOWN.
WHAT ARE YOU AFRAID OF, ISAACS?
WHAT?
WHAT DOES IT MATTER?
JUST SOMETHING THAT'S BEEN ON MY MIND, I GUESS.
SOMETHING TO TALK ABOUT TO PASS THE TIME.
THERE *MUST* BE SOMETHING.
I'M NOT SURE WHAT I'M AFRAID OF, TENNYSON.
SOMETHING.
NOTHING.
WHAT ABOUT YOU?

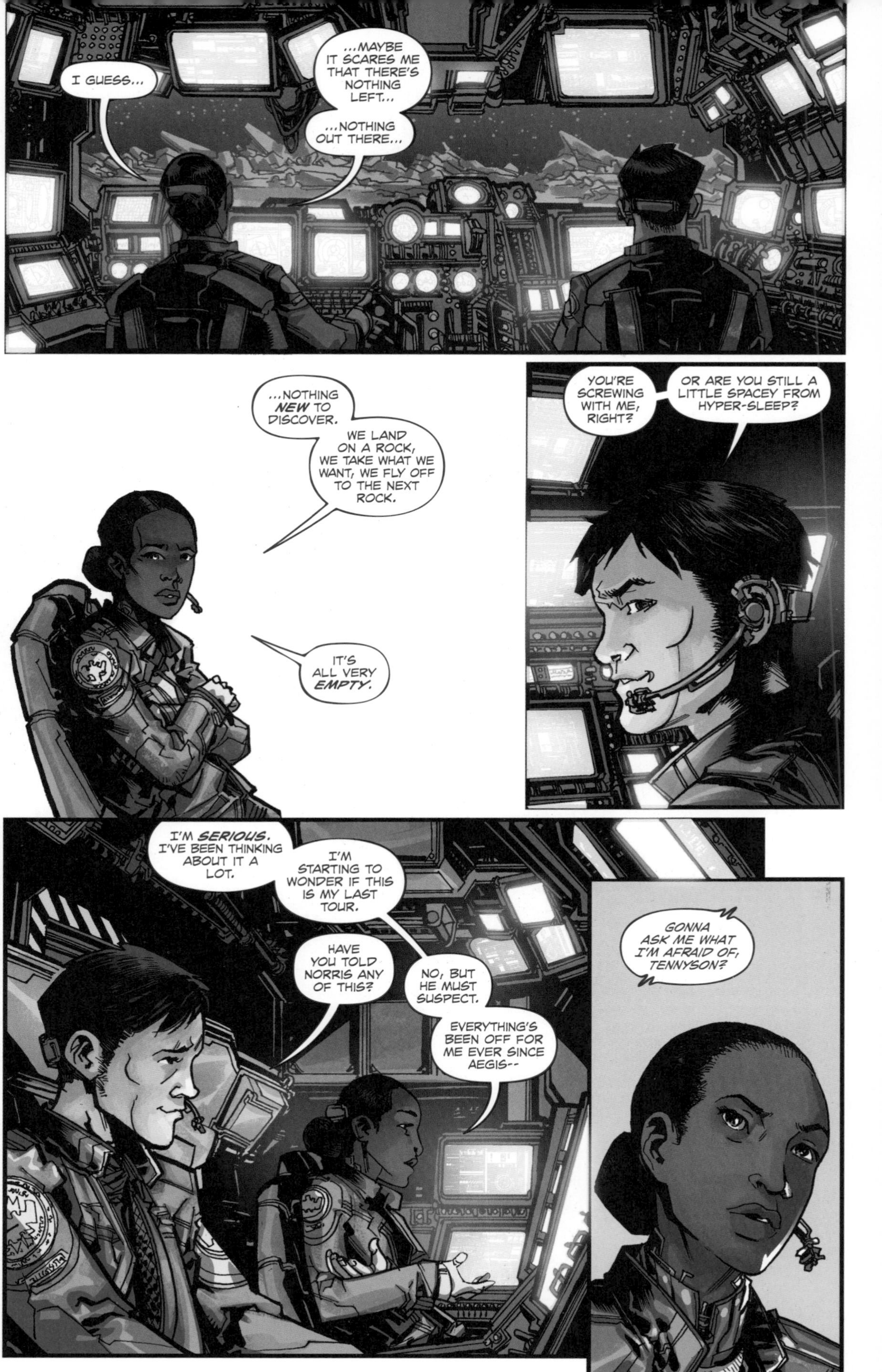
I GUESS...
...MAYBE IT SCARES ME THAT THERE'S NOTHING LEFT...
...NOTHING OUT THERE...
...NOTHING *NEW* TO DISCOVER.
WE LAND ON A ROCK, WE TAKE WHAT WE WANT, WE FLY OFF TO THE NEXT ROCK.
IT'S ALL VERY *EMPTY*.
YOU'RE SCREWING WITH ME, RIGHT?
OR ARE YOU STILL A LITTLE SPACEY FROM HYPER-SLEEP?
I'M *SERIOUS*. I'VE BEEN THINKING ABOUT IT A LOT.
I'M STARTING TO WONDER IF THIS IS MY LAST TOUR.
HAVE YOU TOLD NORRIS ANY OF THIS?
NO, BUT HE MUST SUSPECT.
EVERYTHING'S BEEN OFF FOR ME EVER SINCE AEGIS--
GONNA ASK ME WHAT I'M AFRAID OF, TENNYSON?

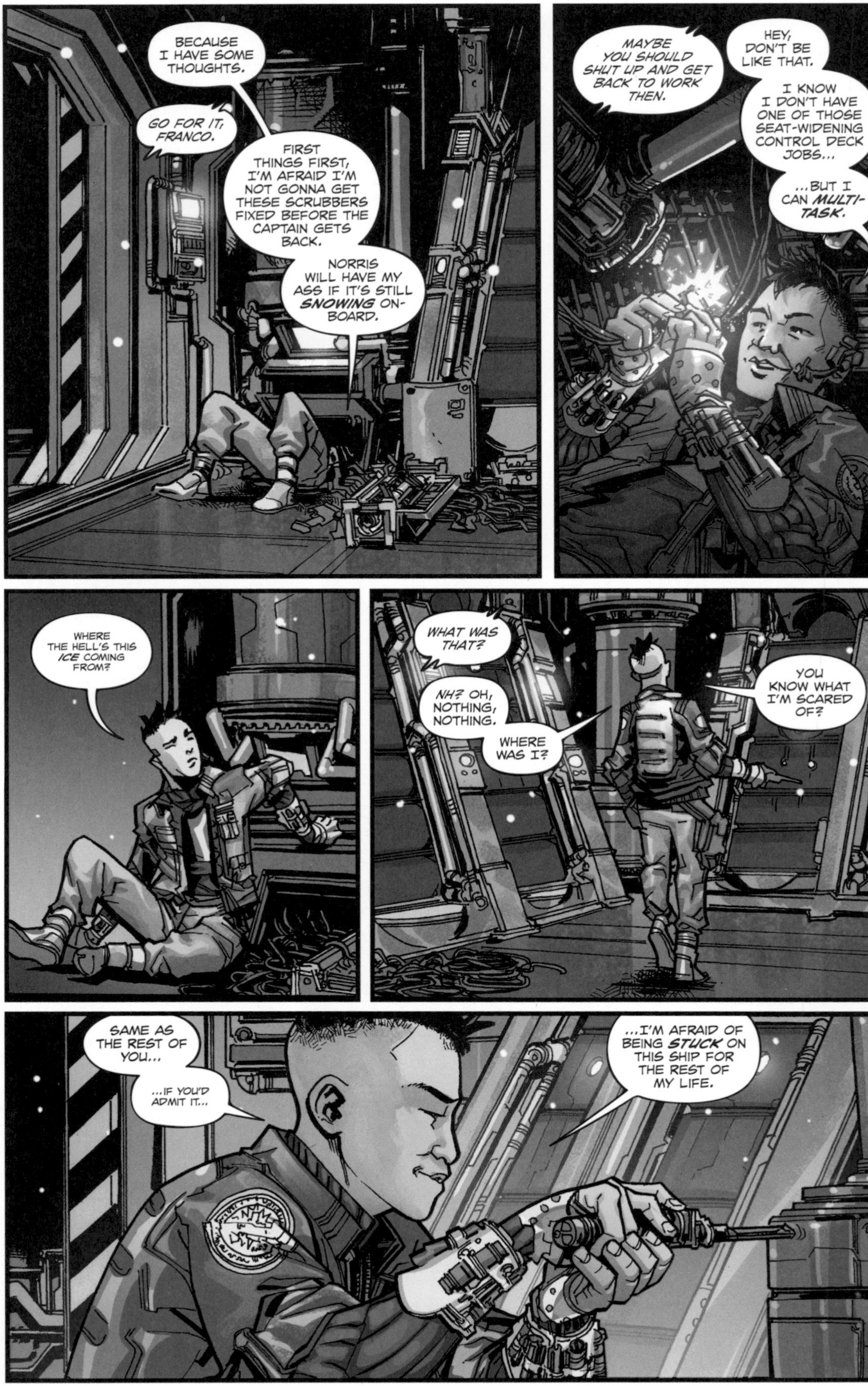
BECAUSE I HAVE SOME THOUGHTS.
GO FOR IT, FRANCO.
FIRST THINGS FIRST, I'M AFRAID I'M NOT GONNA GET THESE SCRUBBERS FIXED BEFORE THE CAPTAIN GETS BACK.
NORRIS WILL HAVE MY ASS IF IT'S STILL SNOWING ON-BOARD.
MAYBE YOU SHOULD SHUT UP AND GET BACK TO WORK THEN.
HEY, DON'T BE LIKE THAT.
I KNOW I DON'T HAVE ONE OF THOSE SEAT-WIDENING CONTROL DECK JOBS...
...BUT I CAN MULTI-TASK.
WHERE THE HELL'S THIS ICE COMING FROM?
WHAT WAS THAT?
NH? OH, NOTHING, NOTHING.
WHERE WAS I?
YOU KNOW WHAT I'M SCARED OF?
SAME AS THE REST OF YOU...
...IF YOU'D ADMIT IT...
...I'M AFRAID OF BEING STUCK ON THIS SHIP FOR THE REST OF MY LIFE.

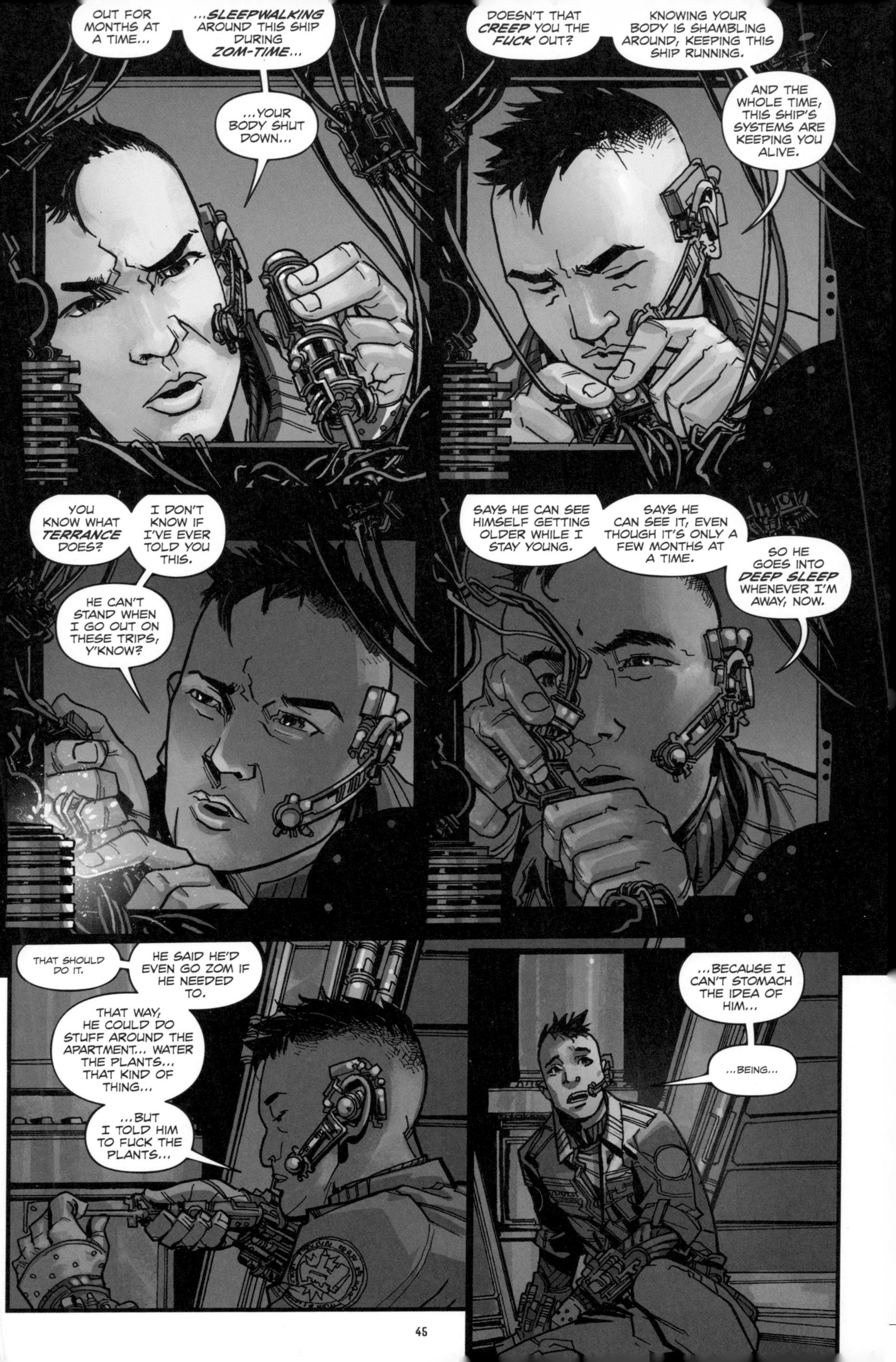
OUT FOR MONTHS AT A TIME...
...SLEEPWALKING AROUND THIS SHIP DURING ZOM-TIME...
...YOUR BODY SHUT DOWN...
DOESN'T THAT CREEP YOU THE FUCK OUT?
KNOWING YOUR BODY IS SHAMBLING AROUND, KEEPING THIS SHIP RUNNING.
AND THE WHOLE TIME, THIS SHIP'S SYSTEMS ARE KEEPING YOU ALIVE.
YOU KNOW WHAT TERRANCE DOES?
I DON'T KNOW IF I'VE EVER TOLD YOU THIS.
HE CAN'T STAND WHEN I GO OUT ON THESE TRIPS, Y'KNOW?
SAYS HE CAN SEE HIMSELF GETTING OLDER WHILE I STAY YOUNG.
SAYS HE CAN SEE IT, EVEN THOUGH IT'S ONLY A FEW MONTHS AT A TIME.
SO HE GOES INTO DEEP SLEEP WHENEVER I'M AWAY, NOW.
THAT SHOULD DO IT.
HE SAID HE'D EVEN GO ZOM IF HE NEEDED TO.
THAT WAY, HE COULD DO STUFF AROUND THE APARTMENT... WATER THE PLANTS... THAT KIND OF THING...
...BUT I TOLD HIM TO FUCK THE PLANTS...
...BECAUSE I CAN'T STOMACH THE IDEA OF HIM...
...BEING...

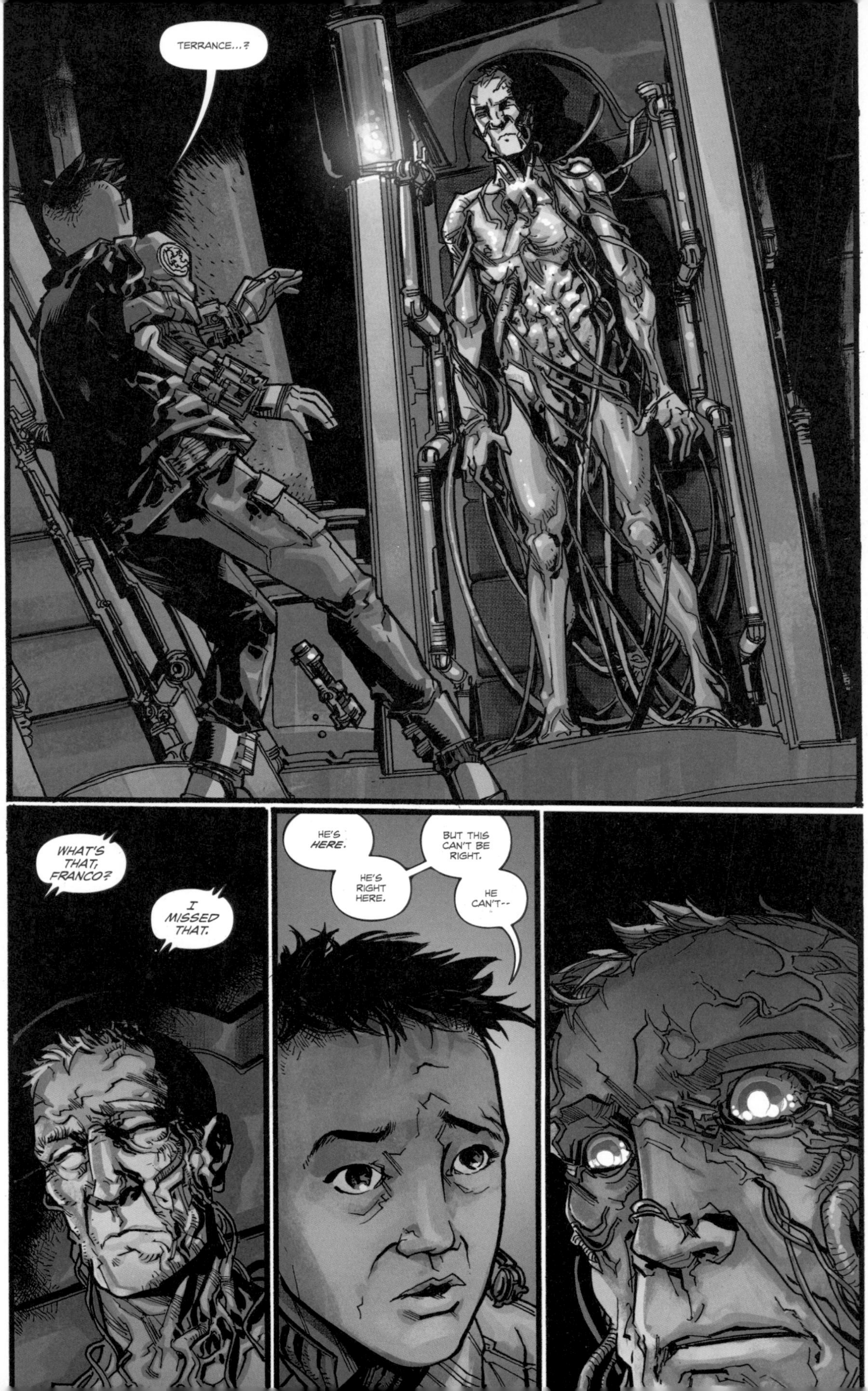

TERRANCE...?
WHAT'S THAT, FRANCO?
I MISSED THAT.
HE'S *HERE.*
HE'S RIGHT HERE.
BUT THIS CAN'T BE RIGHT.
HE CAN'T--

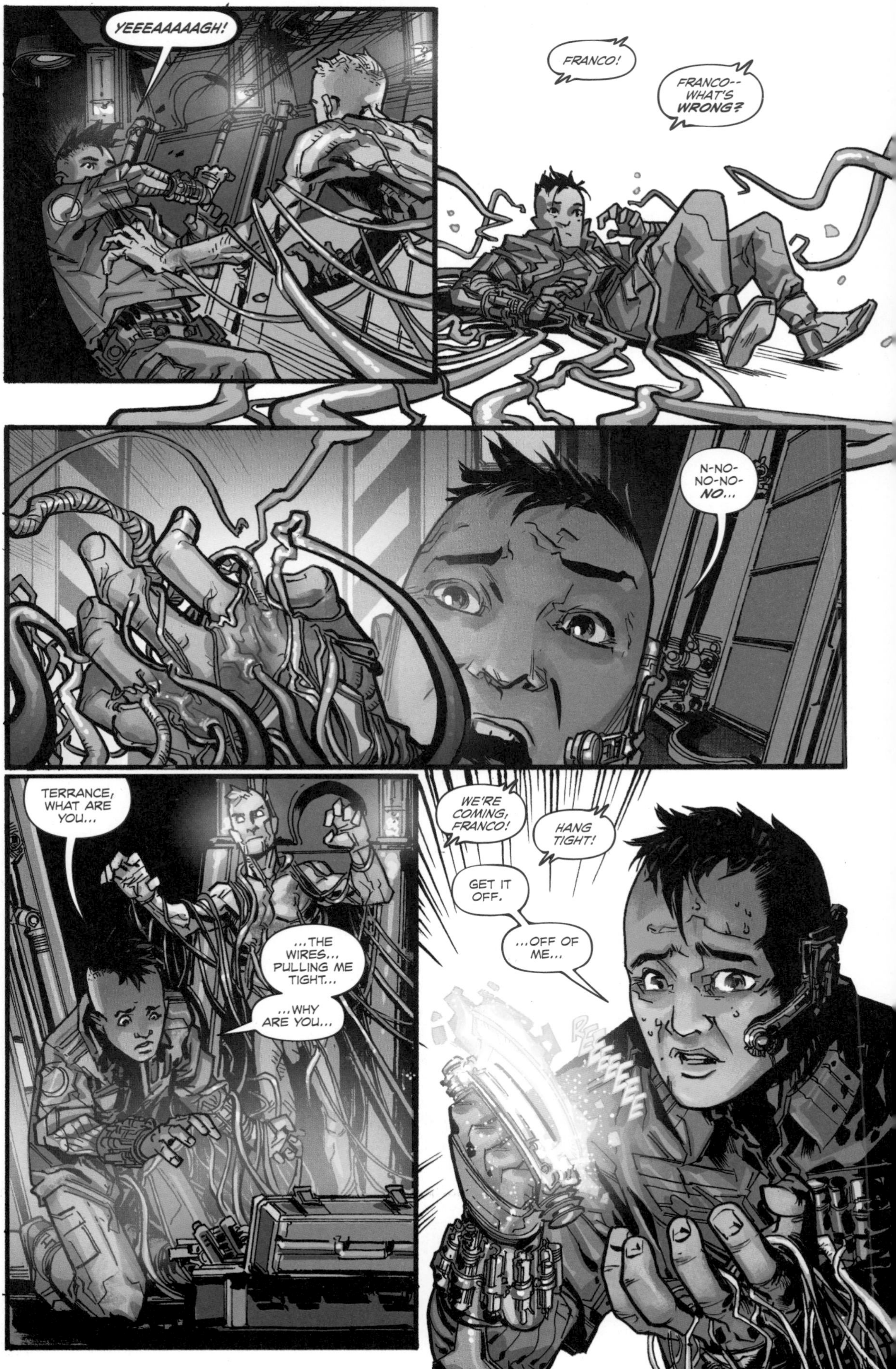
YEEEAAAAAGH!
FRANCO!
FRANCO-- WHAT'S WRONG?
N-NO-NO-NO-NO...
TERRANCE, WHAT ARE YOU...
...THE WIRES... PULLING ME TIGHT...
...WHY ARE YOU...
WE'RE COMING, FRANCO!
HANG TIGHT!
GET IT OFF.
...OFF OF ME...

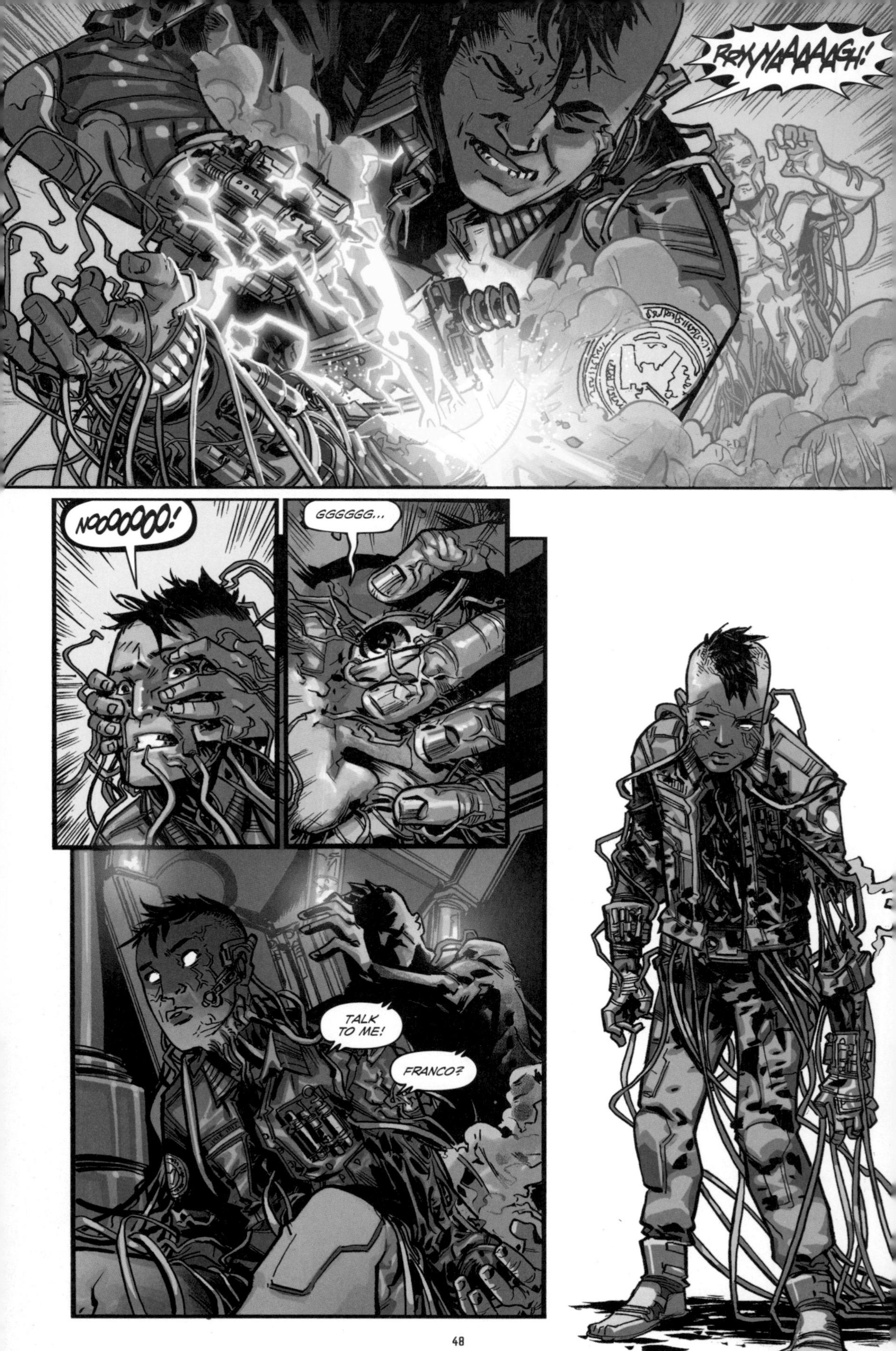
RRKYAAAAAGH!
NOOOOOO!
GGGGGG...
TALK TO ME!
FRANCO?

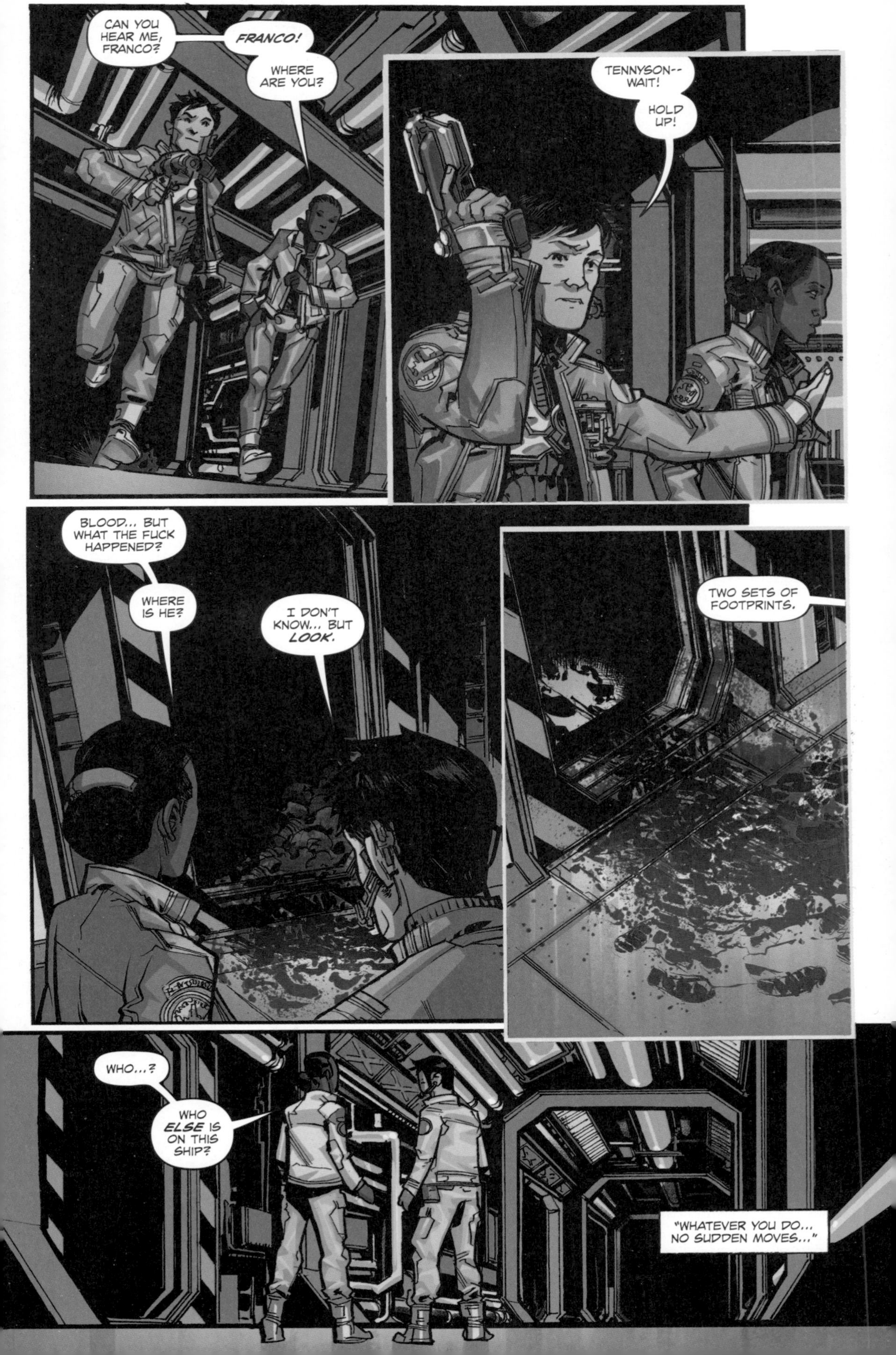
CAN YOU HEAR ME, FRANCO?
FRANCO!
WHERE ARE YOU?
TENNYSON-- WAIT!
HOLD UP!
BLOOD... BUT WHAT THE FUCK HAPPENED?
WHERE IS HE?
I DON'T KNOW... BUT LOOK.
TWO SETS OF FOOTPRINTS.
WHO...?
WHO ELSE IS ON THIS SHIP?
"WHATEVER YOU DO... NO SUDDEN MOVES..."

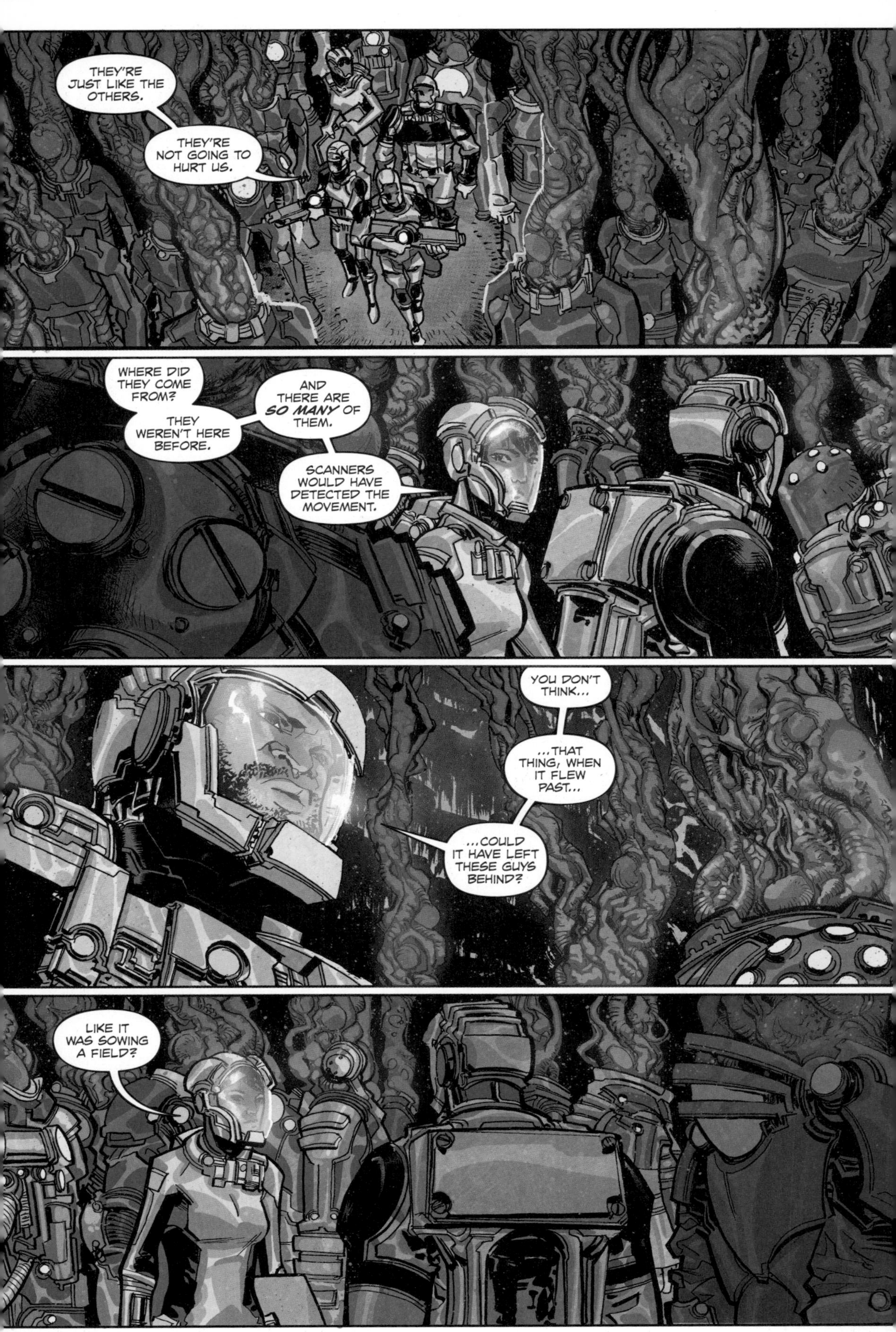
THEY'RE JUST LIKE THE OTHERS.
THEY'RE NOT GOING TO HURT US.
WHERE DID THEY COME FROM?
THEY WEREN'T HERE BEFORE.
AND THERE ARE *SO MANY* OF THEM.
SCANNERS WOULD HAVE DETECTED THE MOVEMENT.
YOU DON'T THINK...
...THAT THING, WHEN IT FLEW PAST...
...COULD IT HAVE LEFT THESE GUYS BEHIND?
LIKE IT WAS SOWING A FIELD?

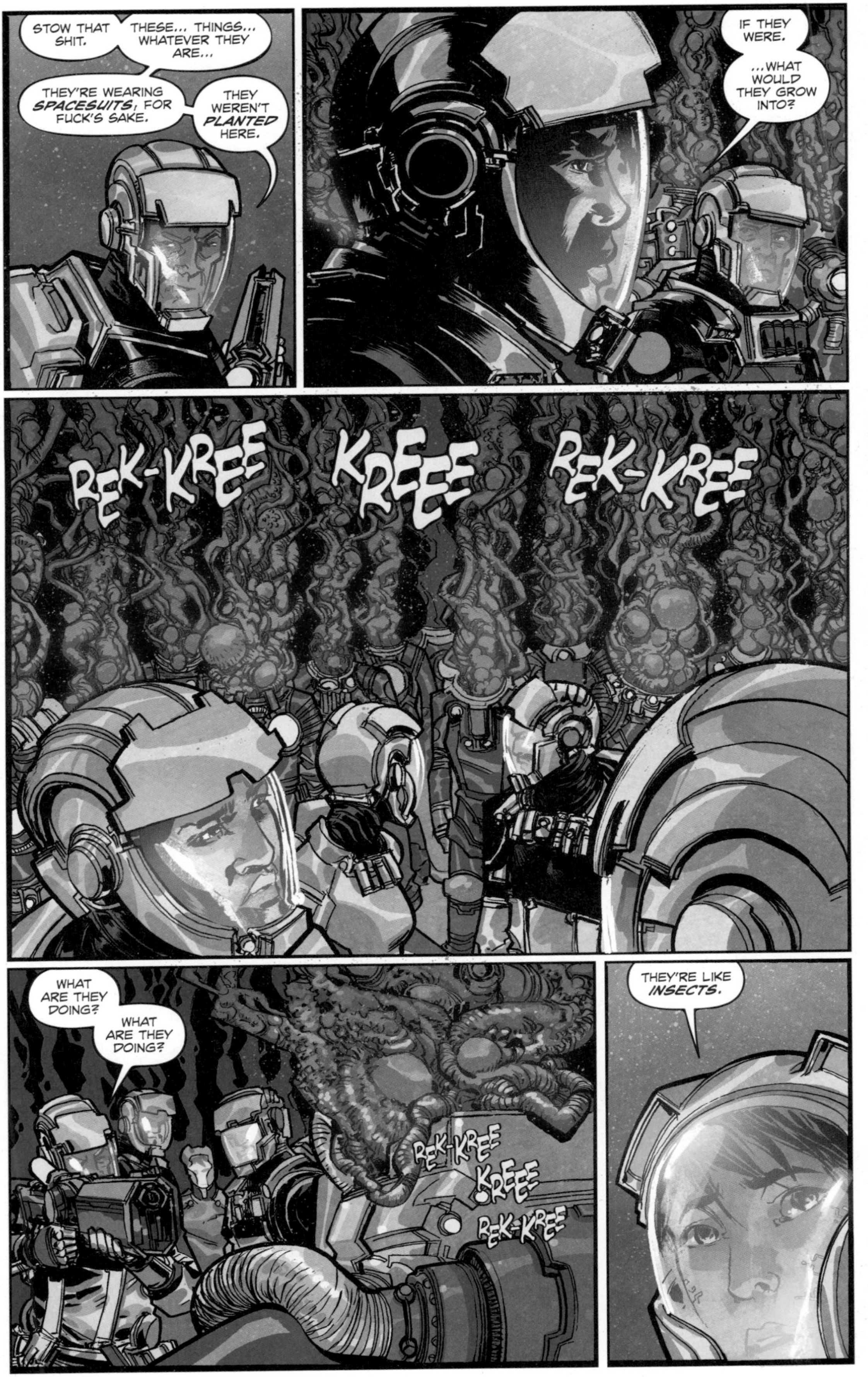

STOW THAT SHIT.
THESE... THINGS... WHATEVER THEY ARE...
THEY'RE WEARING *SPACESUITS*, FOR FUCK'S SAKE.
THEY WEREN'T *PLANTED* HERE.
IF THEY WERE.
...WHAT WOULD THEY GROW INTO?
REK-KREE
KREEE
REK-KREE
WHAT ARE THEY DOING?
WHAT ARE THEY DOING?
REK-KREE
KREEE
REK-KREE
THEY'RE LIKE *INSECTS*.

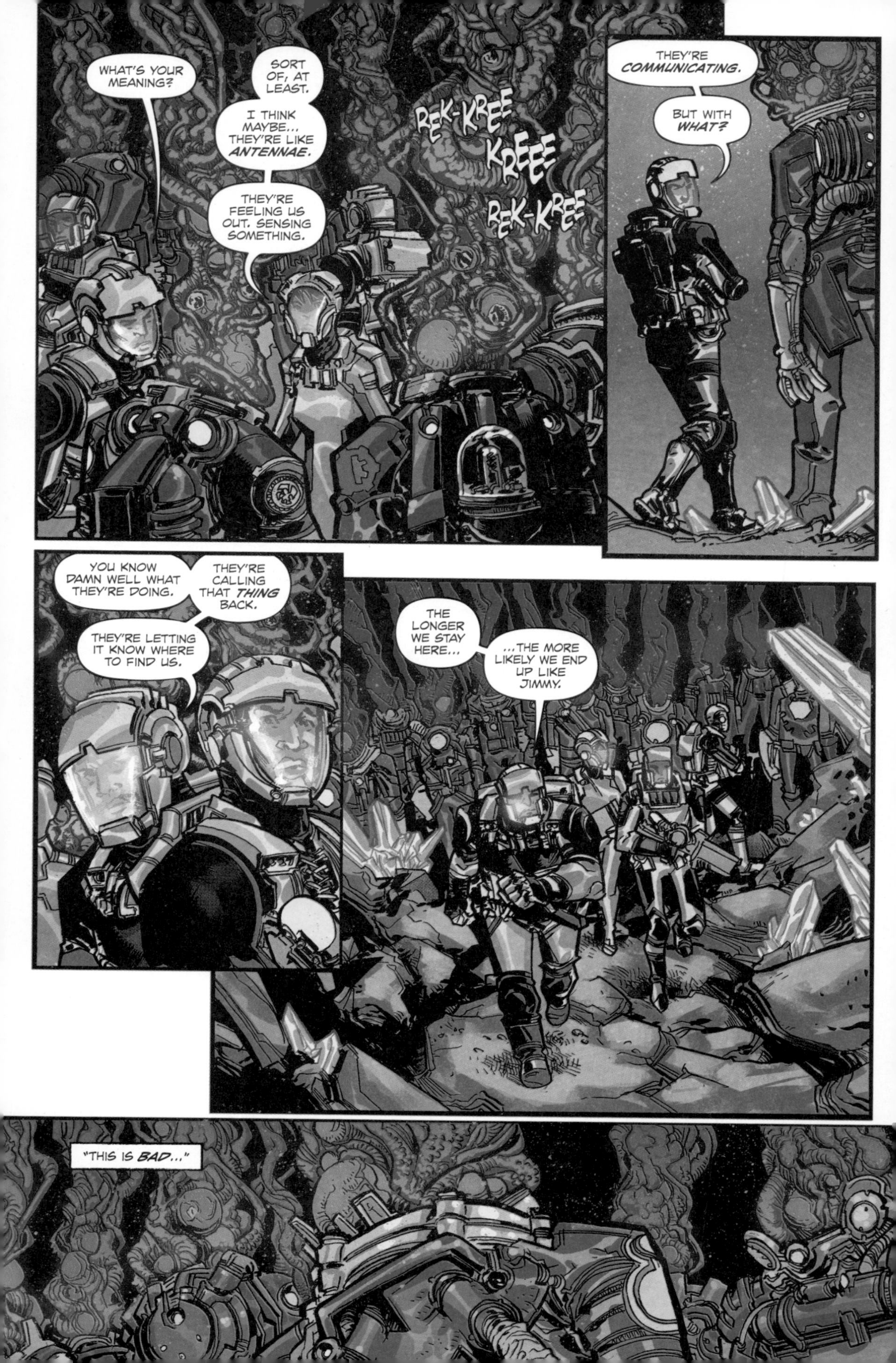
WHAT'S YOUR MEANING?
SORT OF, AT LEAST.
I THINK MAYBE... THEY'RE LIKE *ANTENNAE*.
THEY'RE FEELING US OUT. SENSING SOMETHING.
REK-KREE KREEE REK-KREE
THEY'RE *COMMUNICATING*.
BUT WITH *WHAT?*
YOU KNOW DAMN WELL WHAT THEY'RE DOING.
THEY'RE CALLING THAT *THING* BACK.
THEY'RE LETTING IT KNOW WHERE TO FIND US.
THE LONGER WE STAY HERE...
...THE MORE LIKELY WE END UP LIKE JIMMY.
"THIS IS *BAD*..."

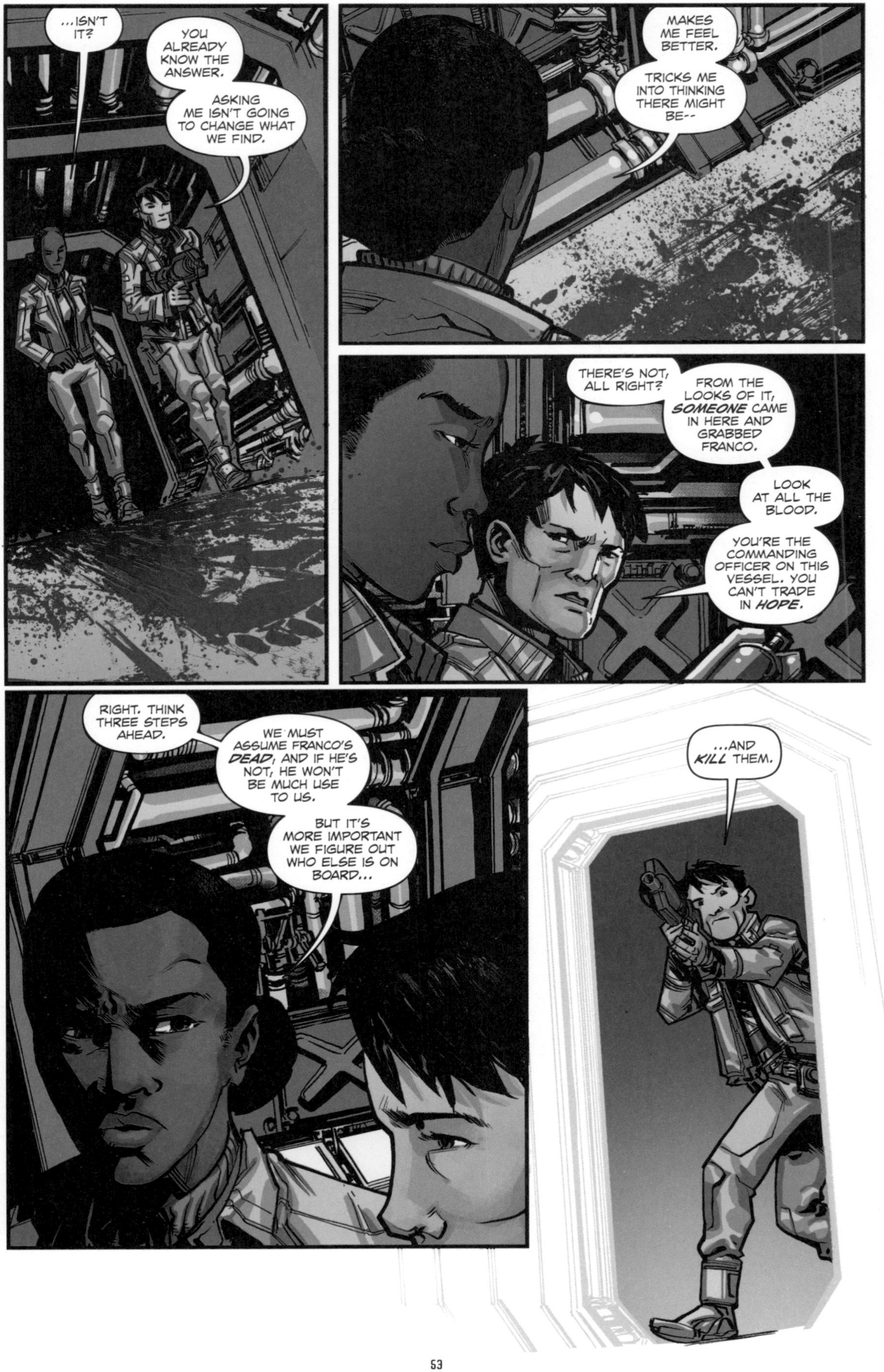
...ISN'T IT?
YOU ALREADY KNOW THE ANSWER.
ASKING ME ISN'T GOING TO CHANGE WHAT WE FIND.
MAKES ME FEEL BETTER.
TRICKS ME INTO THINKING THERE MIGHT BE--
THERE'S NOT, ALL RIGHT?
FROM THE LOOKS OF IT, SOMEONE CAME IN HERE AND GRABBED FRANCO.
LOOK AT ALL THE BLOOD.
YOU'RE THE COMMANDING OFFICER ON THIS VESSEL. YOU CAN'T TRADE IN HOPE.
RIGHT. THINK THREE STEPS AHEAD.
WE MUST ASSUME FRANCO'S DEAD, AND IF HE'S NOT, HE WON'T BE MUCH USE TO US.
BUT IT'S MORE IMPORTANT WE FIGURE OUT WHO ELSE IS ON BOARD...
...AND KILL THEM.

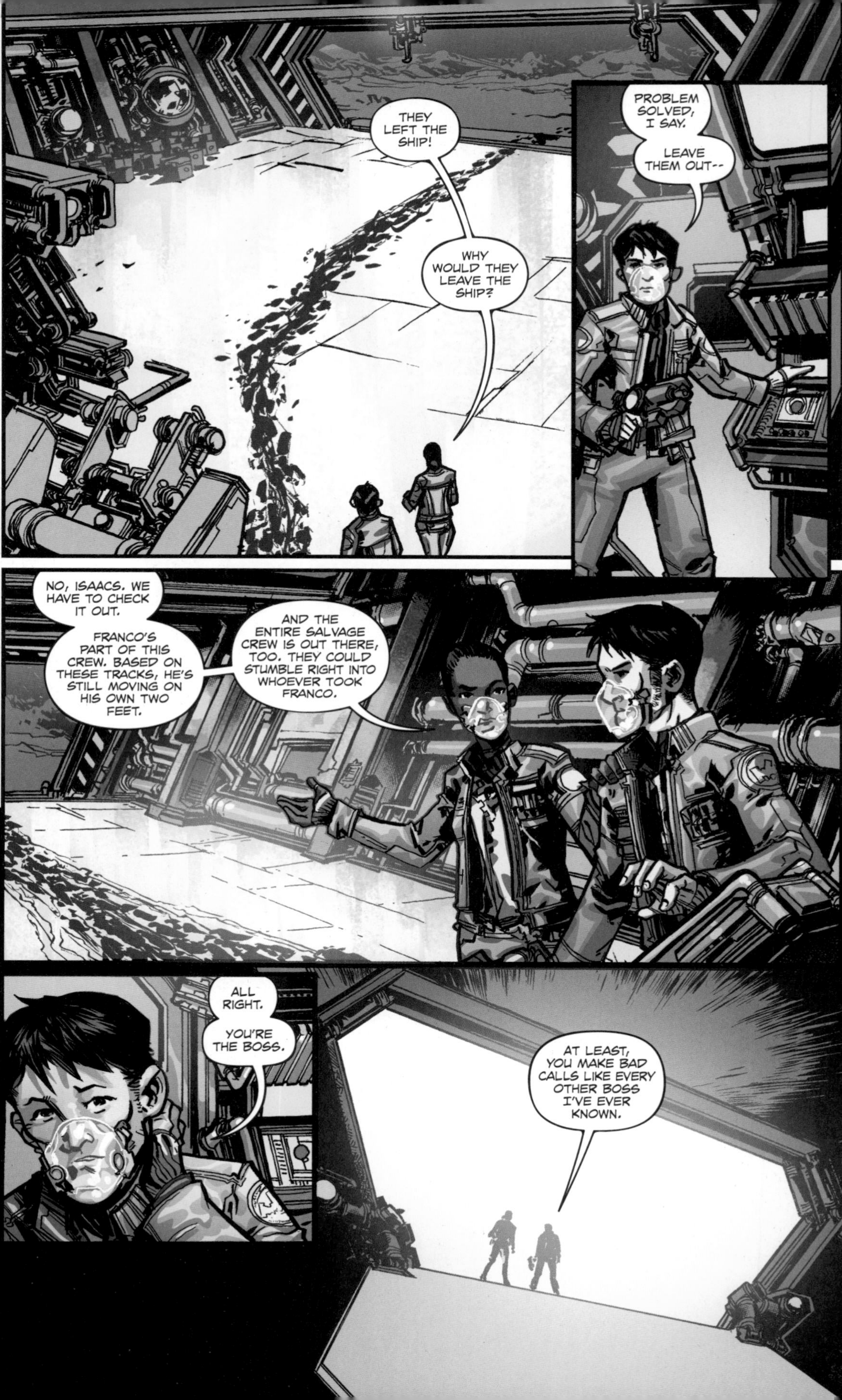
THEY LEFT THE SHIP!
WHY WOULD THEY LEAVE THE SHIP?
PROBLEM SOLVED, I SAY.
LEAVE THEM OUT--
NO, ISAACS. WE HAVE TO CHECK IT OUT.
FRANCO'S PART OF THIS CREW. BASED ON THESE TRACKS, HE'S STILL MOVING ON HIS OWN TWO FEET.
AND THE ENTIRE SALVAGE CREW IS OUT THERE, TOO. THEY COULD STUMBLE RIGHT INTO WHOEVER TOOK FRANCO.
ALL RIGHT.
YOU'RE THE BOSS.
AT LEAST, YOU MAKE BAD CALLS LIKE EVERY OTHER BOSS I'VE EVER KNOWN.

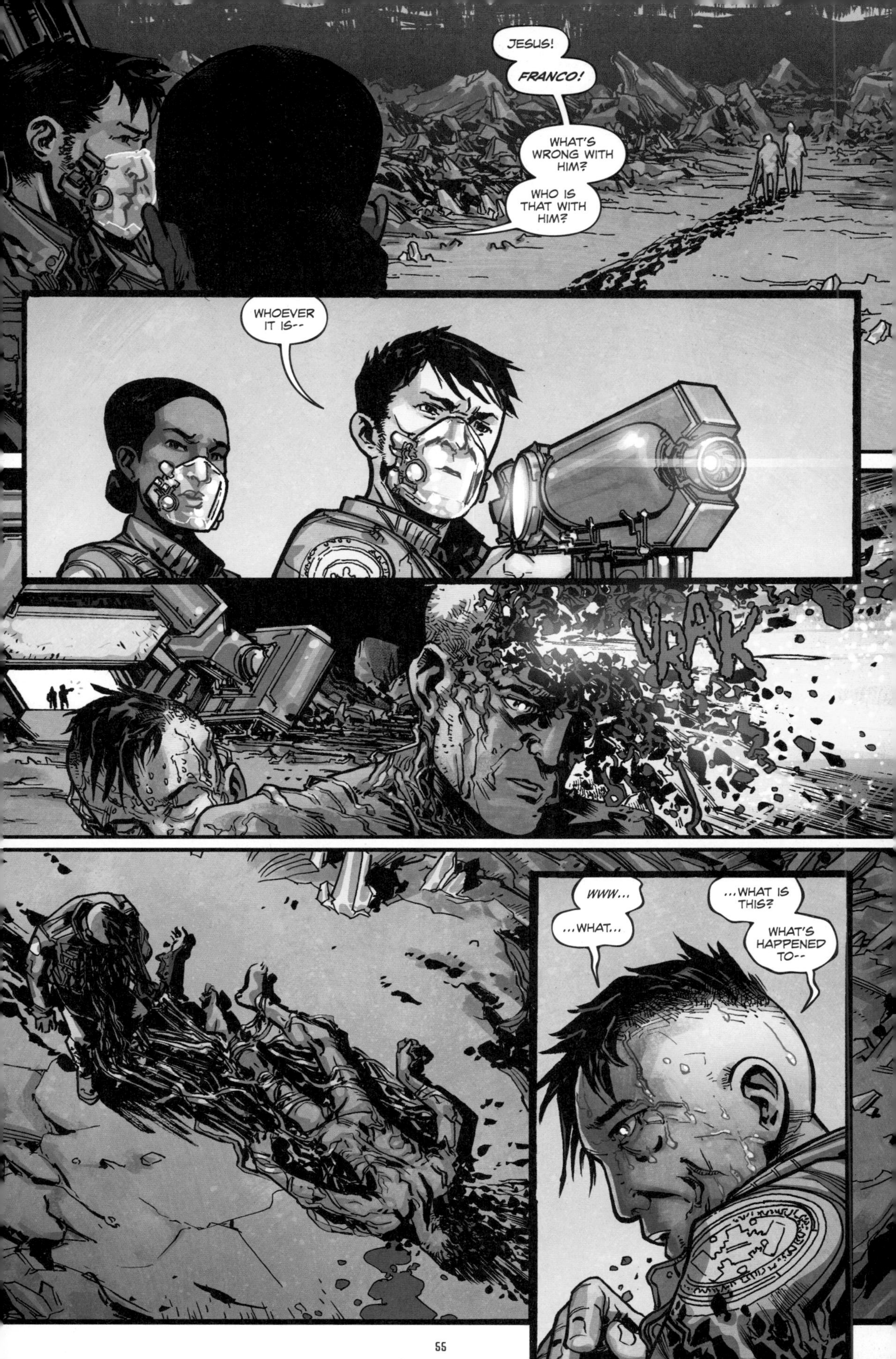
JESUS!
FRANCO!
WHAT'S WRONG WITH HIM?
WHO IS THAT WITH HIM?
WHOEVER IT IS--
VRAK
WWW...
...WHAT...
...WHAT IS THIS?
WHAT'S HAPPENED TO--

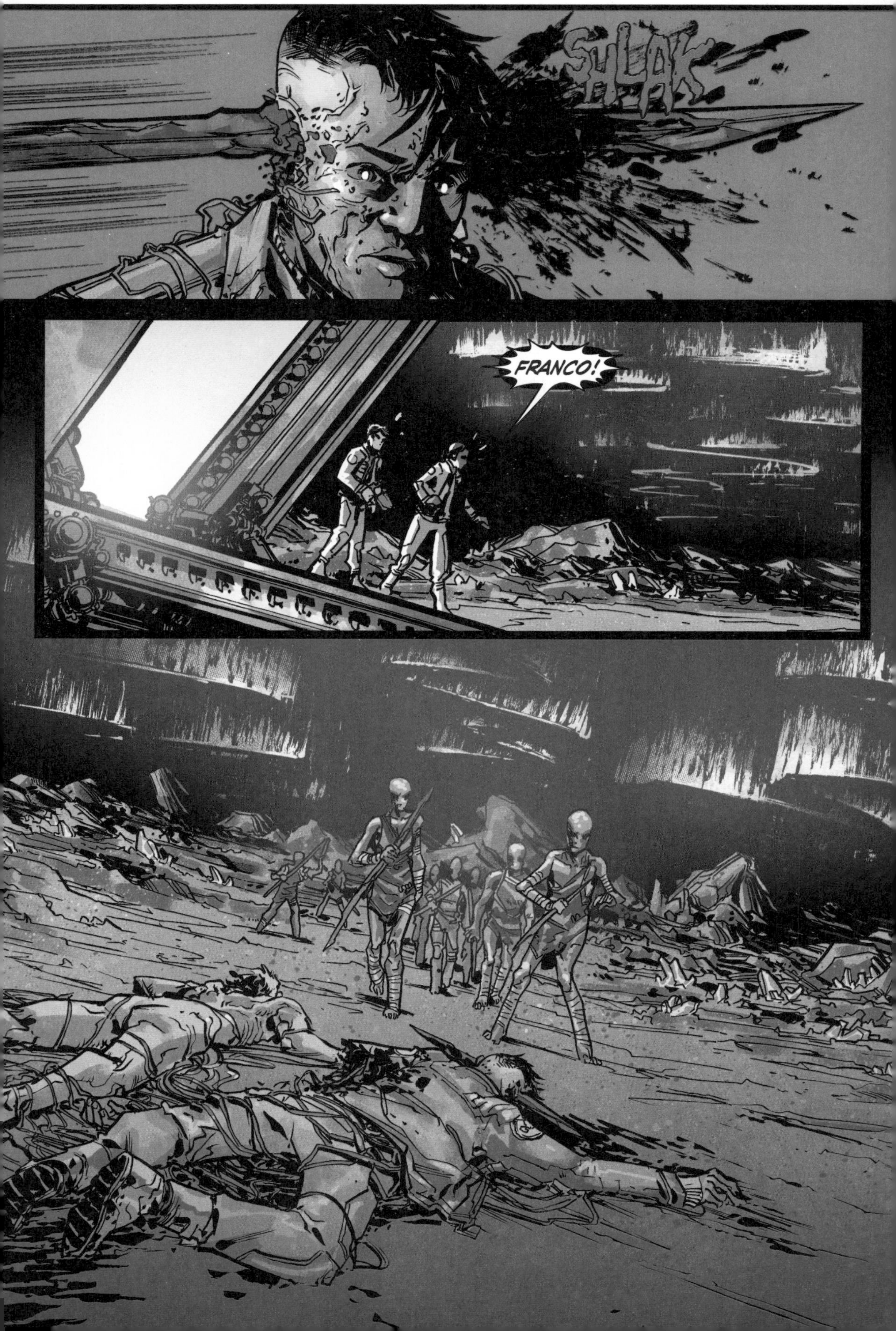
SHLAK
FRANCO!

CHAPTER 03

FEAR NOT

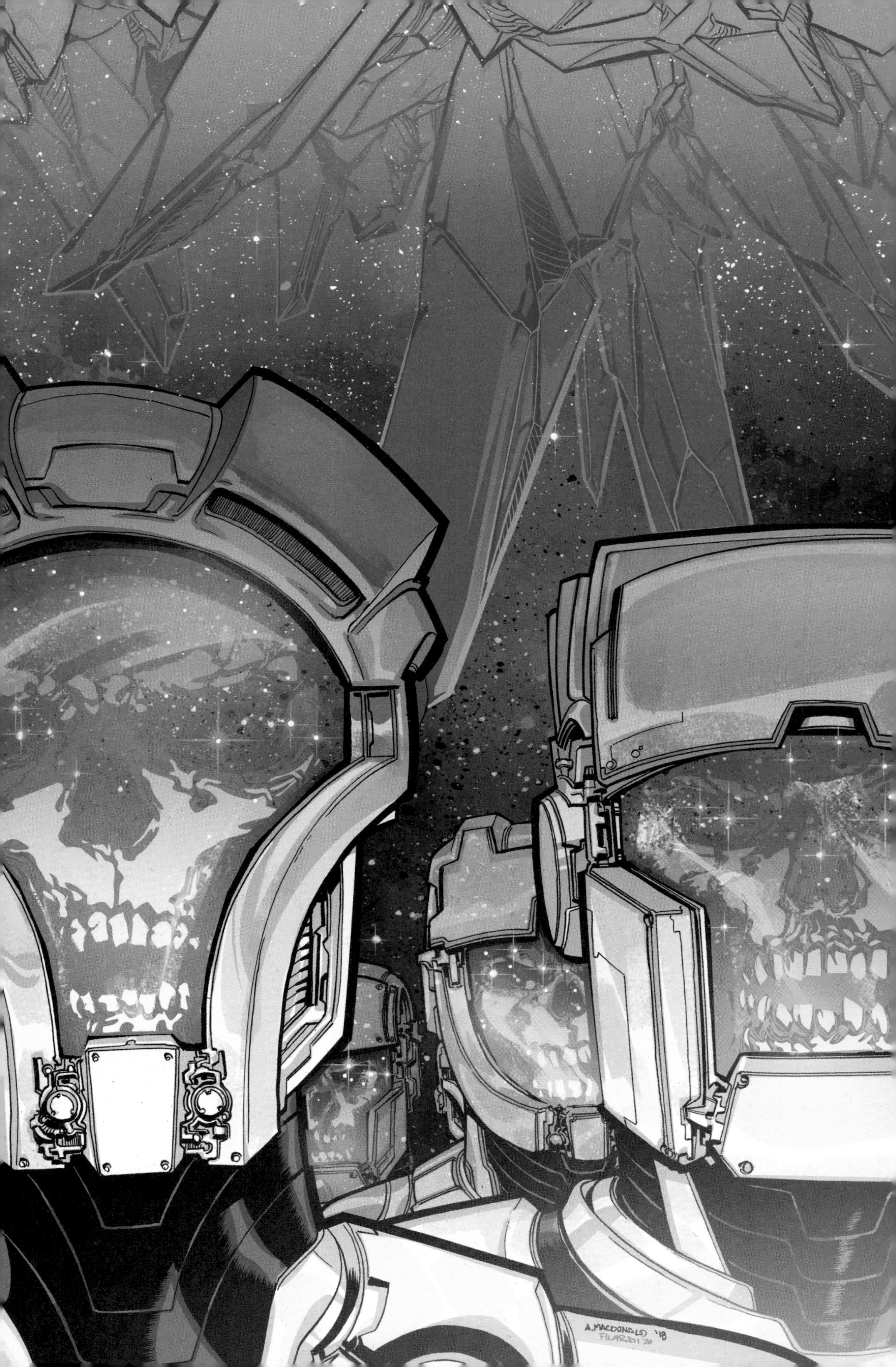
A.MACDONALD '18
FILARDI '20

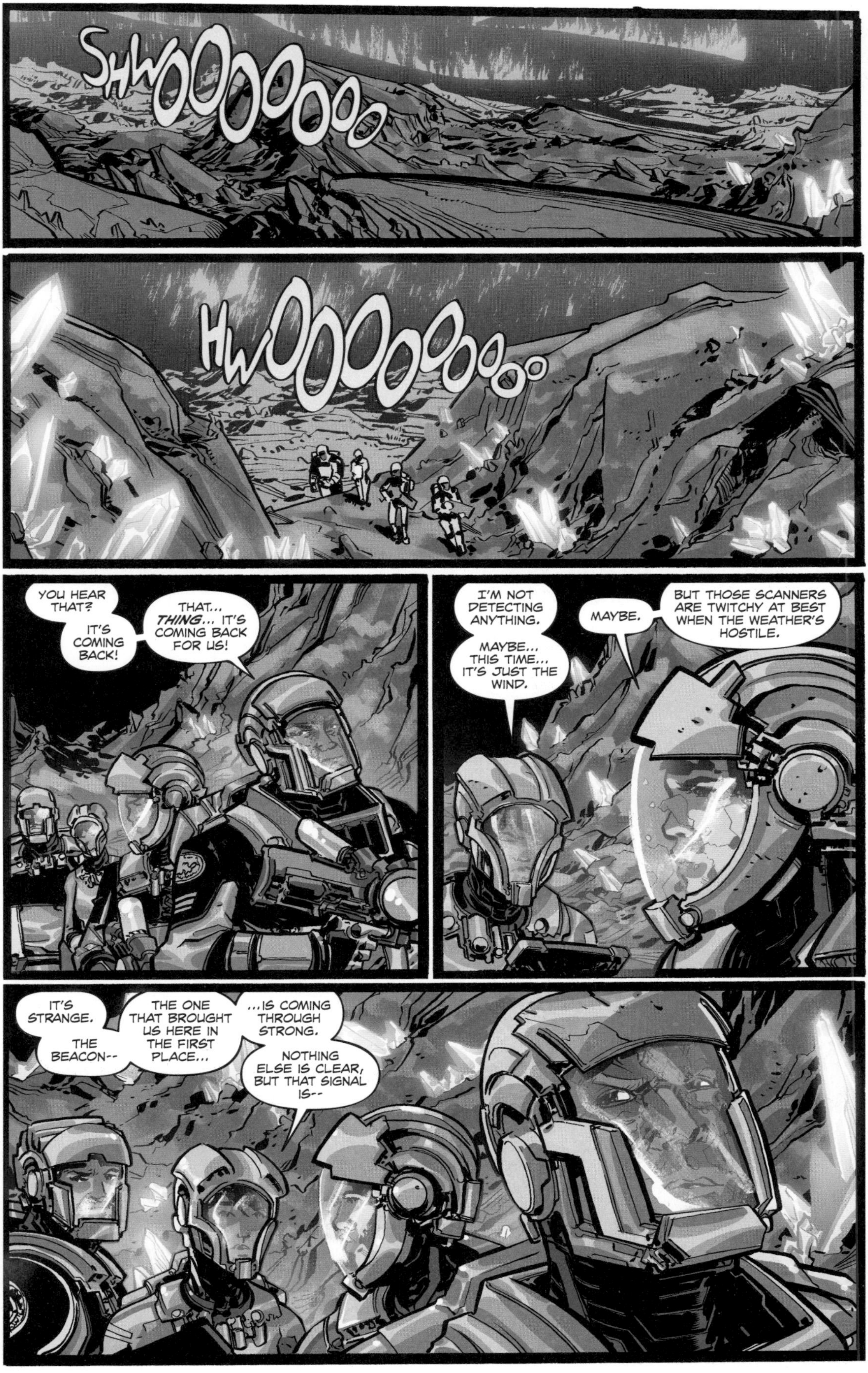
SHWOOOOOOOO
HWOOOOOOOOOO
YOU HEAR THAT?
IT'S COMING BACK!
THAT... *THING*... IT'S COMING BACK FOR US!
I'M NOT DETECTING ANYTHING.
MAYBE... THIS TIME... IT'S JUST THE WIND.
MAYBE.
BUT THOSE SCANNERS ARE TWITCHY AT BEST WHEN THE WEATHER'S HOSTILE.
IT'S STRANGE.
THE BEACON--
THE ONE THAT BROUGHT US HERE IN THE FIRST PLACE...
...IS COMING THROUGH STRONG.
NOTHING ELSE IS CLEAR, BUT THAT SIGNAL IS--

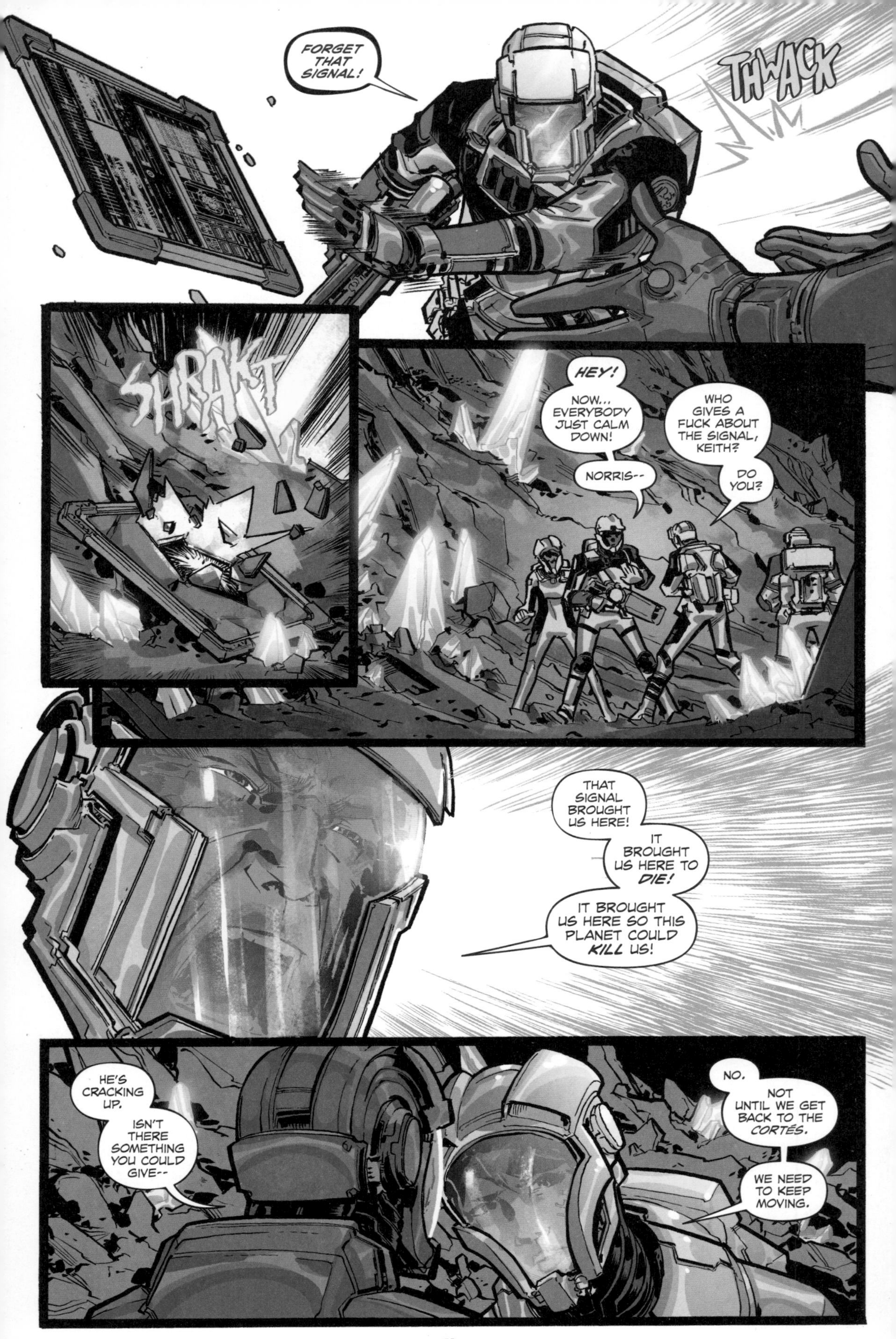
FORGET THAT SIGNAL!
THWACK
SHRAKT
HEY!
NOW... EVERYBODY JUST CALM DOWN!
NORRIS--
WHO GIVES A FUCK ABOUT THE SIGNAL, KEITH?
DO YOU?
THAT SIGNAL BROUGHT US HERE!
IT BROUGHT US HERE TO *DIE!*
IT BROUGHT US HERE SO THIS PLANET COULD *KILL* US!
HE'S CRACKING UP.
ISN'T THERE SOMETHING YOU COULD GIVE--
NO.
NOT UNTIL WE GET BACK TO THE *CORTÉS*.
WE NEED TO KEEP MOVING.

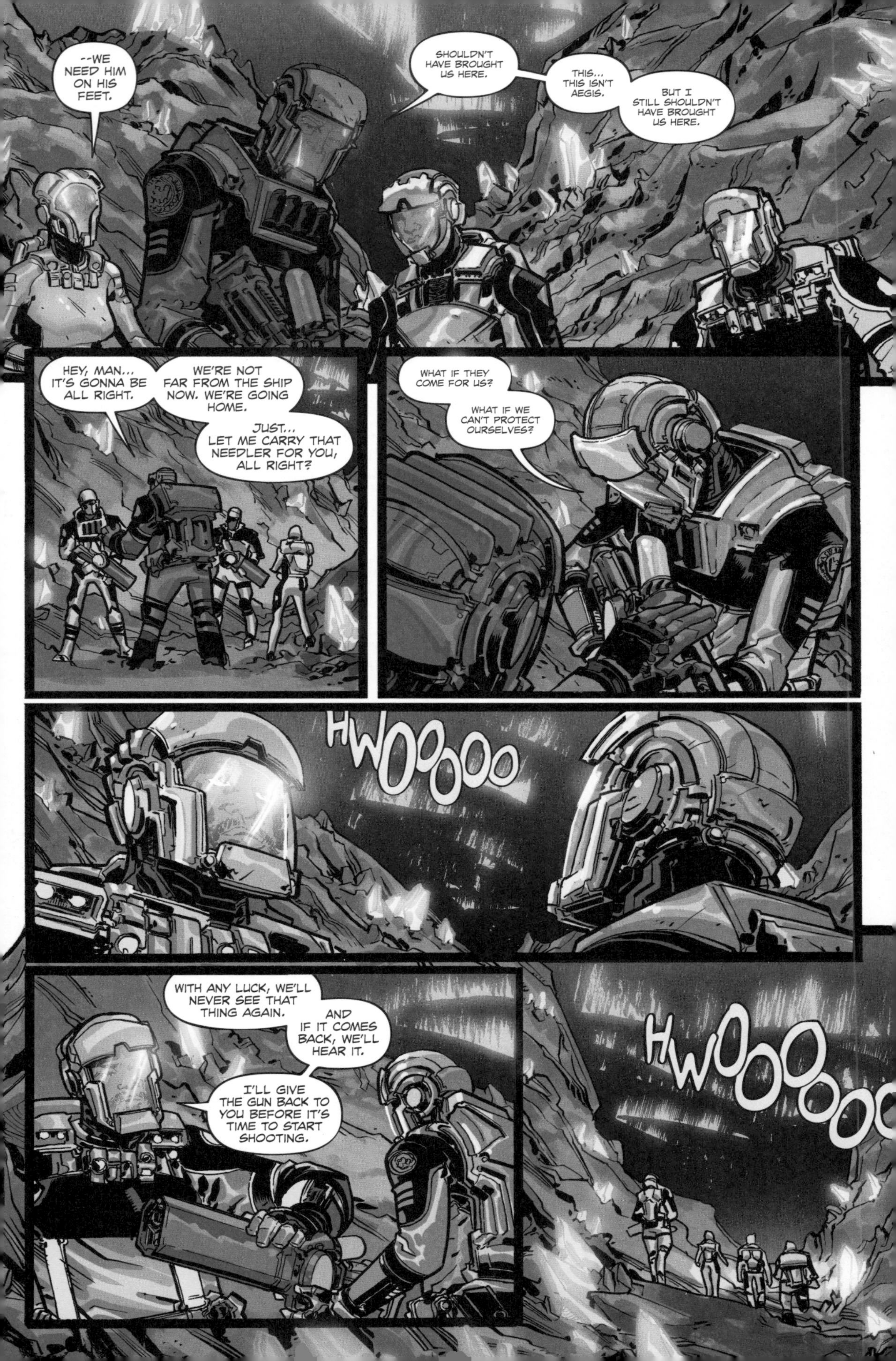
--WE NEED HIM ON HIS FEET.
SHOULDN'T HAVE BROUGHT US HERE.
THIS... THIS ISN'T AEGIS.
BUT I STILL SHOULDN'T HAVE BROUGHT US HERE.
HEY, MAN... IT'S GONNA BE ALL RIGHT.
WE'RE NOT FAR FROM THE SHIP NOW. WE'RE GOING HOME.
JUST... LET ME CARRY THAT NEEDLER FOR YOU, ALL RIGHT?
WHAT IF THEY COME FOR US?
WHAT IF WE CAN'T PROTECT OURSELVES?
HWOOOOO
WITH ANY LUCK, WE'LL NEVER SEE THAT THING AGAIN.
AND IF IT COMES BACK, WE'LL HEAR IT.
I'LL GIVE THE GUN BACK TO YOU BEFORE IT'S TIME TO START SHOOTING.
HWOOOOOO

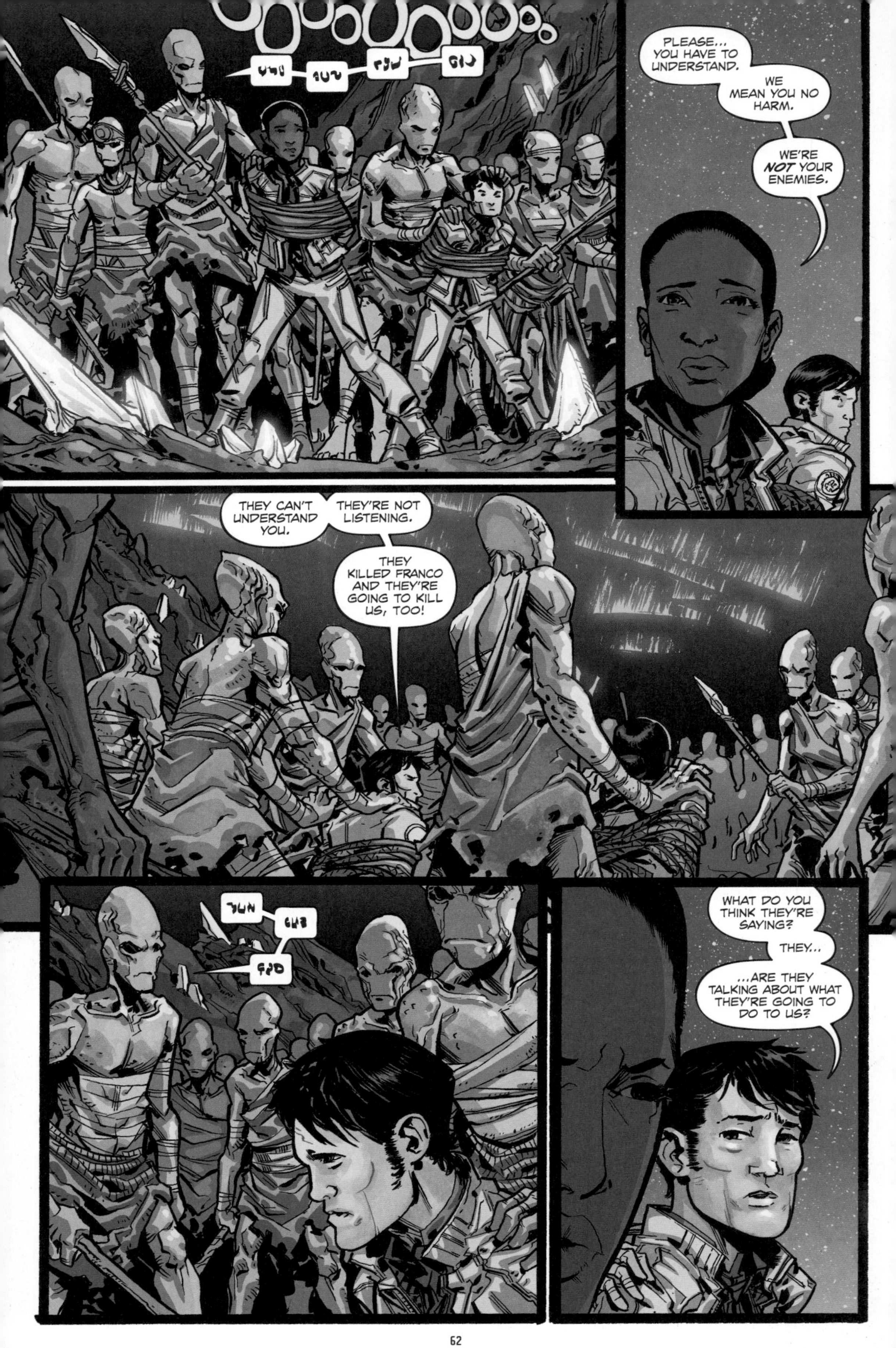
PLEASE... YOU HAVE TO UNDERSTAND.
WE MEAN YOU NO HARM.
WE'RE NOT YOUR ENEMIES.
THEY CAN'T UNDERSTAND YOU.
THEY'RE NOT LISTENING.
THEY KILLED FRANCO AND THEY'RE GOING TO KILL US, TOO!
WHAT DO YOU THINK THEY'RE SAYING?
THEY...
...ARE THEY TALKING ABOUT WHAT THEY'RE GOING TO DO TO US?

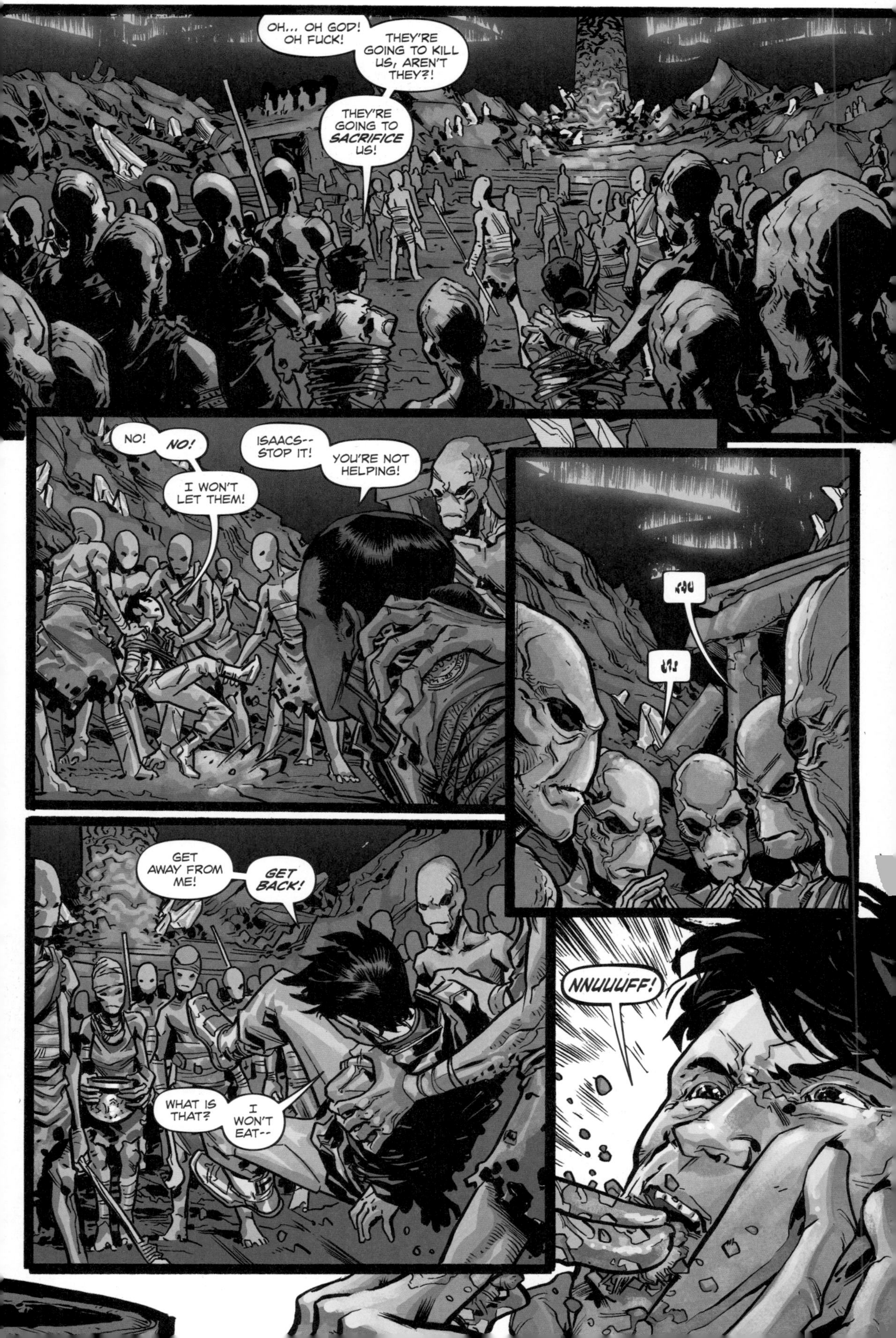
OH... OH GOD! OH FUCK!
THEY'RE GOING TO KILL US, AREN'T THEY?!
THEY'RE GOING TO SACRIFICE US!
NO! NO!
I WON'T LET THEM!
ISAACS-- STOP IT!
YOU'RE NOT HELPING!
GET AWAY FROM ME!
GET BACK!
WHAT IS THAT?
I WON'T EAT--
NNUUUFF!

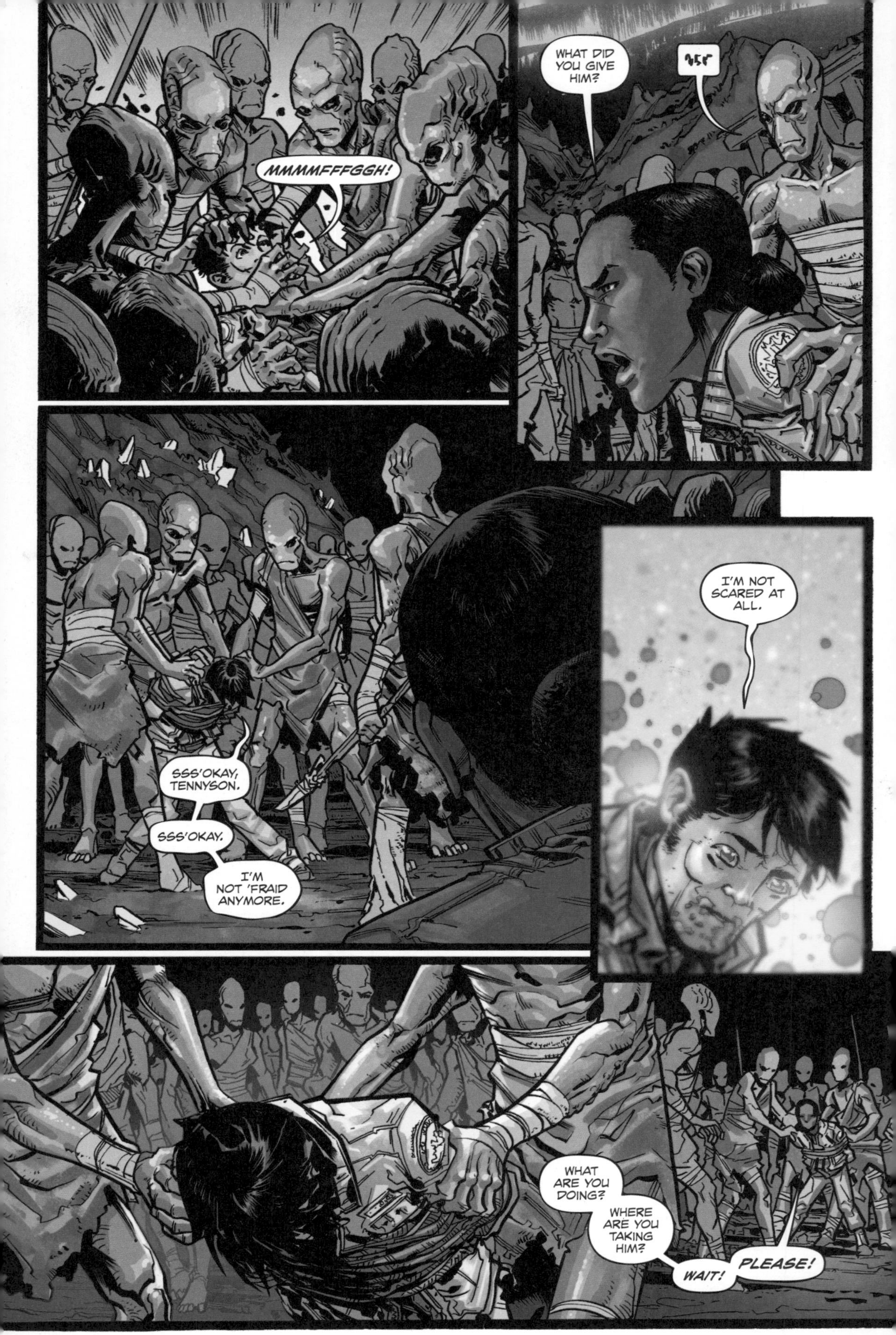
MMMMFFFGGH!
WHAT DID YOU GIVE HIM?
SSS'OKAY, TENNYSON.
SSS'OKAY.
I'M NOT 'FRAID ANYMORE.
I'M NOT SCARED AT ALL.
WHAT ARE YOU DOING?
WHERE ARE YOU TAKING HIM?
WAIT!
PLEASE!

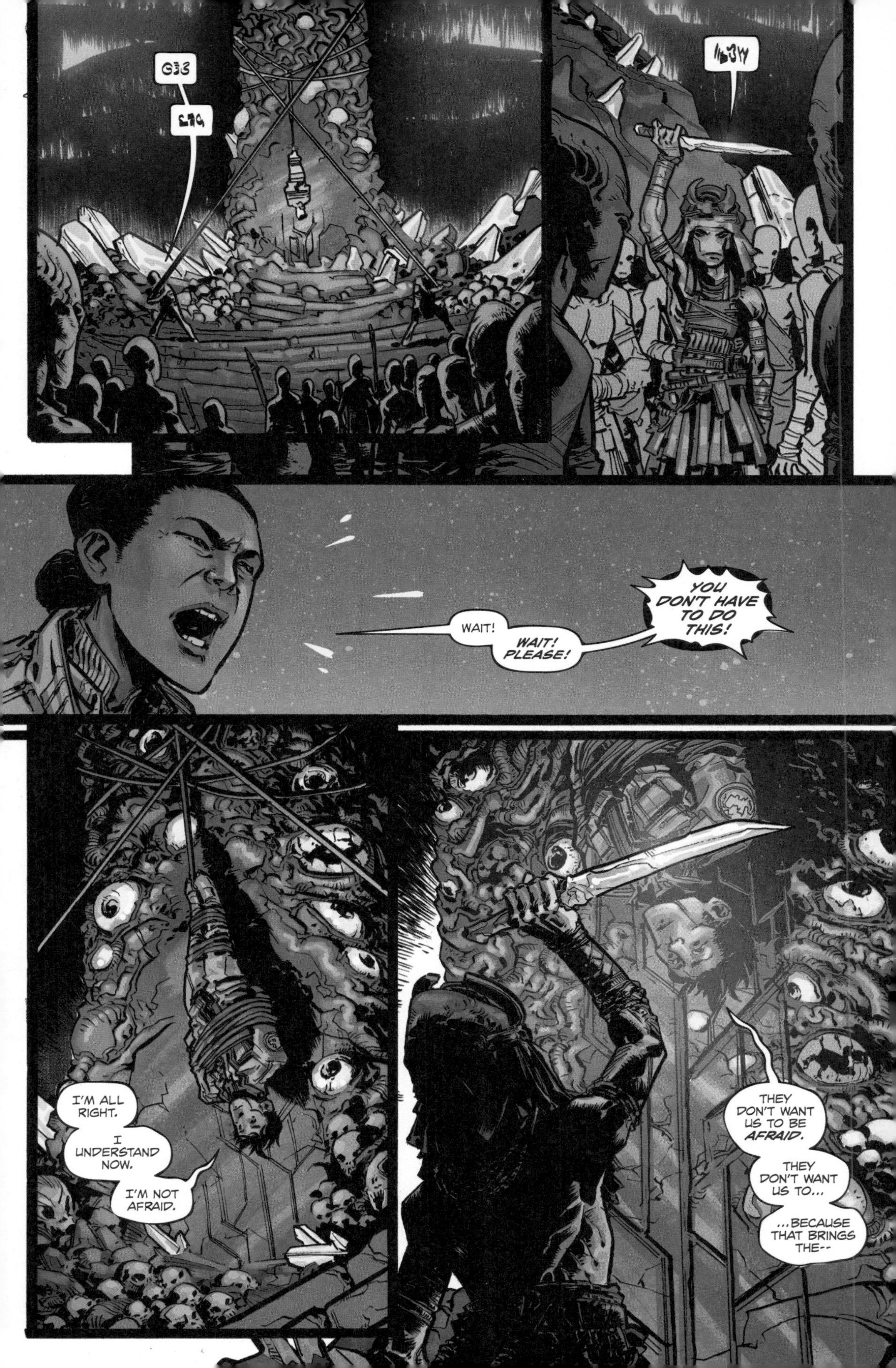
WAIT!
WAIT! PLEASE!
YOU DON'T HAVE TO DO THIS!
I'M ALL RIGHT.
I UNDERSTAND NOW.
I'M NOT AFRAID.
THEY DON'T WANT US TO BE AFRAID.
THEY DON'T WANT US TO...
...BECAUSE THAT BRINGS THE--

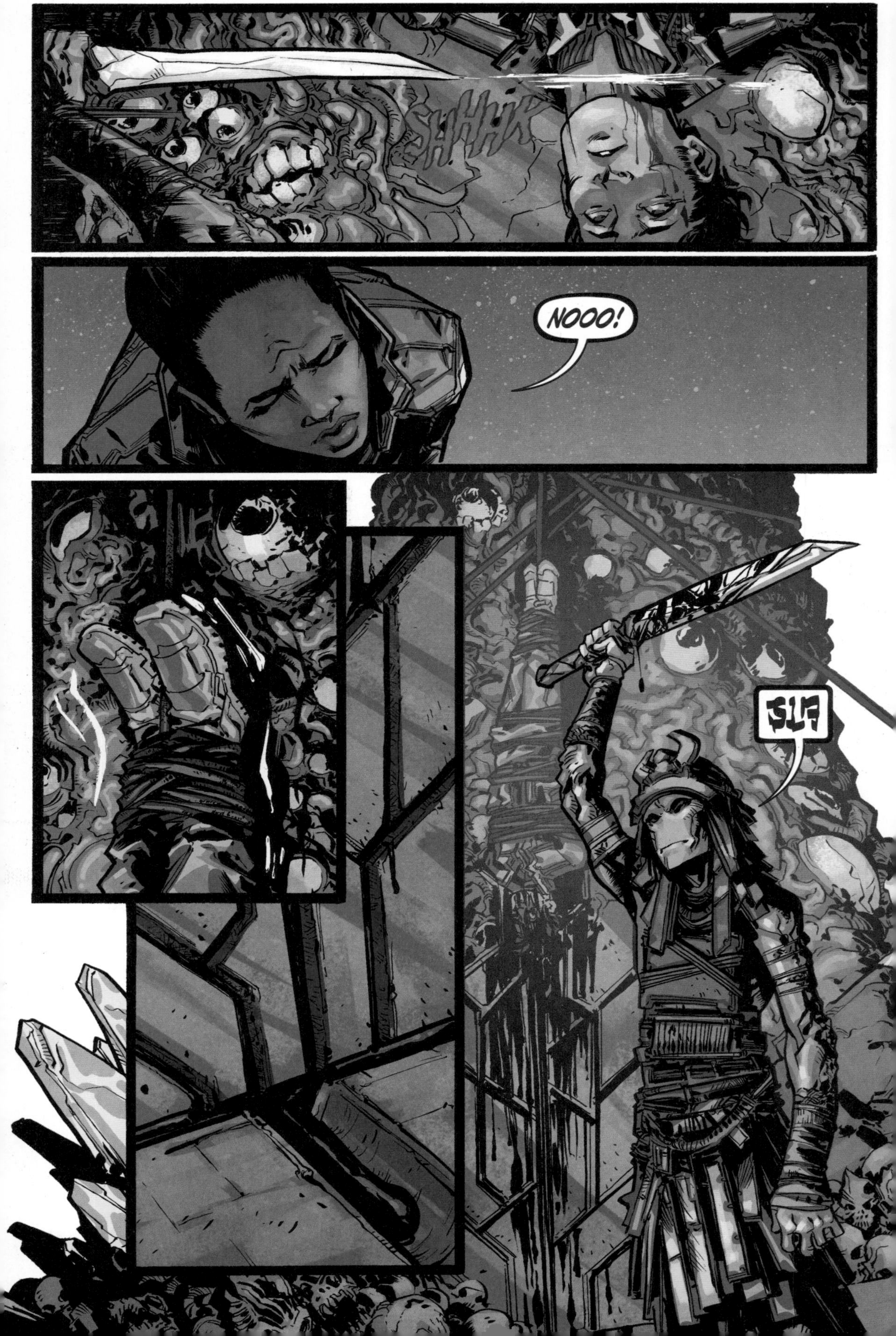
SHHHK
NOOO!

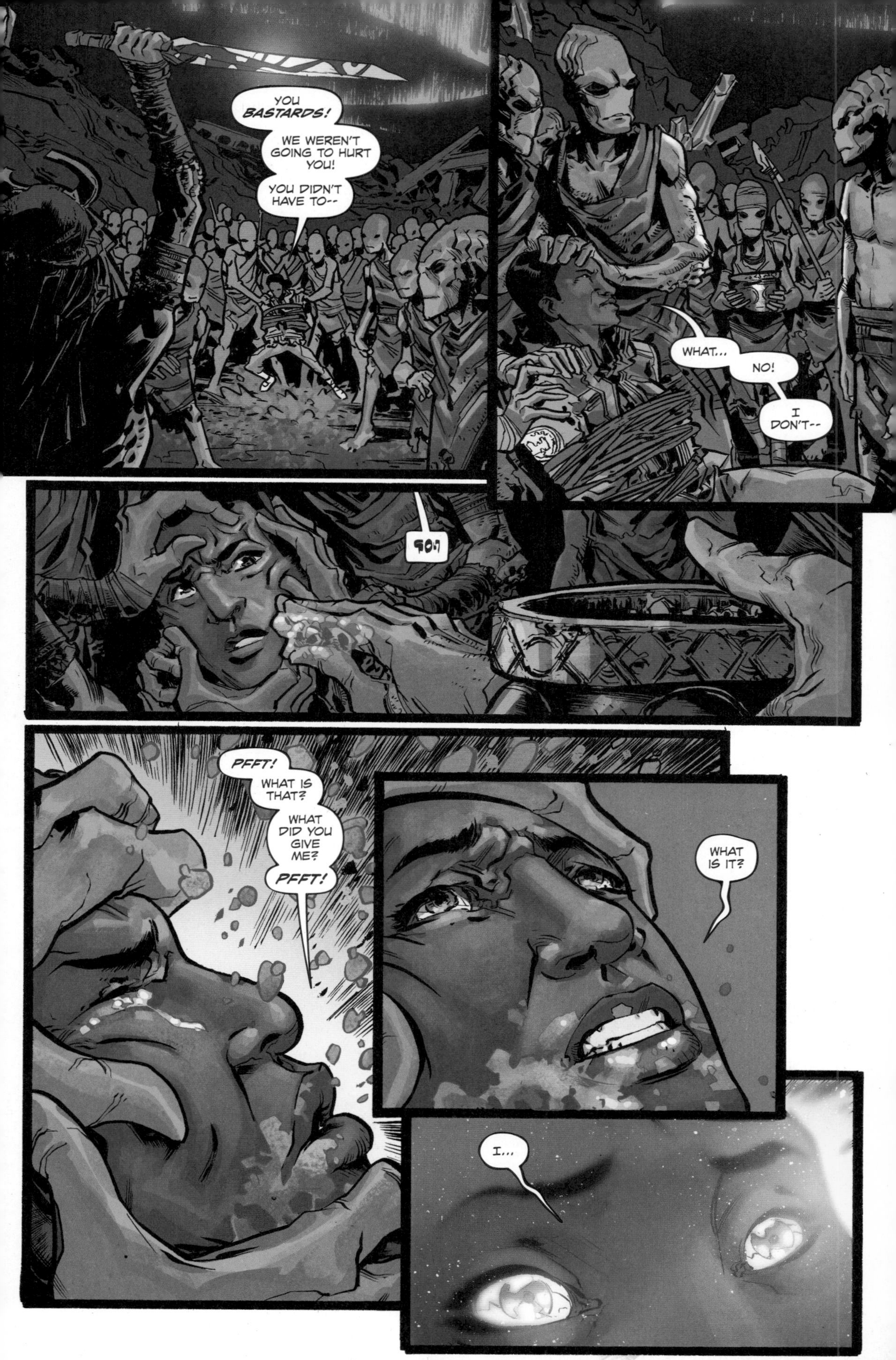
YOU BASTARDS!
WE WEREN'T GOING TO HURT YOU!
YOU DIDN'T HAVE TO--
WHAT...
NO!
I DON'T--
PFFT!
WHAT IS THAT?
WHAT DID YOU GIVE ME?
PFFT!
WHAT IS IT?
I...

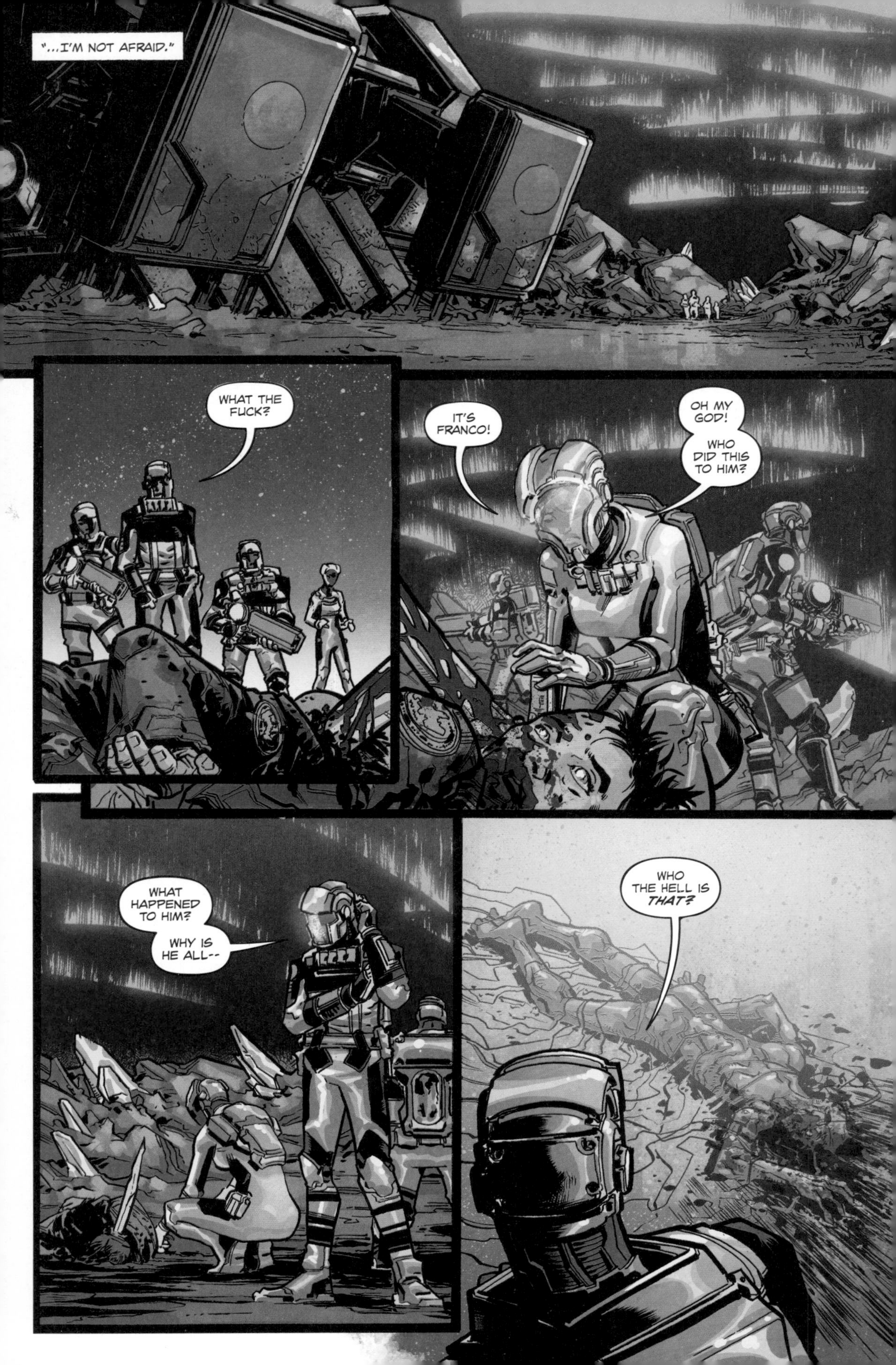
"...I'M NOT AFRAID."
WHAT THE FUCK?
IT'S FRANCO!
OH MY GOD!
WHO DID THIS TO HIM?
WHAT HAPPENED TO HIM?
WHY IS HE ALL--
WHO THE HELL IS *THAT?*

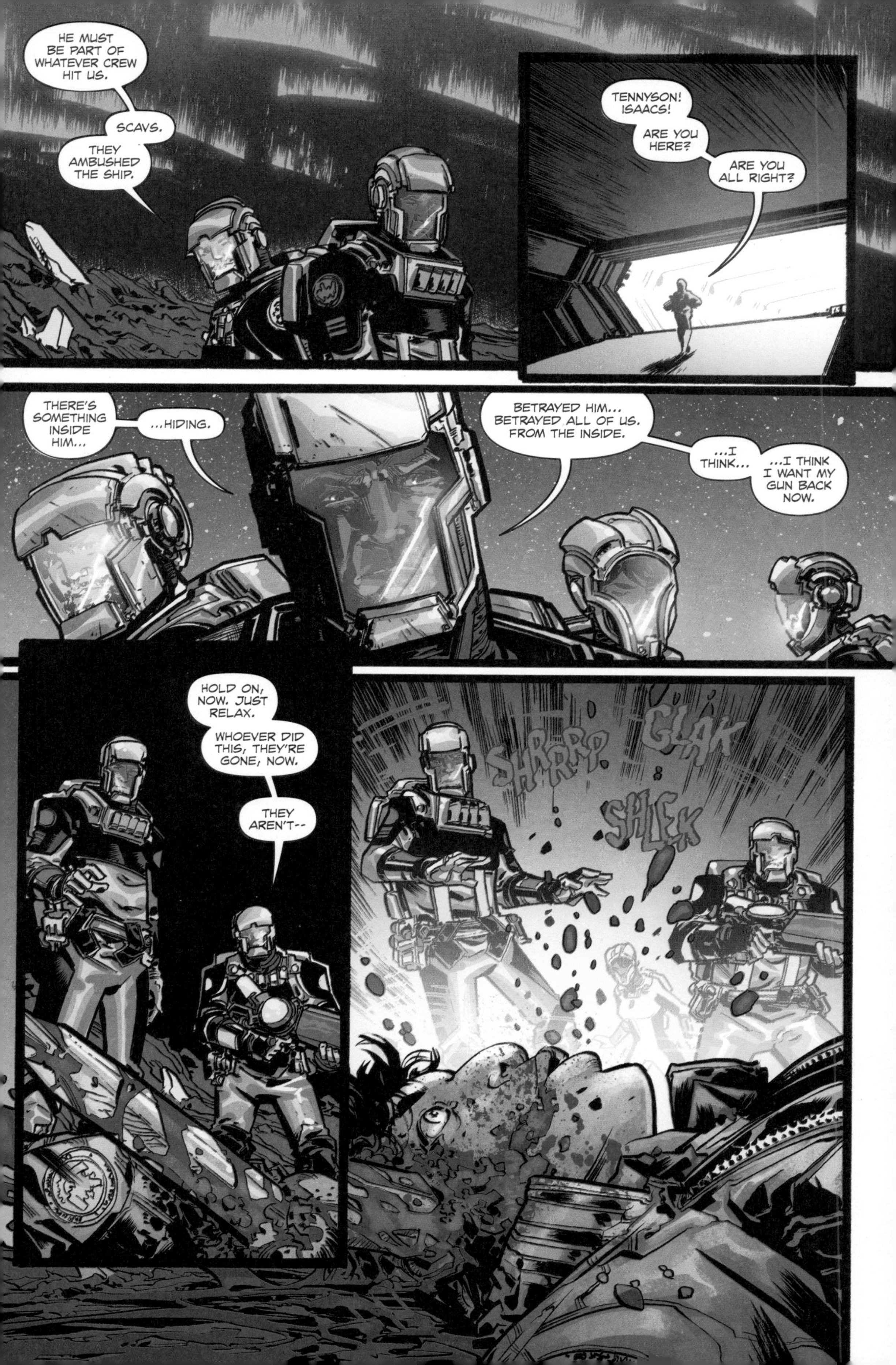
HE MUST BE PART OF WHATEVER CREW HIT US.
SCAVS.
THEY AMBUSHED THE SHIP.
TENNYSON! ISAACS!
ARE YOU HERE?
ARE YOU ALL RIGHT?
THERE'S SOMETHING INSIDE HIM...
...HIDING.
BETRAYED HIM... BETRAYED ALL OF US. FROM THE INSIDE.
...I THINK...
...I THINK I WANT MY GUN BACK NOW.
HOLD ON, NOW. JUST RELAX.
WHOEVER DID THIS, THEY'RE GONE, NOW.
THEY AREN'T--
SHRRP
GLAK
SHLEK

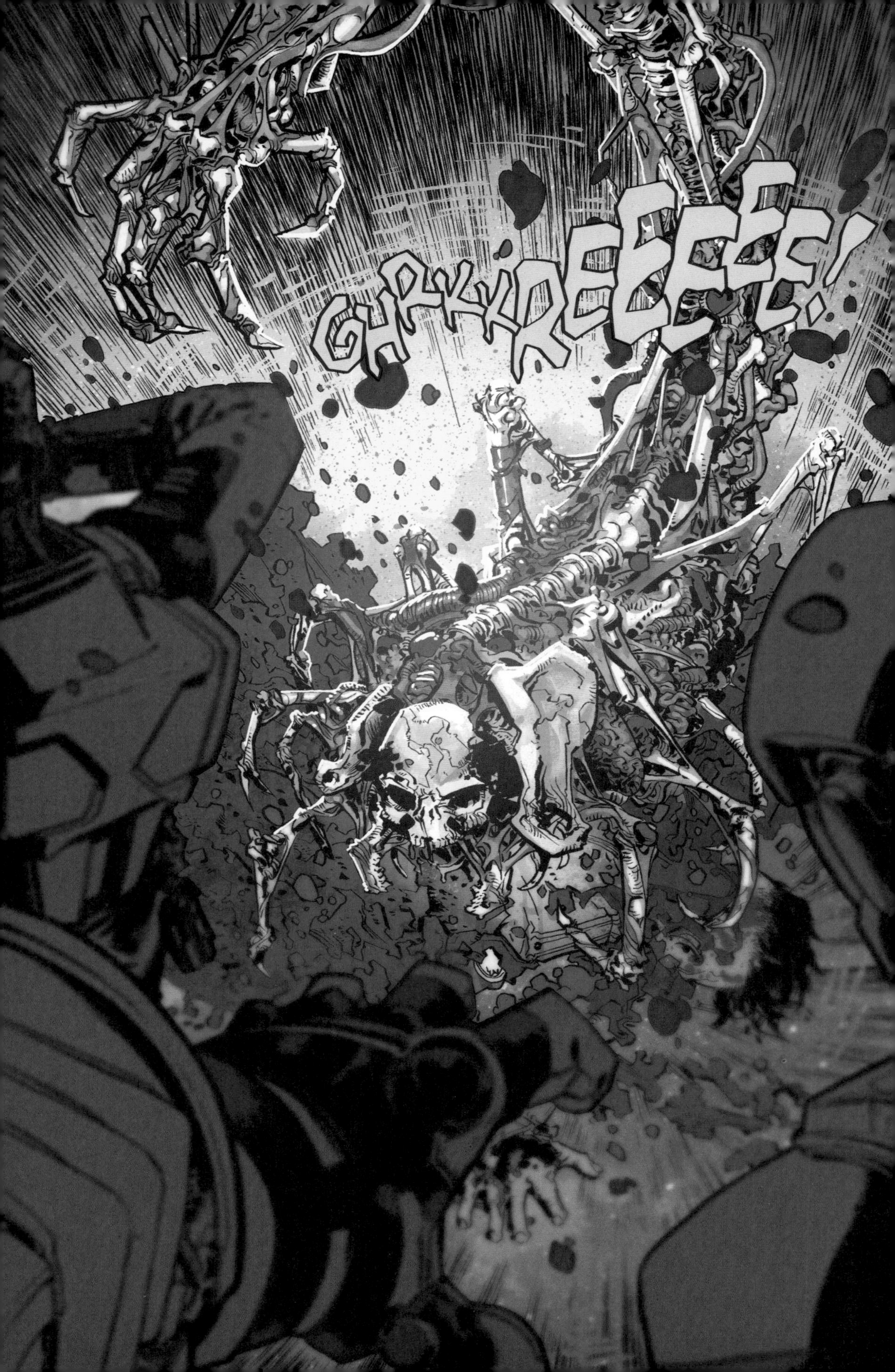
GHRKKREEEEEE!!

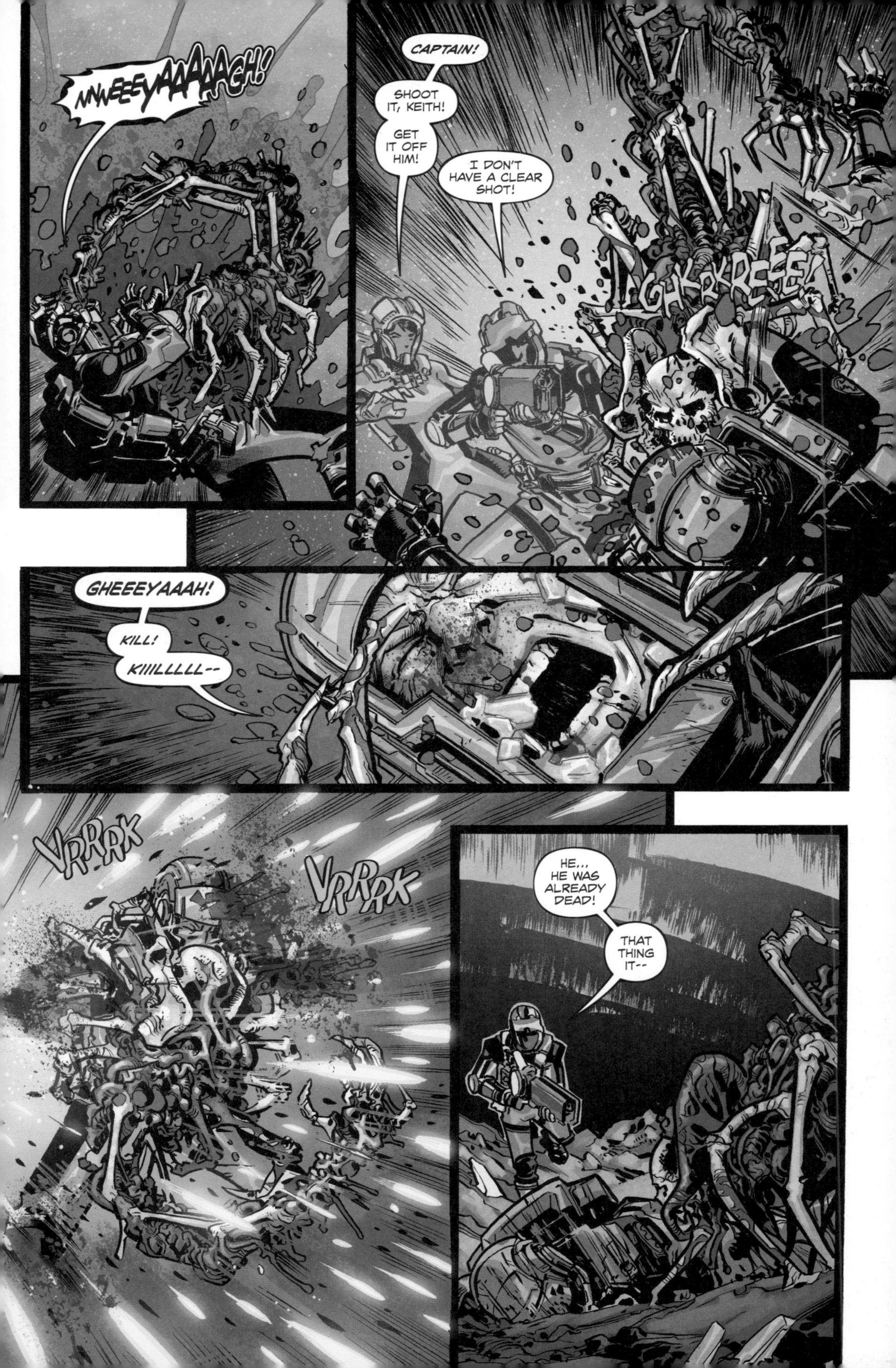
NNWEEEYAAAAAGH!
CAPTAIN!
SHOOT IT, KEITH!
GET IT OFF HIM!
I DON'T HAVE A CLEAR SHOT!
GHKKREEE!
GHEEEYAAAH!
KILL!
KIIILLLLL--
VRRRK
VRRRK
HE... HE WAS ALREADY DEAD!
THAT THING IT--

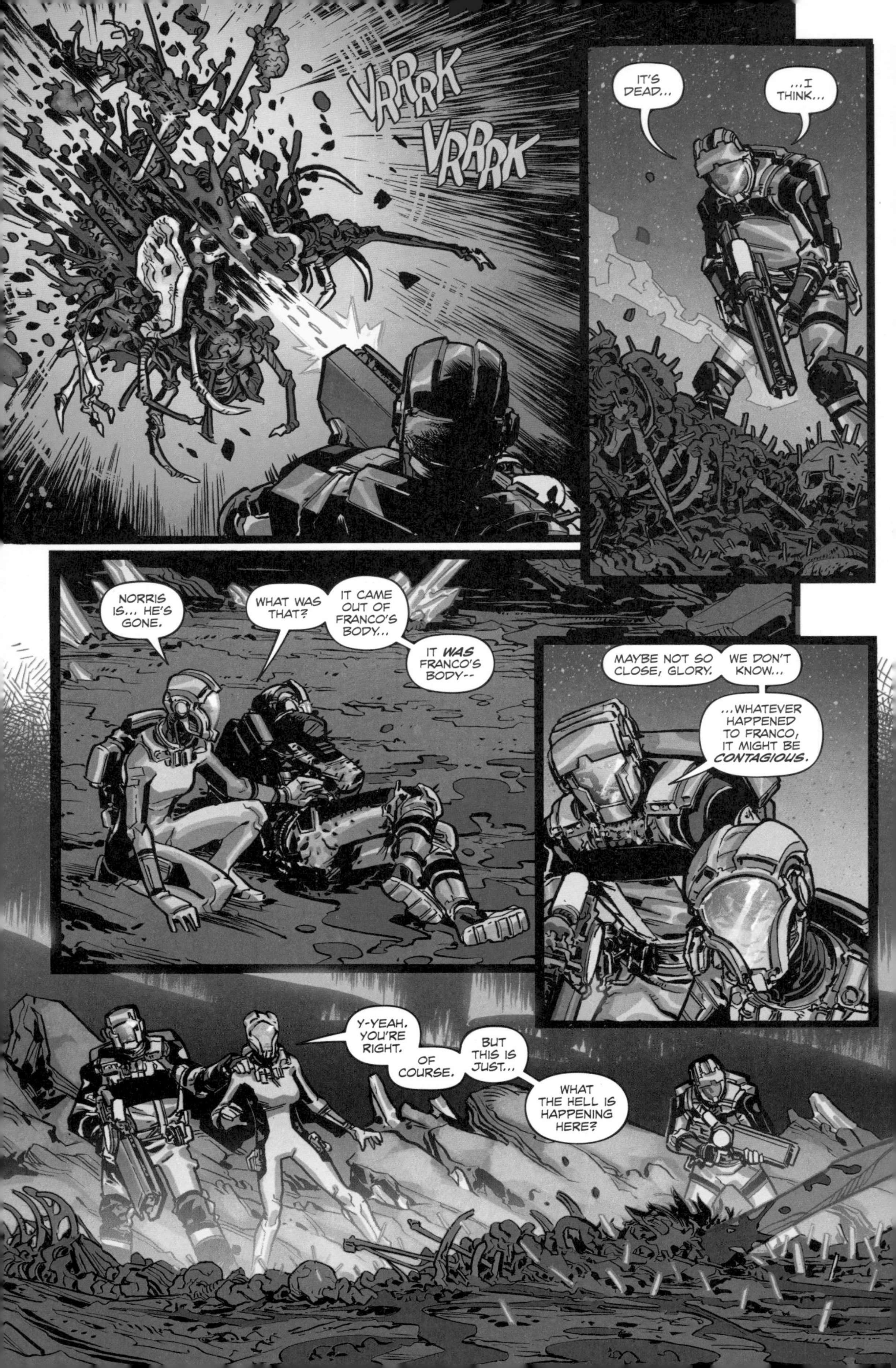
VRRRK
VRRRK
IT'S DEAD...
...I THINK...
NORRIS IS... HE'S GONE.
WHAT WAS THAT?
IT CAME OUT OF FRANCO'S BODY...
IT *WAS* FRANCO'S BODY--
MAYBE NOT SO CLOSE, GLORY.
WE DON'T KNOW...
...WHATEVER HAPPENED TO FRANCO, IT MIGHT BE *CONTAGIOUS*.
Y-YEAH. YOU'RE RIGHT.
OF COURSE.
BUT THIS IS JUST...
WHAT THE HELL IS HAPPENING HERE?

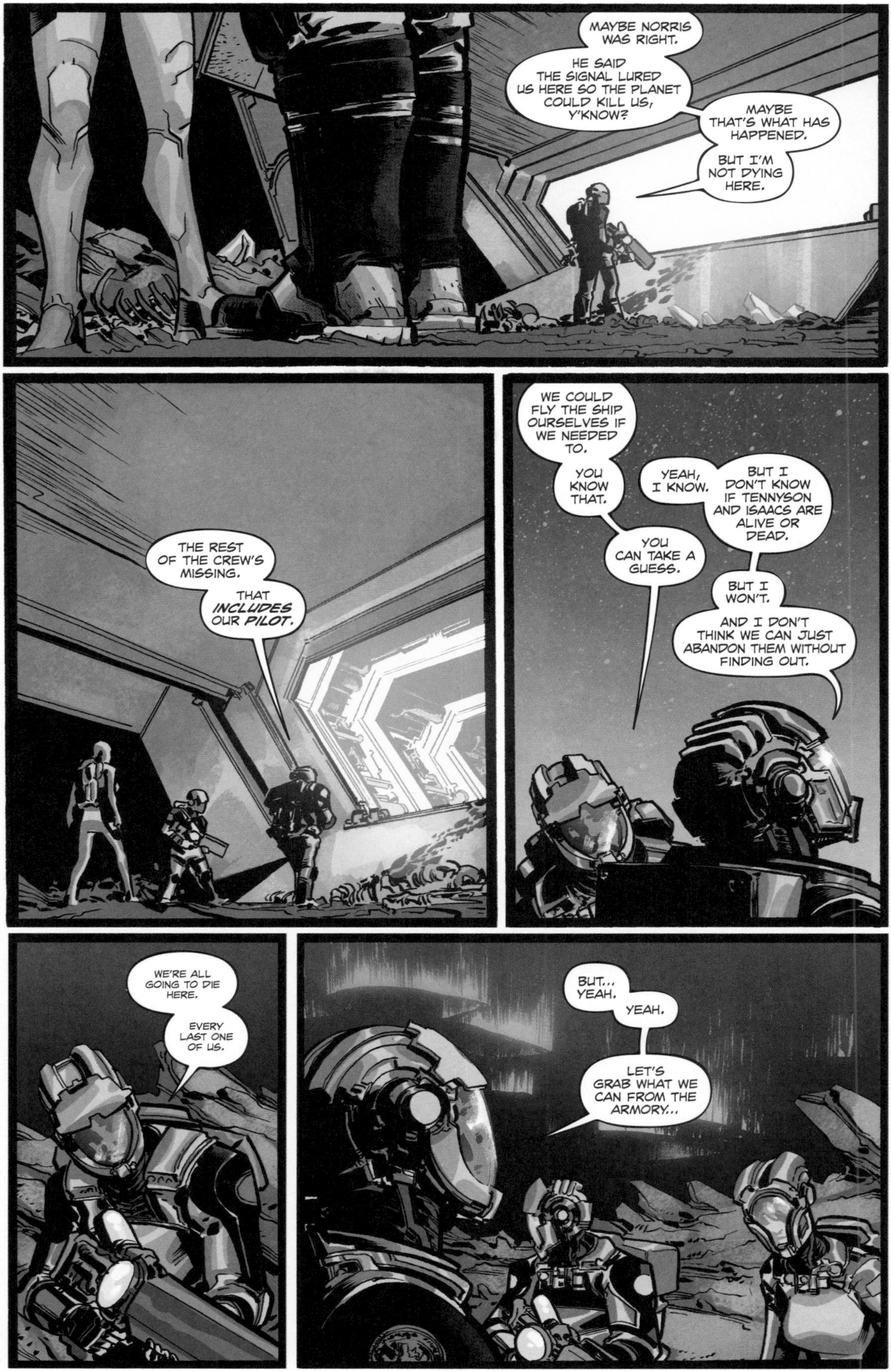
MAYBE NORRIS WAS RIGHT.
HE SAID THE SIGNAL LURED US HERE SO THE PLANET COULD KILL US, Y'KNOW?
MAYBE THAT'S WHAT HAS HAPPENED.
BUT I'M NOT DYING HERE.
THE REST OF THE CREW'S MISSING.
THAT *INCLUDES* OUR *PILOT*.
WE COULD FLY THE SHIP OURSELVES IF WE NEEDED TO.
YOU KNOW THAT.
YEAH, I KNOW.
BUT I DON'T KNOW IF TENNYSON AND ISAACS ARE ALIVE OR DEAD.
YOU CAN TAKE A GUESS.
BUT I WON'T.
AND I DON'T THINK WE CAN JUST ABANDON THEM WITHOUT FINDING OUT.
WE'RE ALL GOING TO DIE HERE.
EVERY LAST ONE OF US.
BUT... YEAH.
YEAH.
LET'S GRAB WHAT WE CAN FROM THE ARMORY...

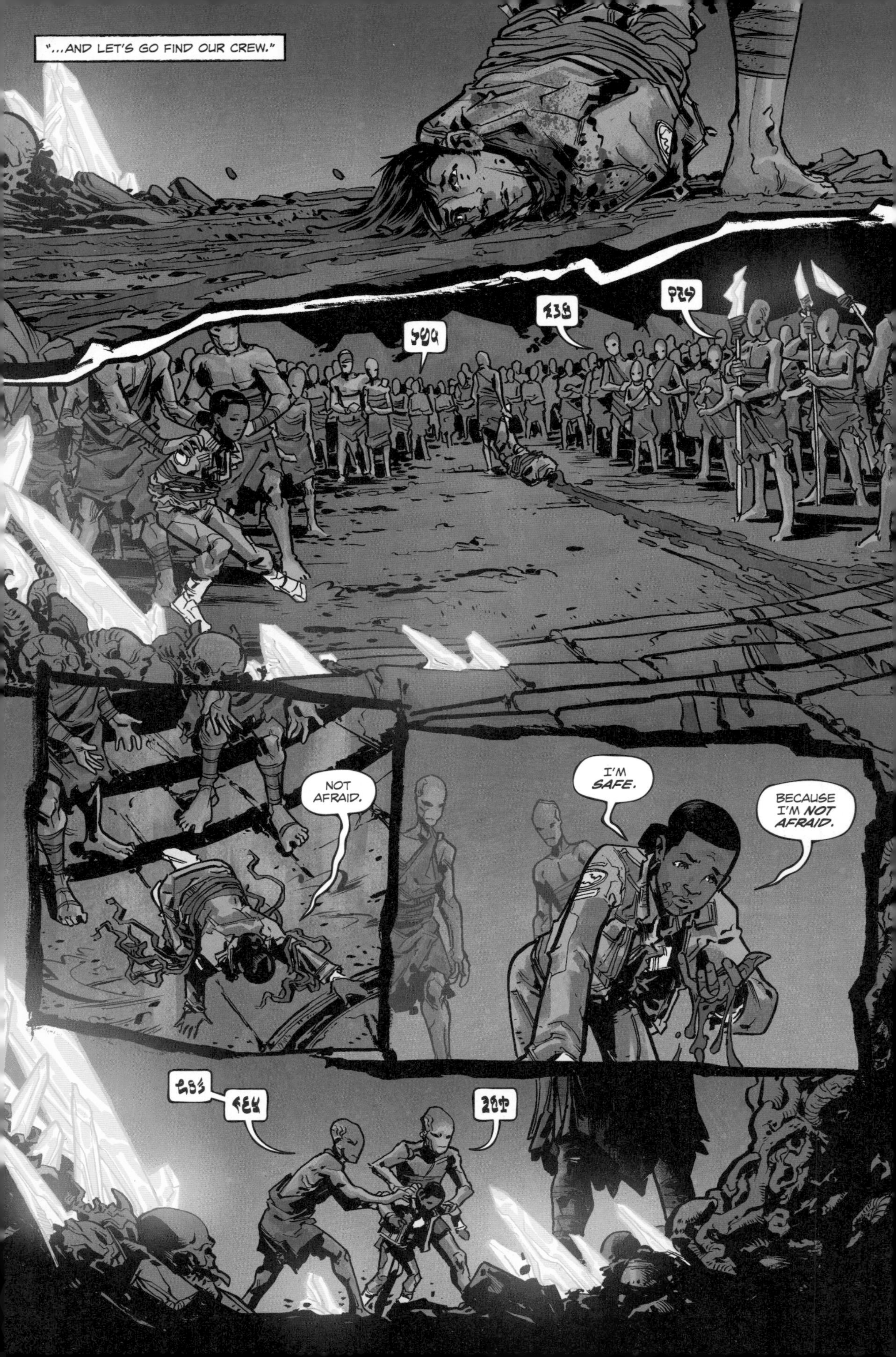
"...AND LET'S GO FIND OUR CREW."
NOT AFRAID.
I'M SAFE.
BECAUSE I'M NOT AFRAID.

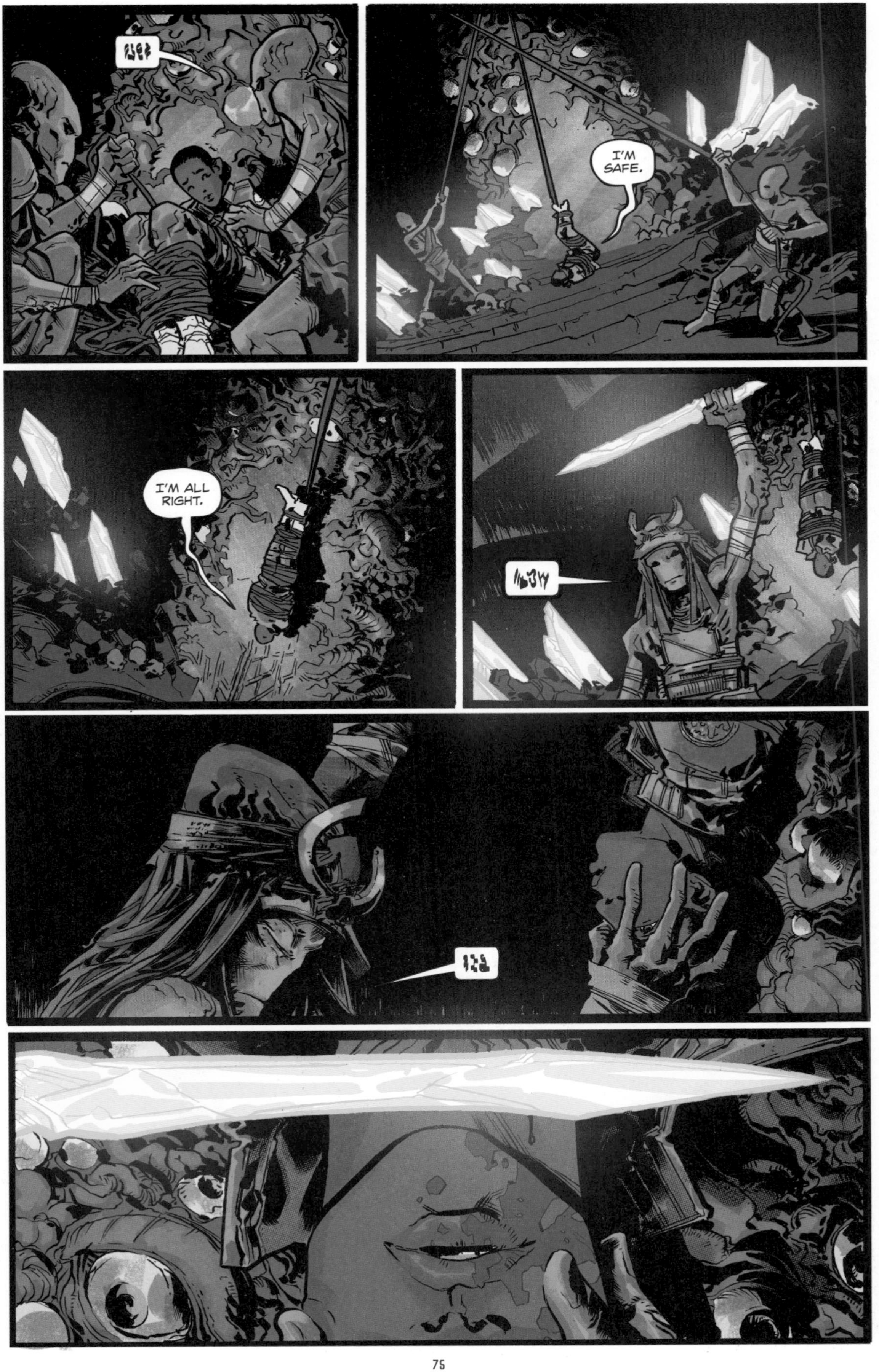
I'M SAFE.
I'M ALL RIGHT.

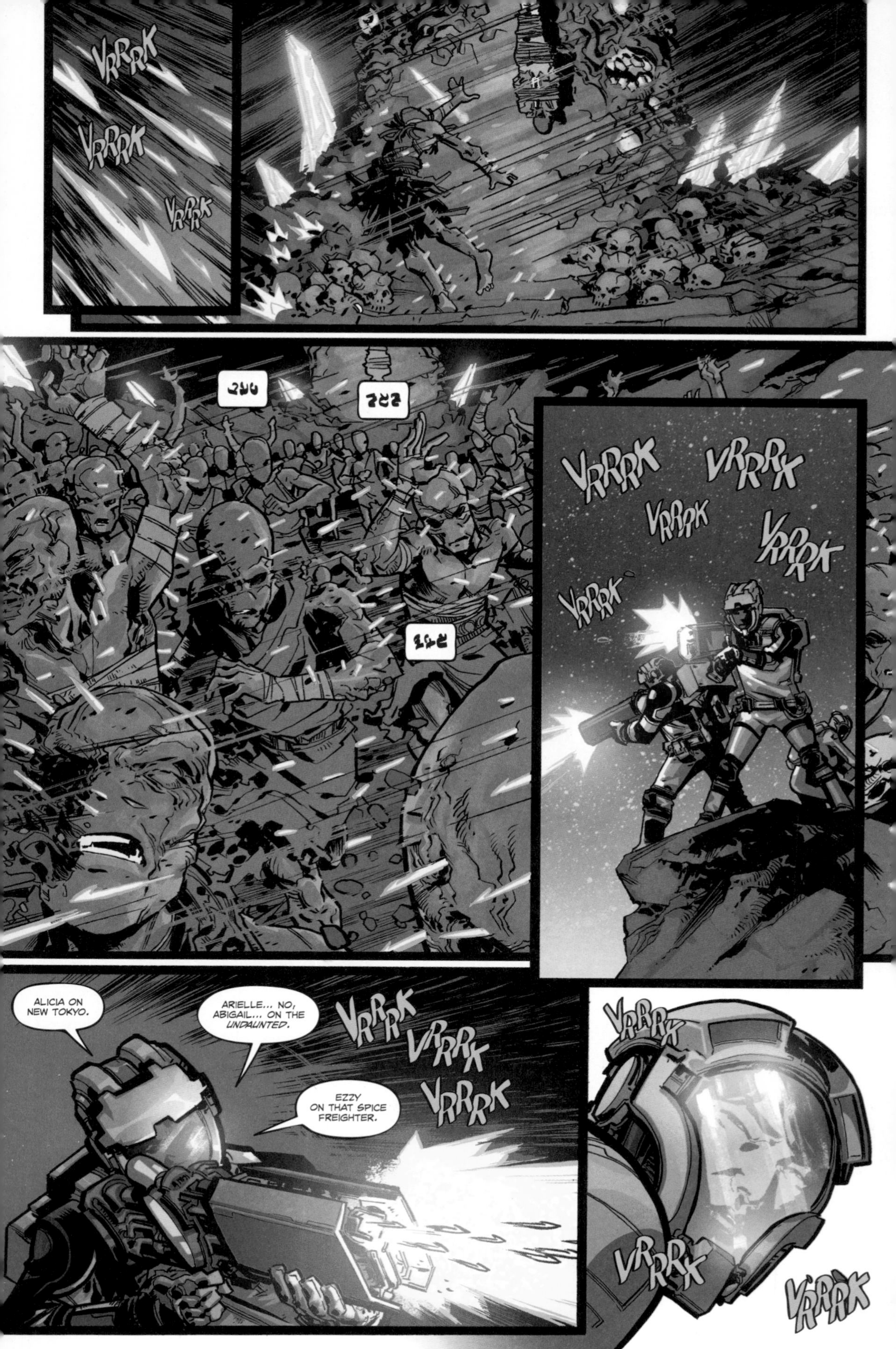
VRRRK
VRRRK
VRRRK
VRRRK
VRRRK
VRRRK
VRRRK
VRRRK
ALICIA ON NEW TOKYO.
ARIELLE... NO, ABIGAIL... ON THE *UNDAUNTED*.
EZZY ON THAT SPICE FREIGHTER.
VRRRK
VRRRK
VRRRK
VRRRK
VRRRK
VRRRK

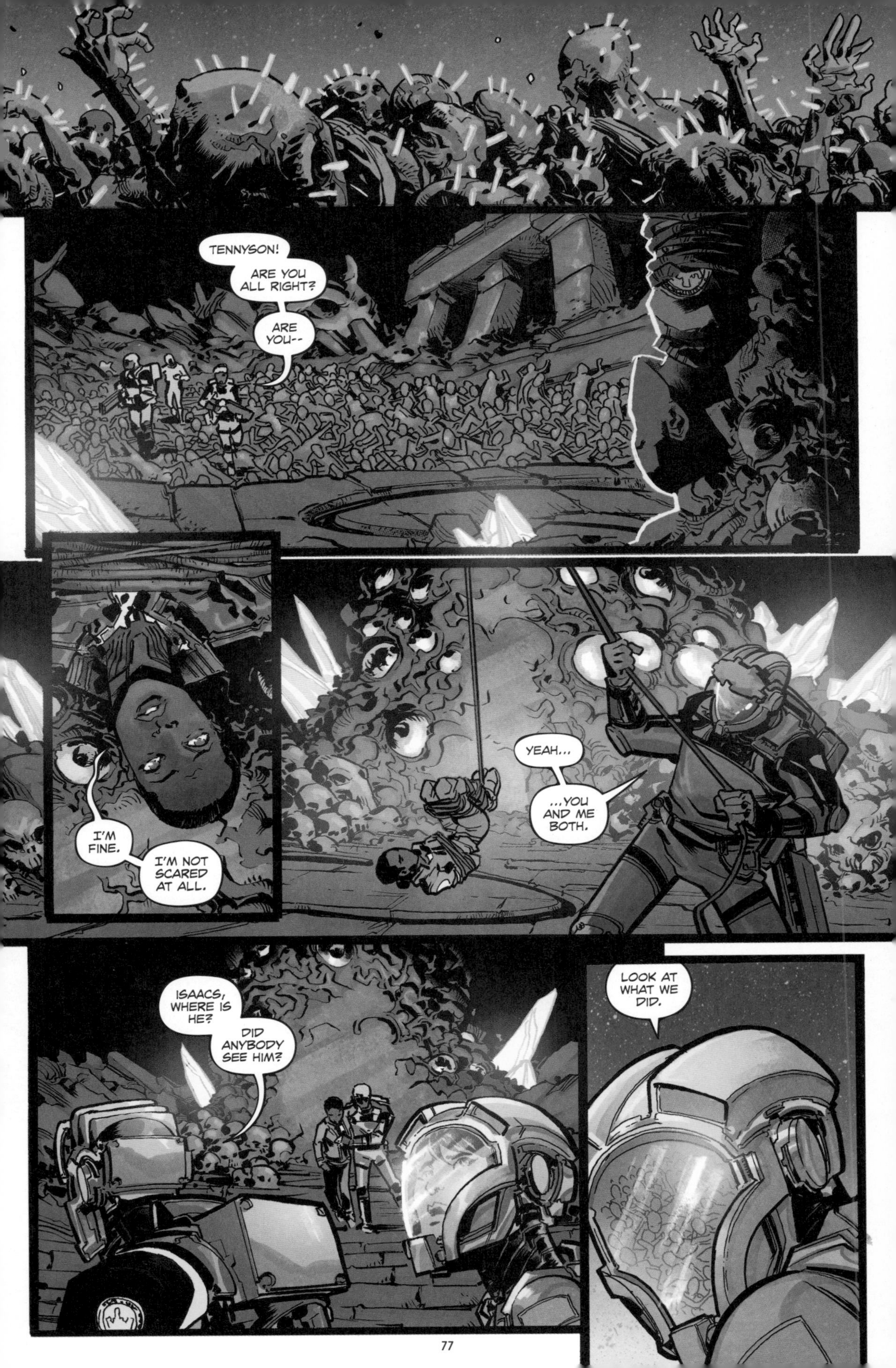
TENNYSON!
ARE YOU ALL RIGHT?
ARE YOU--
I'M FINE.
I'M NOT SCARED AT ALL.
YEAH...
...YOU AND ME BOTH.
ISAACS, WHERE IS HE?
DID ANYBODY SEE HIM?
LOOK AT WHAT WE DID.

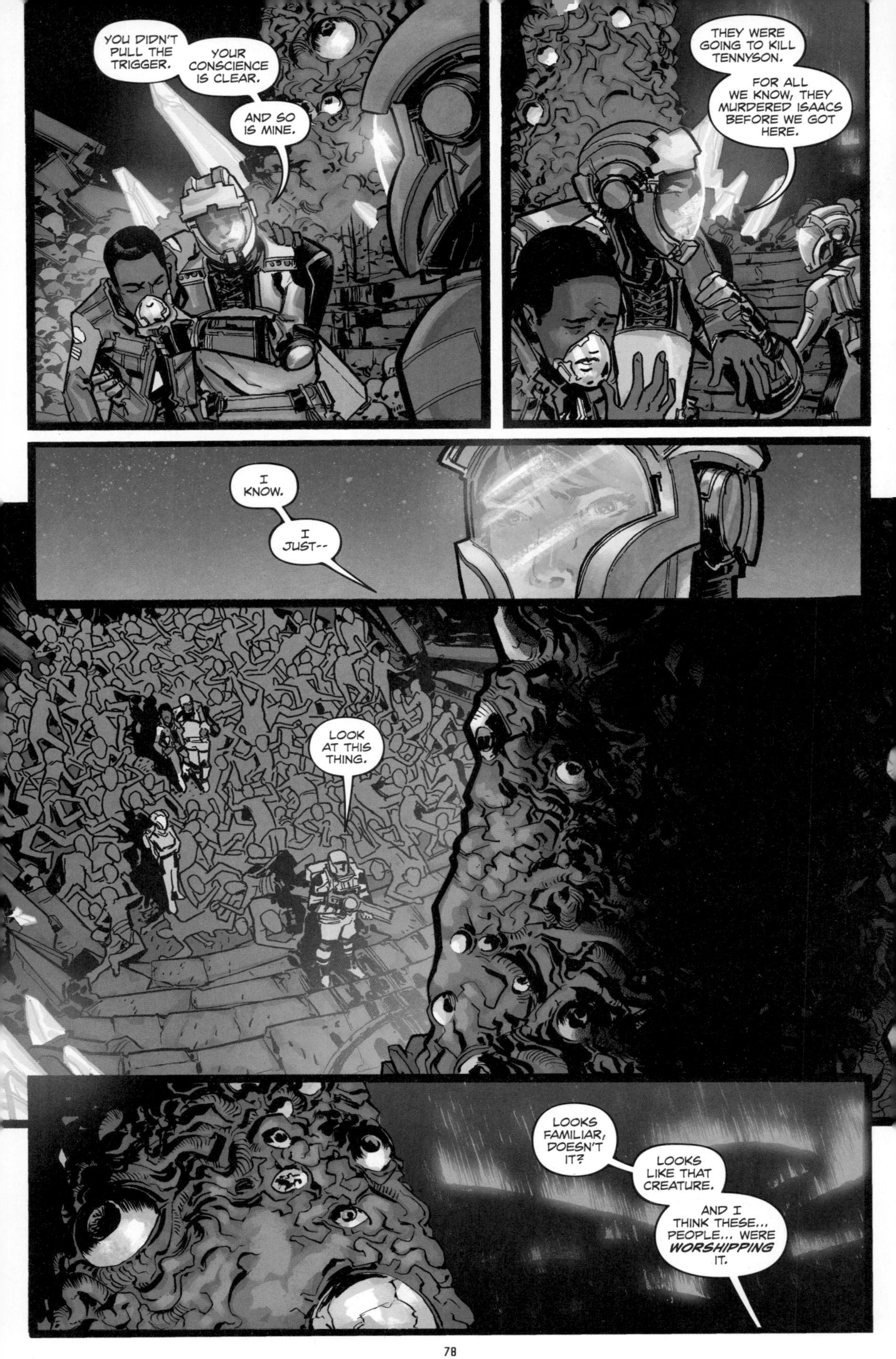
YOU DIDN'T PULL THE TRIGGER.
YOUR CONSCIENCE IS CLEAR.
AND SO IS MINE.
THEY WERE GOING TO KILL TENNYSON.
FOR ALL WE KNOW, THEY MURDERED ISAACS BEFORE WE GOT HERE.
I KNOW.
I JUST--
LOOK AT THIS THING.
LOOKS FAMILIAR, DOESN'T IT?
LOOKS LIKE THAT CREATURE.
AND I THINK THESE... PEOPLE... WERE *WORSHIPPING* IT.

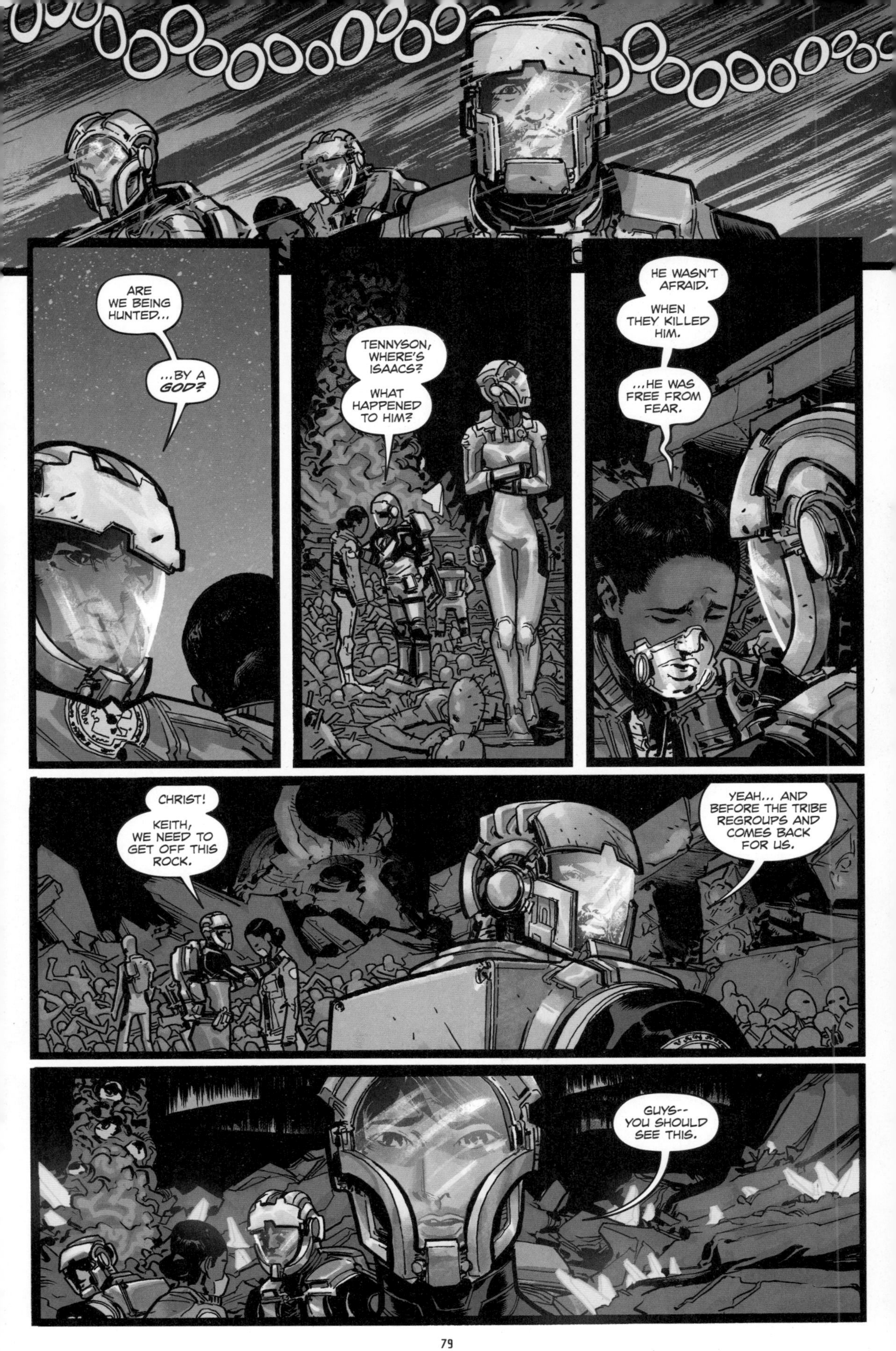
OOOOOOOOOOOOOOOOOOOOOOOOOOOOOOO
ARE WE BEING HUNTED...
...BY A *GOD?*
TENNYSON, WHERE'S ISAACS?
WHAT HAPPENED TO HIM?
HE WASN'T AFRAID.
WHEN THEY KILLED HIM.
...HE WAS FREE FROM FEAR.
CHRIST!
KEITH, WE NEED TO GET OFF THIS ROCK.
YEAH... AND BEFORE THE TRIBE REGROUPS AND COMES BACK FOR US.
GUYS-- YOU SHOULD SEE THIS.

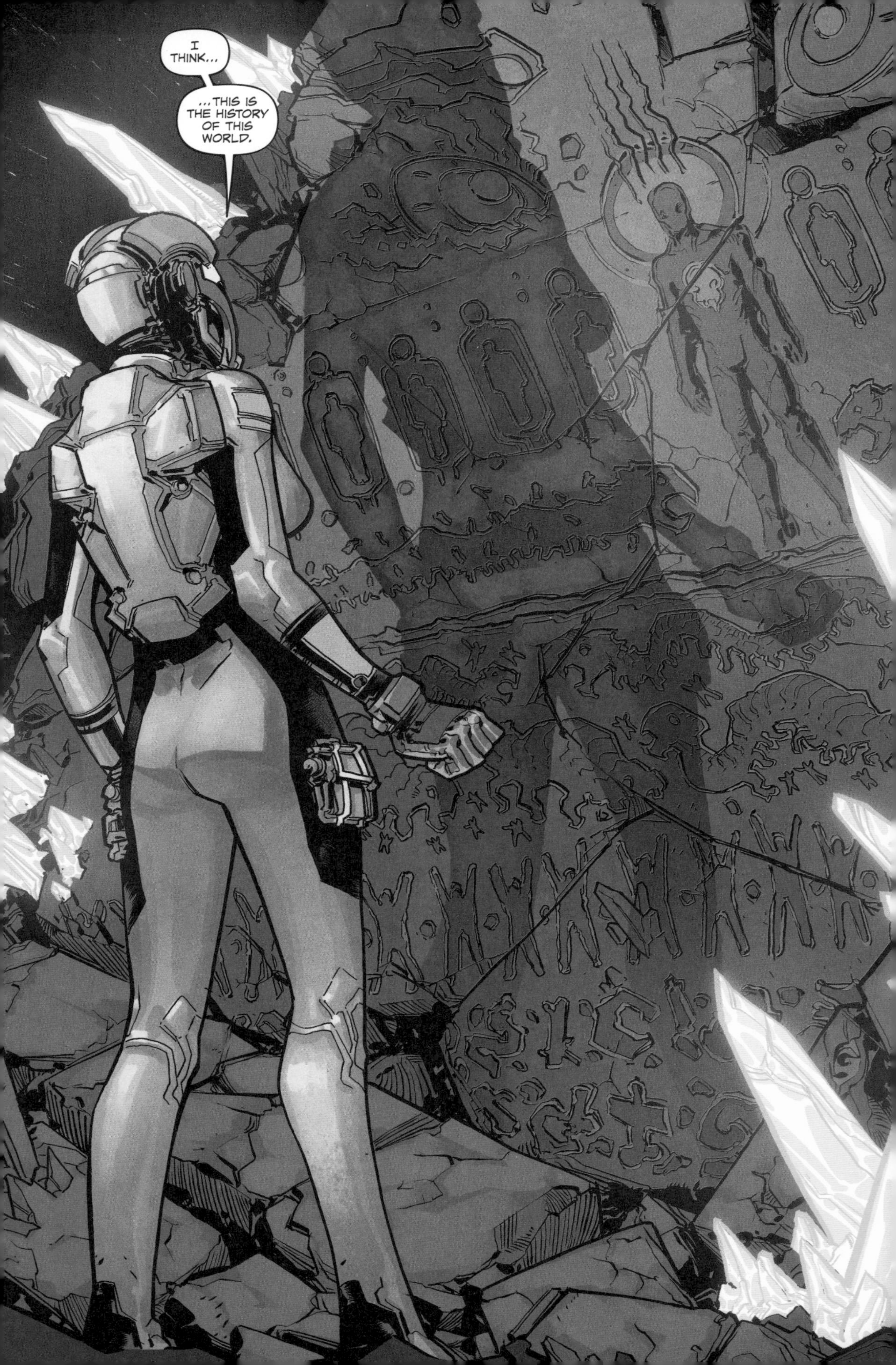
I THINK...
...THIS IS THE HISTORY OF THIS WORLD.

CHAPTER 04

ESCAPE

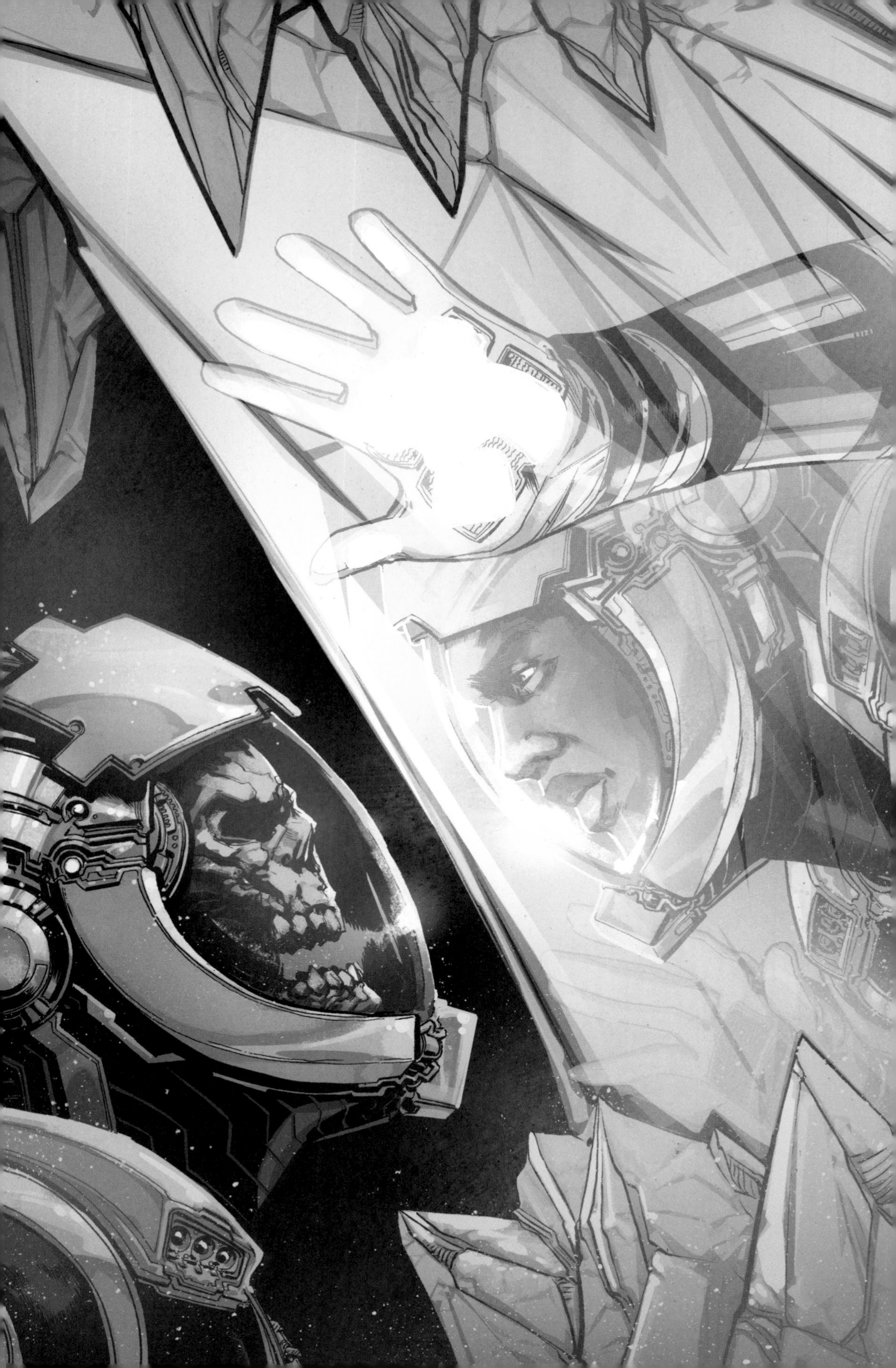

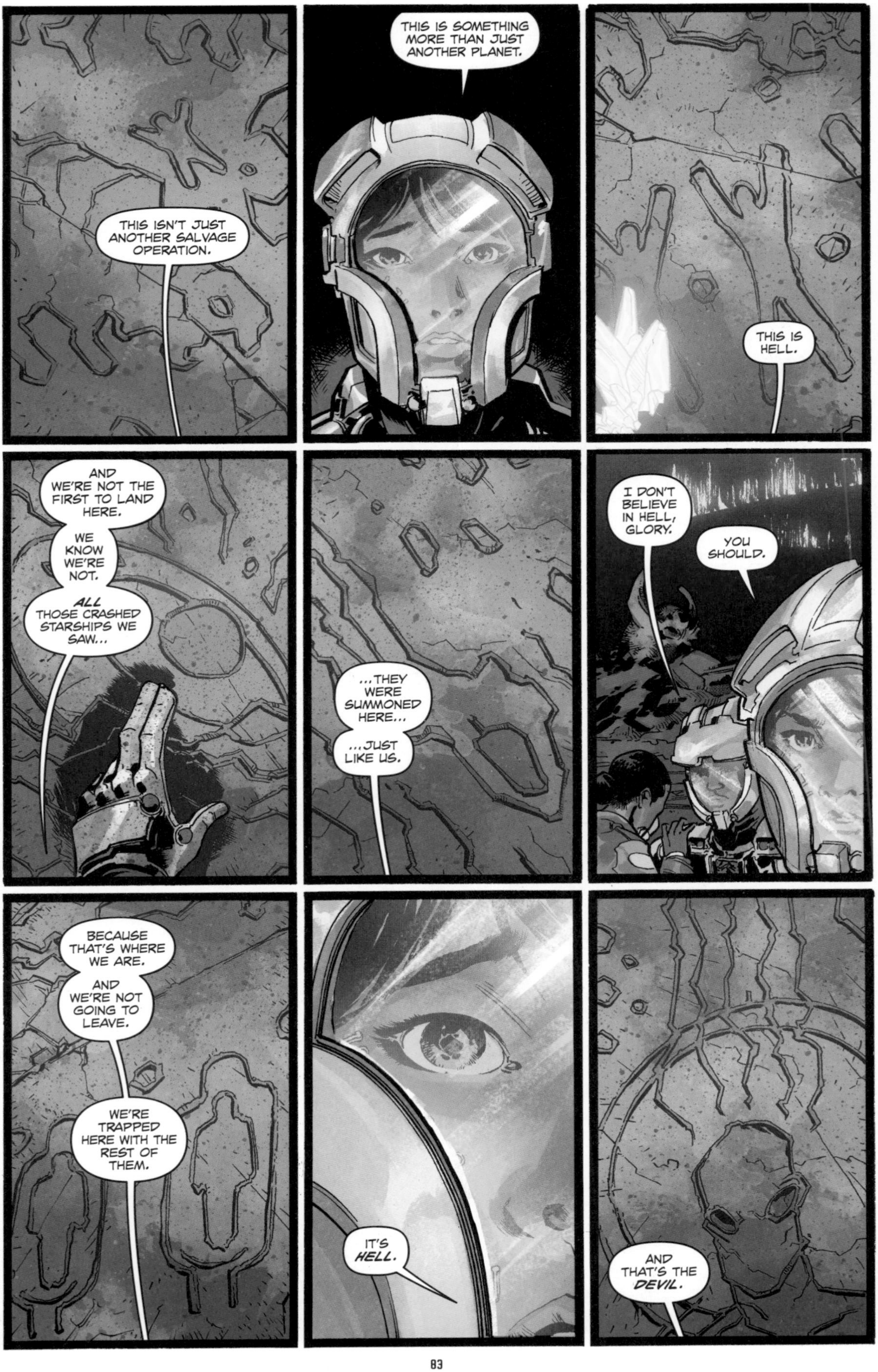
THIS ISN'T JUST ANOTHER SALVAGE OPERATION.
THIS IS SOMETHING MORE THAN JUST ANOTHER PLANET.
THIS IS HELL.
AND WE'RE NOT THE FIRST TO LAND HERE.
WE KNOW WE'RE NOT.
ALL THOSE CRASHED STARSHIPS WE SAW...
...THEY WERE SUMMONED HERE...
...JUST LIKE US.
I DON'T BELIEVE IN HELL, GLORY.
YOU SHOULD.
BECAUSE THAT'S WHERE WE ARE.
AND WE'RE NOT GOING TO LEAVE.
WE'RE TRAPPED HERE WITH THE REST OF THEM.
IT'S HELL.
AND THAT'S THE DEVIL.

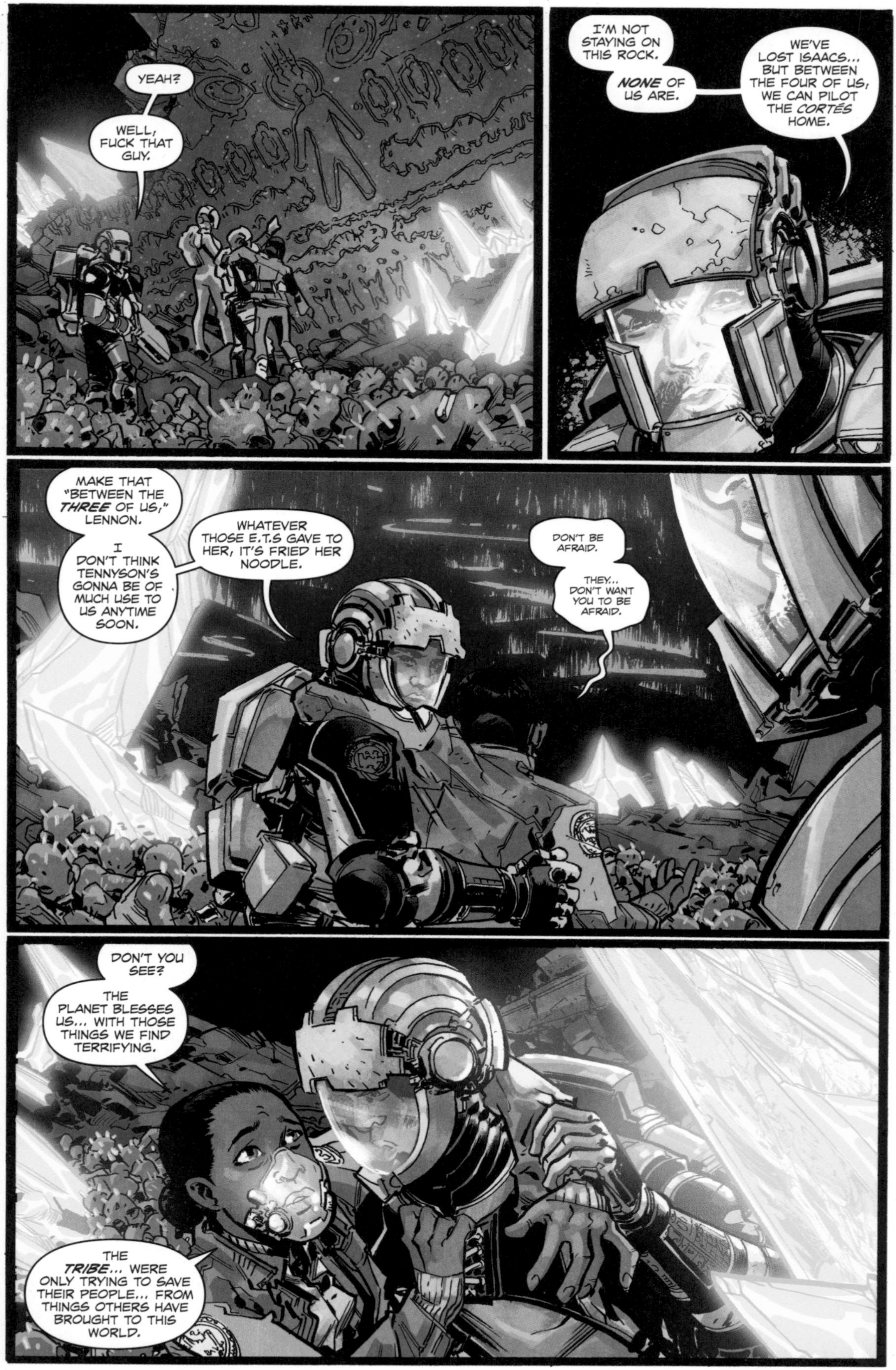
YEAH?
WELL, FUCK THAT GUY.
I'M NOT STAYING ON THIS ROCK.
NONE OF US ARE.
WE'VE LOST ISAACS... BUT BETWEEN THE FOUR OF US, WE CAN PILOT THE *CORTÉS* HOME.
MAKE THAT "BETWEEN THE *THREE* OF US," LENNON.
I DON'T THINK TENNYSON'S GONNA BE OF MUCH USE TO US ANYTIME SOON.
WHATEVER THOSE E.T.S GAVE TO HER, IT'S FRIED HER NOODLE.
DON'T BE AFRAID.
THEY... DON'T WANT YOU TO BE AFRAID.
DON'T YOU SEE?
THE PLANET BLESSES US... WITH THOSE THINGS WE FIND TERRIFYING.
THE *TRIBE*... WERE ONLY TRYING TO SAVE THEIR PEOPLE... FROM THINGS OTHERS HAVE BROUGHT TO THIS WORLD.

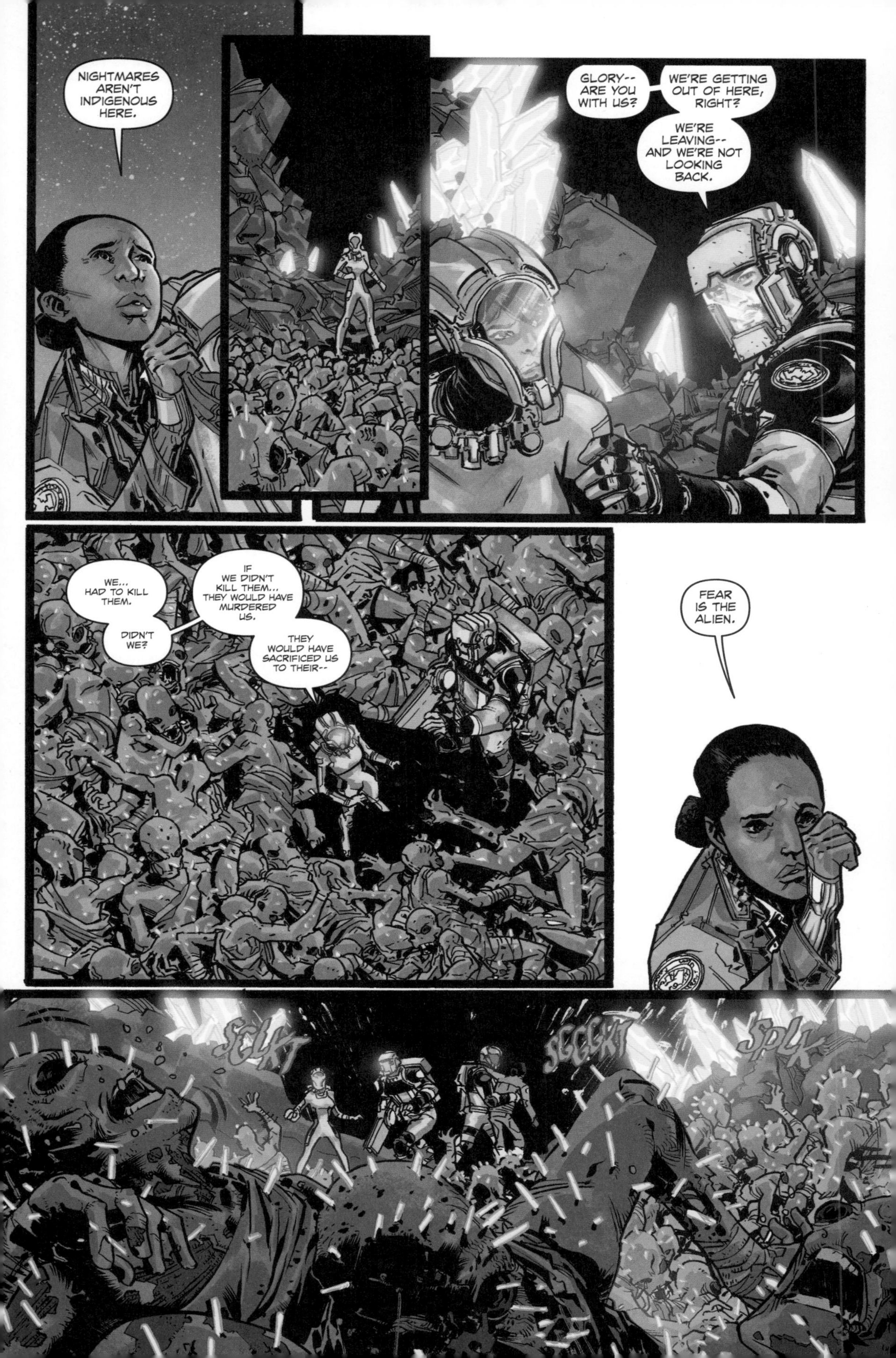
NIGHTMARES AREN'T INDIGENOUS HERE.
GLORY-- ARE YOU WITH US?
WE'RE GETTING OUT OF HERE, RIGHT?
WE'RE LEAVING-- AND WE'RE NOT LOOKING BACK.
WE... HAD TO KILL THEM.
DIDN'T WE?
IF WE DIDN'T KILL THEM... THEY WOULD HAVE MURDERED US.
THEY WOULD HAVE SACRIFICED US TO THEIR--
FEAR IS THE ALIEN.
SCLKT
SCCCKT
SPLK

HHHRRRRRRNNNNNNN

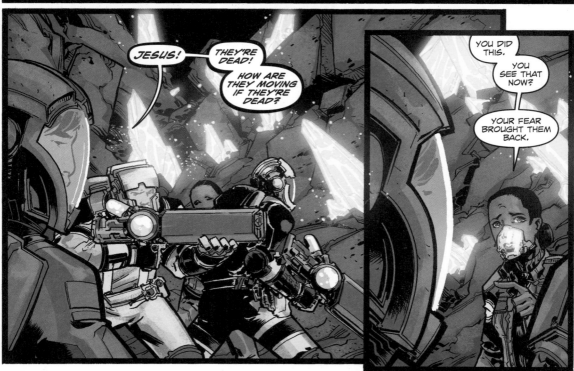

JESUS!

THEY'RE DEAD!

HOW ARE THEY MOVING IF THEY'RE DEAD?

YOU DID THIS. YOU SEE THAT NOW?

YOUR FEAR BROUGHT THEM BACK.

HRRRGAAAAAHUH

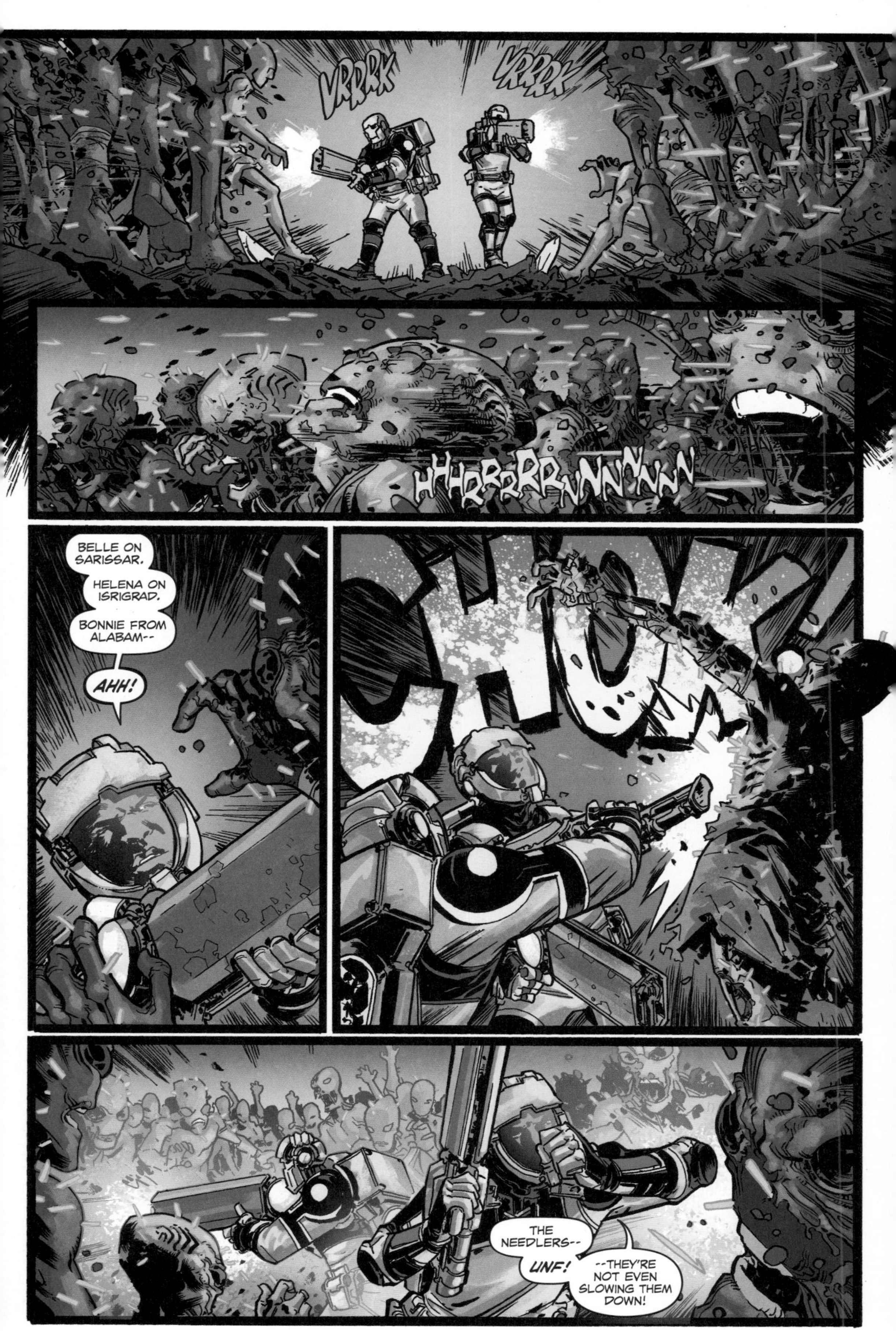
VRRRK
VRRRK
HHHRRRRRNNNNNNN
BELLE ON SARISSAR.
HELENA ON ISRIGRAD.
BONNIE FROM ALABAM--
AHH!
THE NEEDLERS--
UNF!
--THEY'RE NOT EVEN SLOWING THEM DOWN!

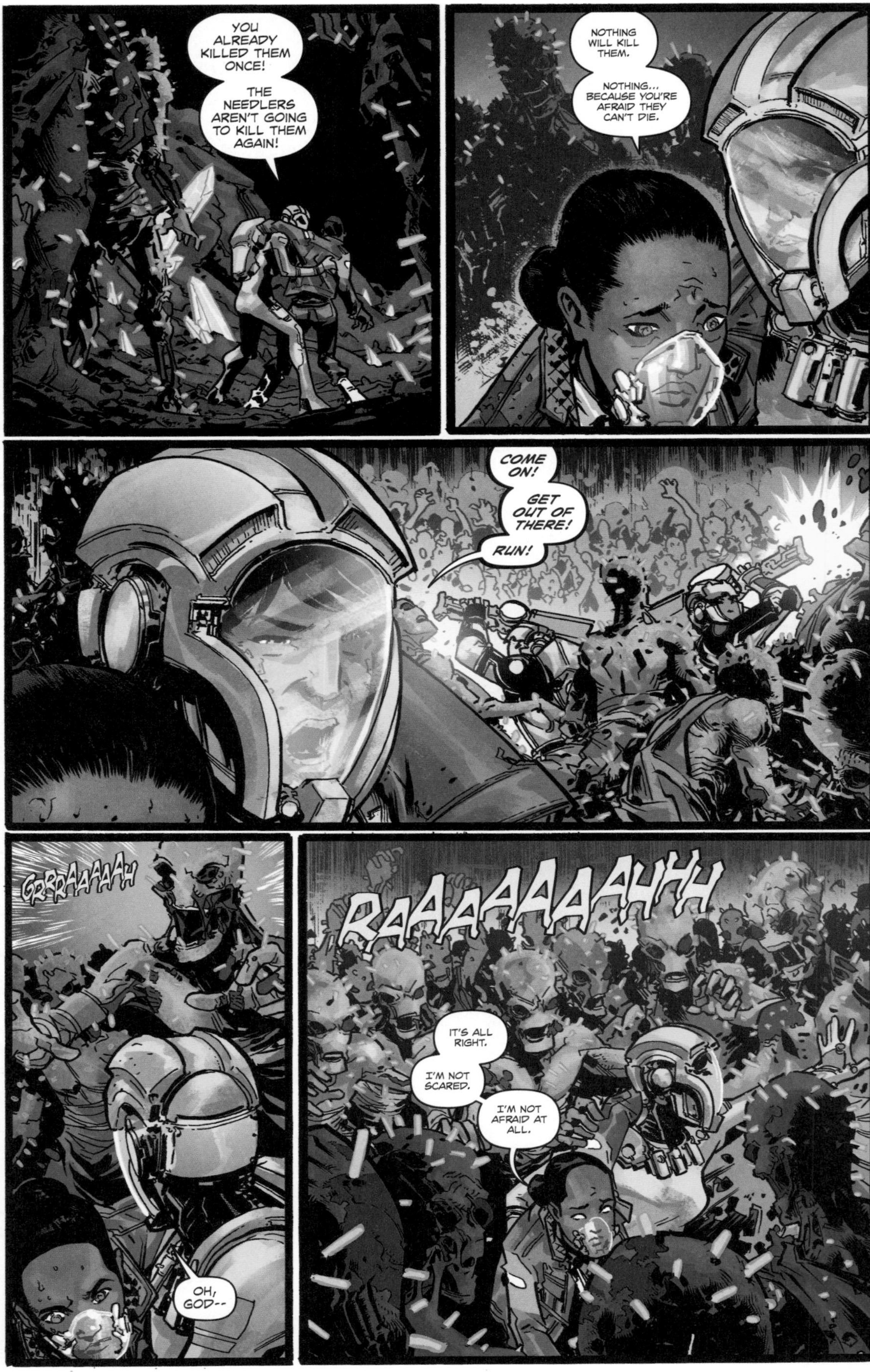
YOU ALREADY KILLED THEM ONCE!
THE NEEDLERS AREN'T GOING TO KILL THEM AGAIN!
NOTHING WILL KILL THEM.
NOTHING... BECAUSE YOU'RE AFRAID THEY CAN'T DIE.
COME ON!
GET OUT OF THERE!
RUN!
GRRRAAAAAH
OH, GOD--
RAAAAAAAAHH
IT'S ALL RIGHT.
I'M NOT SCARED.
I'M NOT AFRAID AT ALL.

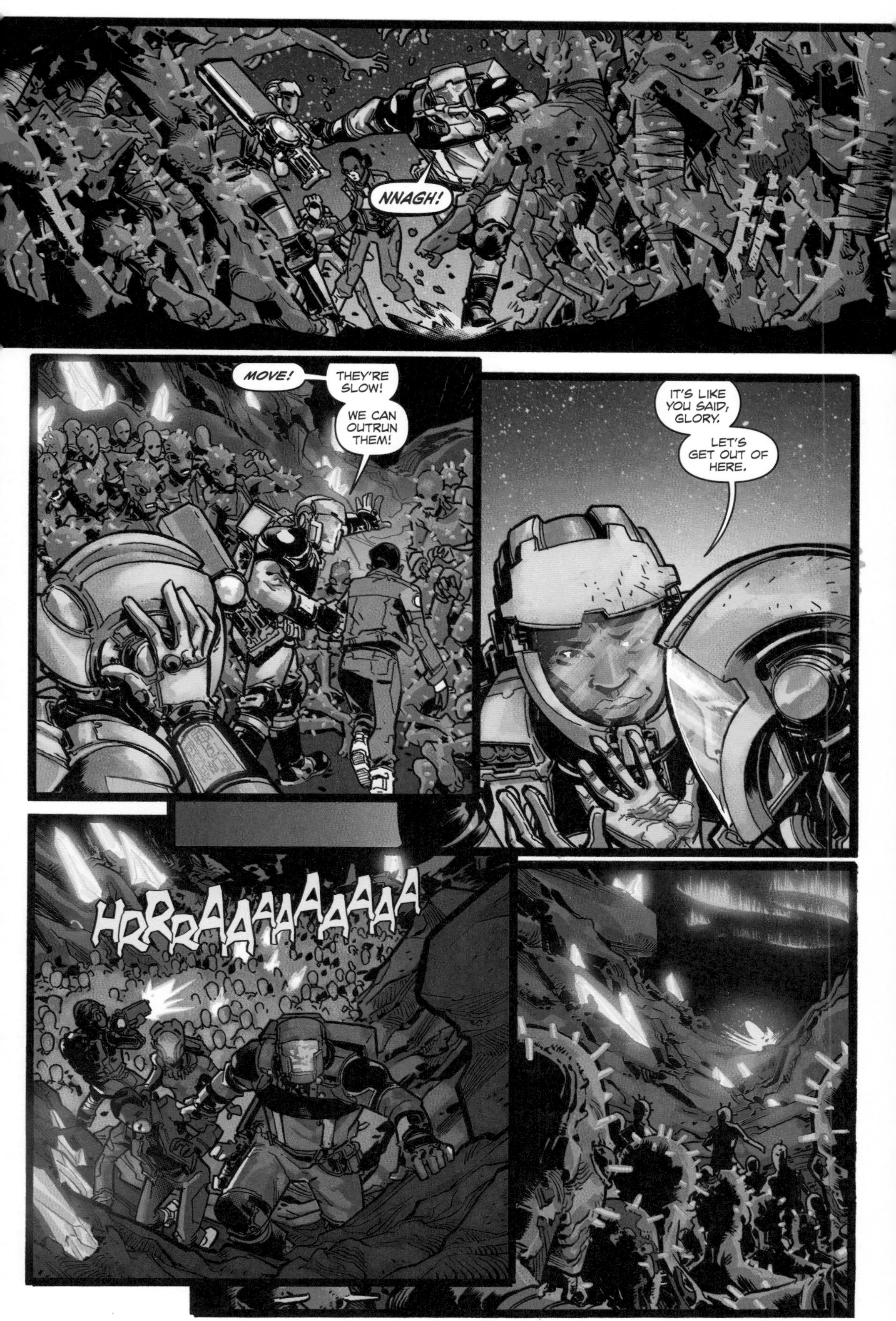
NNAGH!
MOVE!
THEY'RE SLOW!
WE CAN OUTRUN THEM!
IT'S LIKE YOU SAID, GLORY.
LET'S GET OUT OF HERE.
HRRRAAAAAAAAAA

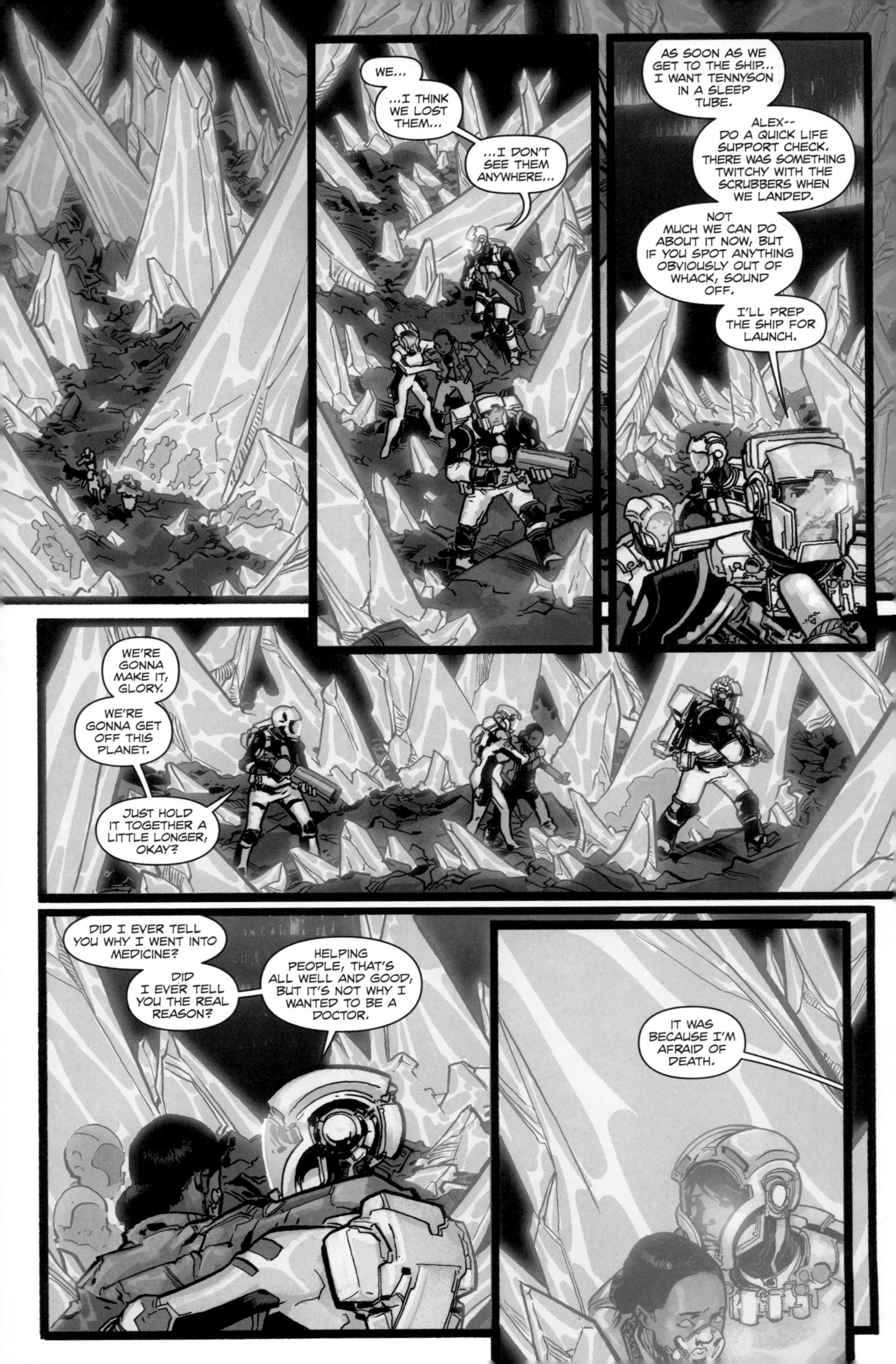
WE...
...I THINK WE LOST THEM...
...I DON'T SEE THEM ANYWHERE...
AS SOON AS WE GET TO THE SHIP... I WANT TENNYSON IN A SLEEP TUBE.
ALEX-- DO A QUICK LIFE SUPPORT CHECK. THERE WAS SOMETHING TWITCHY WITH THE SCRUBBERS WHEN WE LANDED.
NOT MUCH WE CAN DO ABOUT IT NOW, BUT IF YOU SPOT ANYTHING OBVIOUSLY OUT OF WHACK, SOUND OFF.
I'LL PREP THE SHIP FOR LAUNCH.
WE'RE GONNA MAKE IT, GLORY.
WE'RE GONNA GET OFF THIS PLANET.
JUST HOLD IT TOGETHER A LITTLE LONGER, OKAY?
DID I EVER TELL YOU WHY I WENT INTO MEDICINE?
DID I EVER TELL YOU THE REAL REASON?
HELPING PEOPLE, THAT'S ALL WELL AND GOOD, BUT IT'S NOT WHY I WANTED TO BE A DOCTOR.
IT WAS BECAUSE I'M AFRAID OF DEATH.

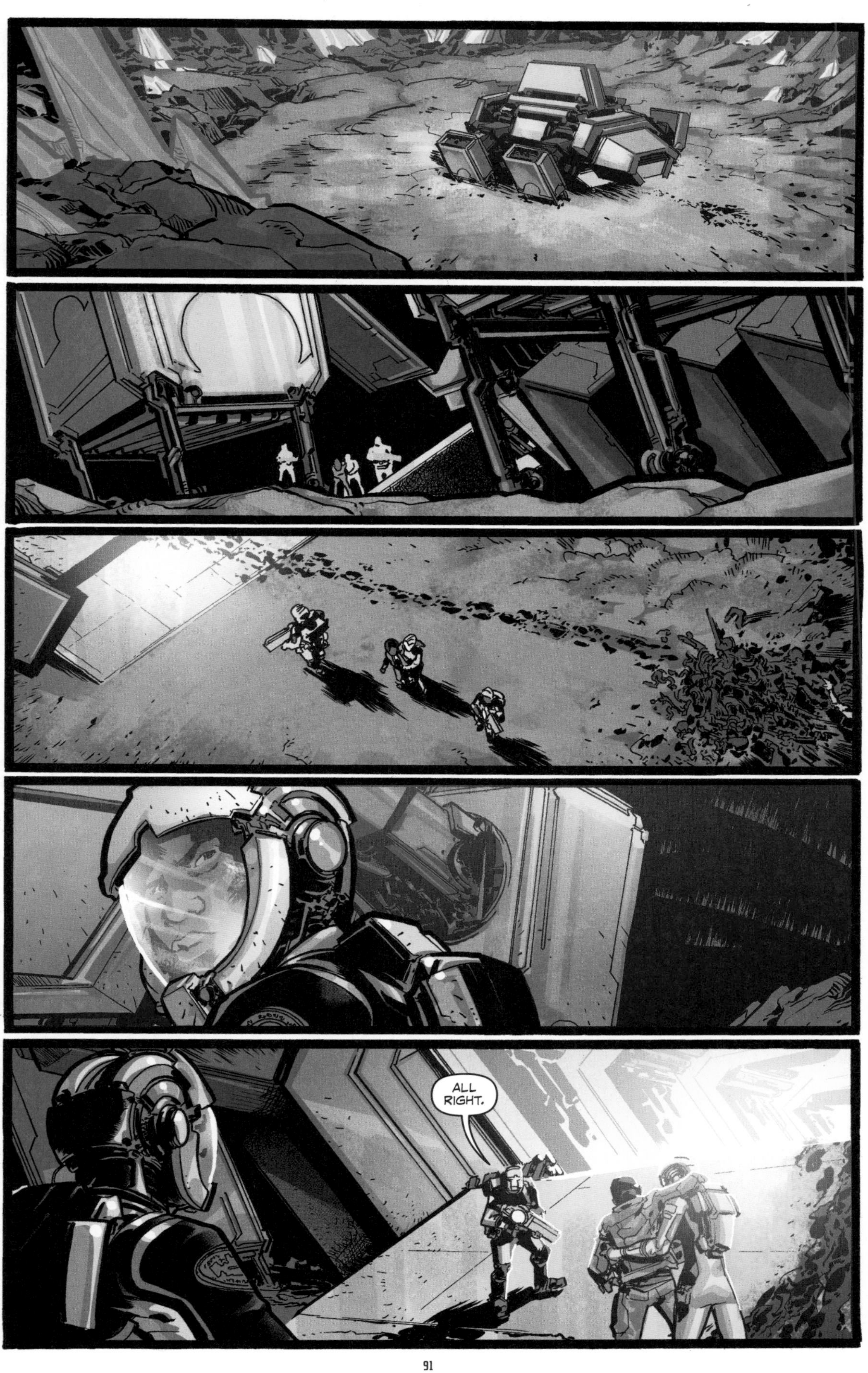
ALL RIGHT.

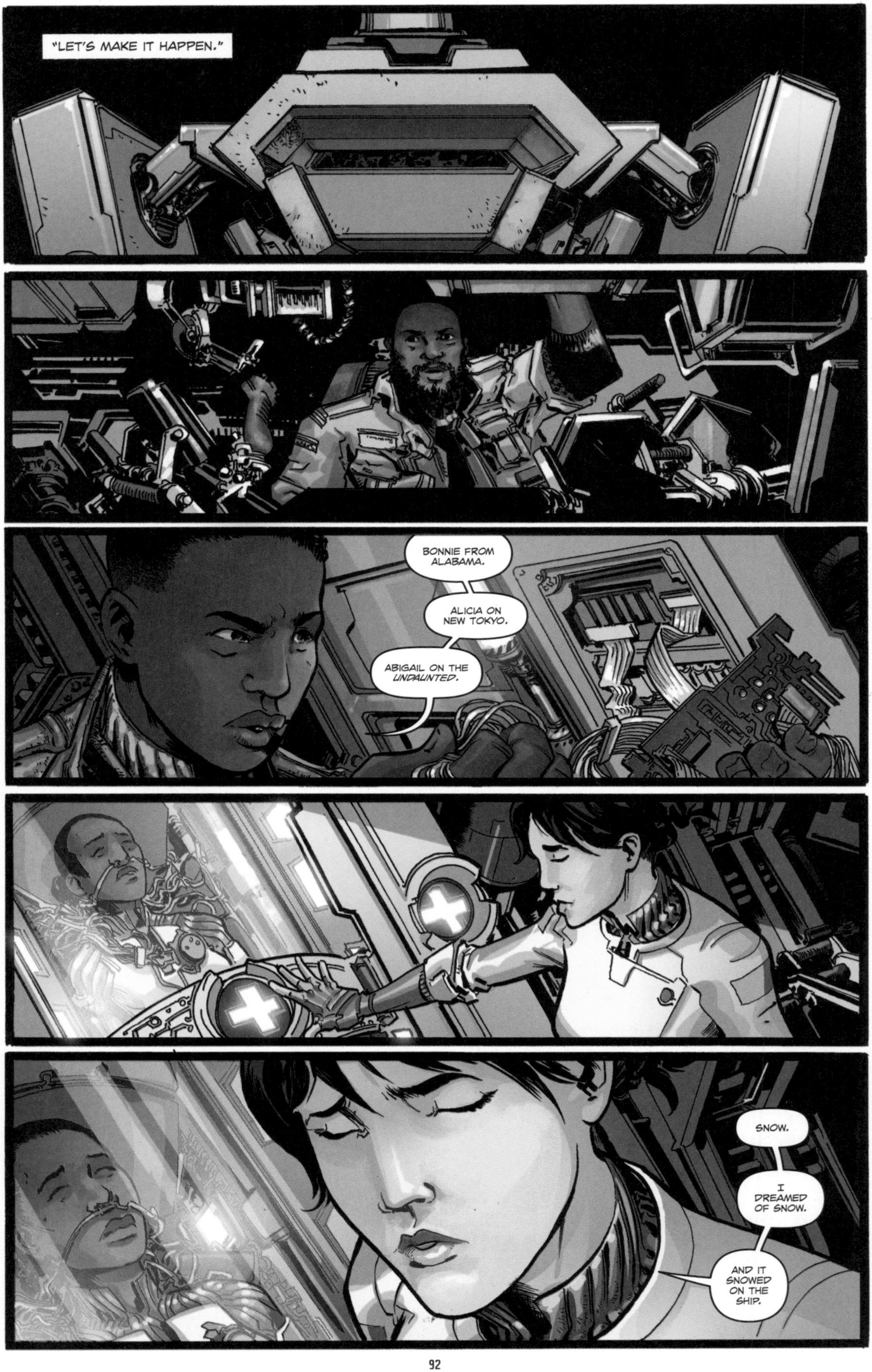
"LET'S MAKE IT HAPPEN."
BONNIE FROM ALABAMA.
ALICIA ON NEW TOKYO.
ABIGAIL ON THE *UNDAUNTED*.
SNOW.
I DREAMED OF SNOW.
AND IT SNOWED ON THE SHIP.

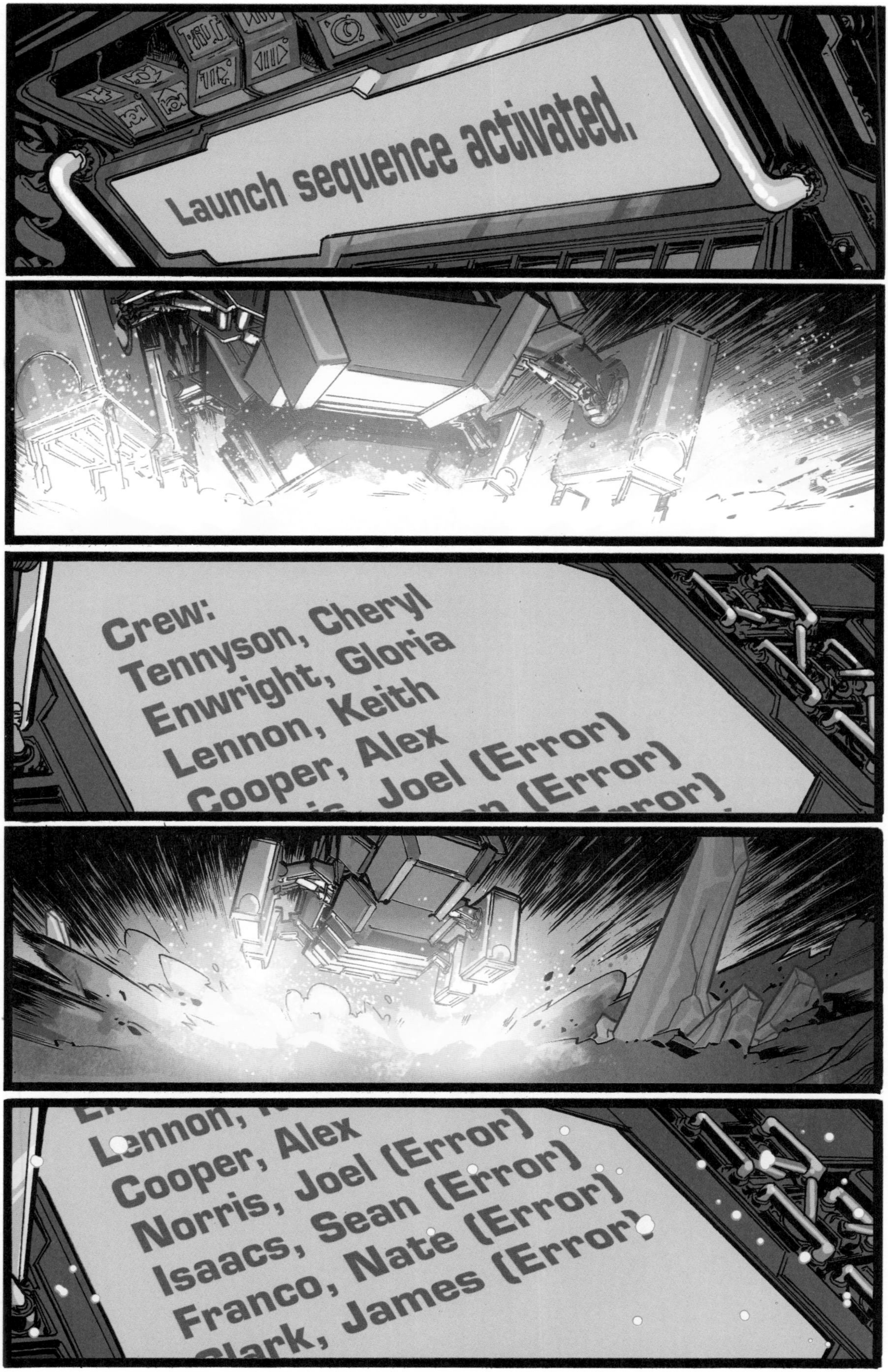

Launch sequence activated.
Crew:
Tennyson, Cheryl
Enwright, Gloria
Lennon, Keith
Cooper, Alex
Cooper, Alex
Norris, Joel (Error)
Isaacs, Sean (Error)
Franco, Nate (Error)
Clark, James (Error)

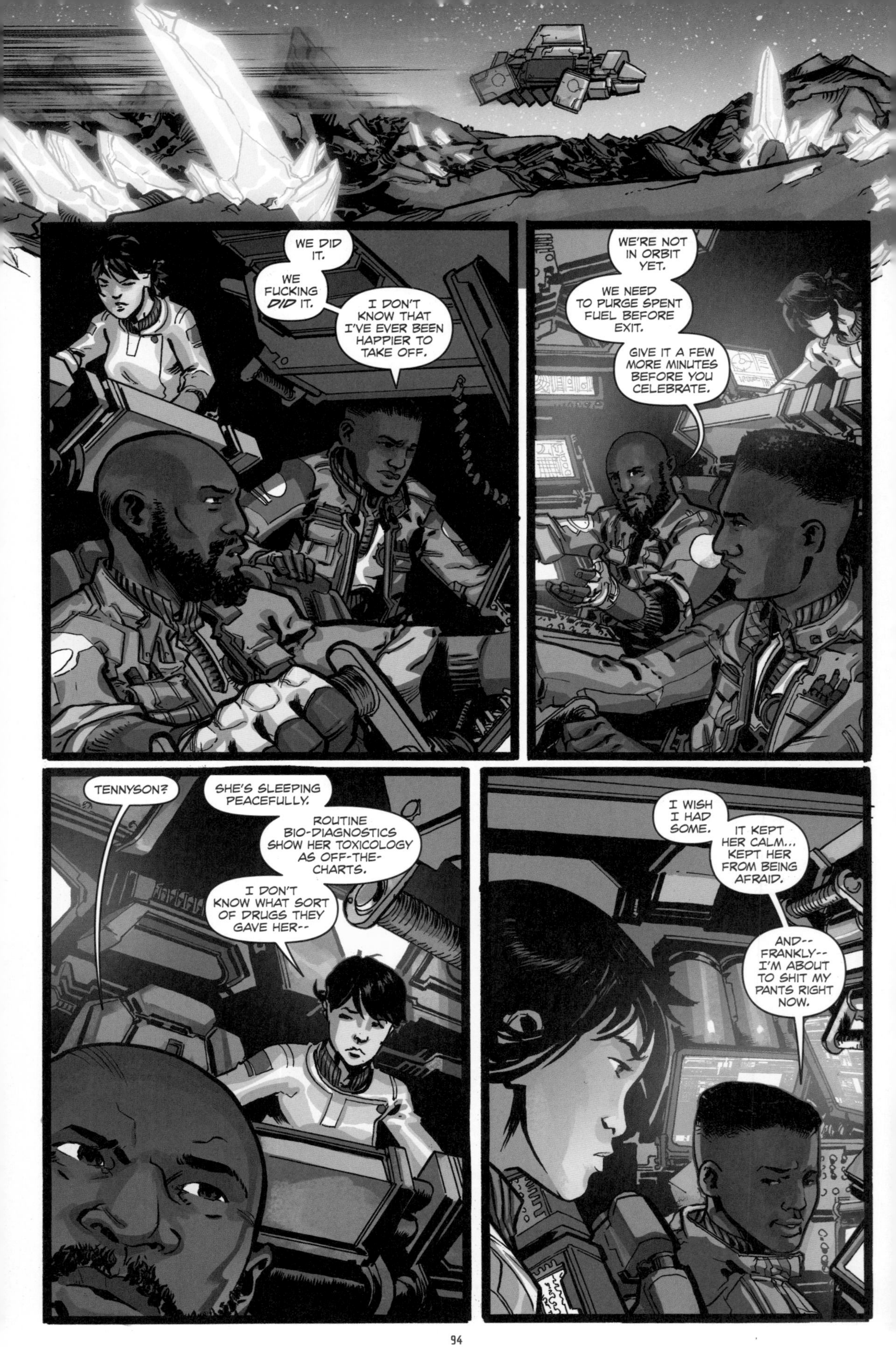
WE DID IT.
WE FUCKING *DID* IT.
I DON'T KNOW THAT I'VE EVER BEEN HAPPIER TO TAKE OFF.
WE'RE NOT IN ORBIT YET.
WE NEED TO PURGE SPENT FUEL BEFORE EXIT.
GIVE IT A FEW MORE MINUTES BEFORE YOU CELEBRATE.
TENNYSON?
SHE'S SLEEPING PEACEFULLY.
ROUTINE BIO-DIAGNOSTICS SHOW HER TOXICOLOGY AS OFF-THE-CHARTS.
I DON'T KNOW WHAT SORT OF DRUGS THEY GAVE HER--
I WISH I HAD SOME.
IT KEPT HER CALM... KEPT HER FROM BEING AFRAID.
AND--FRANKLY--I'M ABOUT TO SHIT MY PANTS RIGHT NOW.

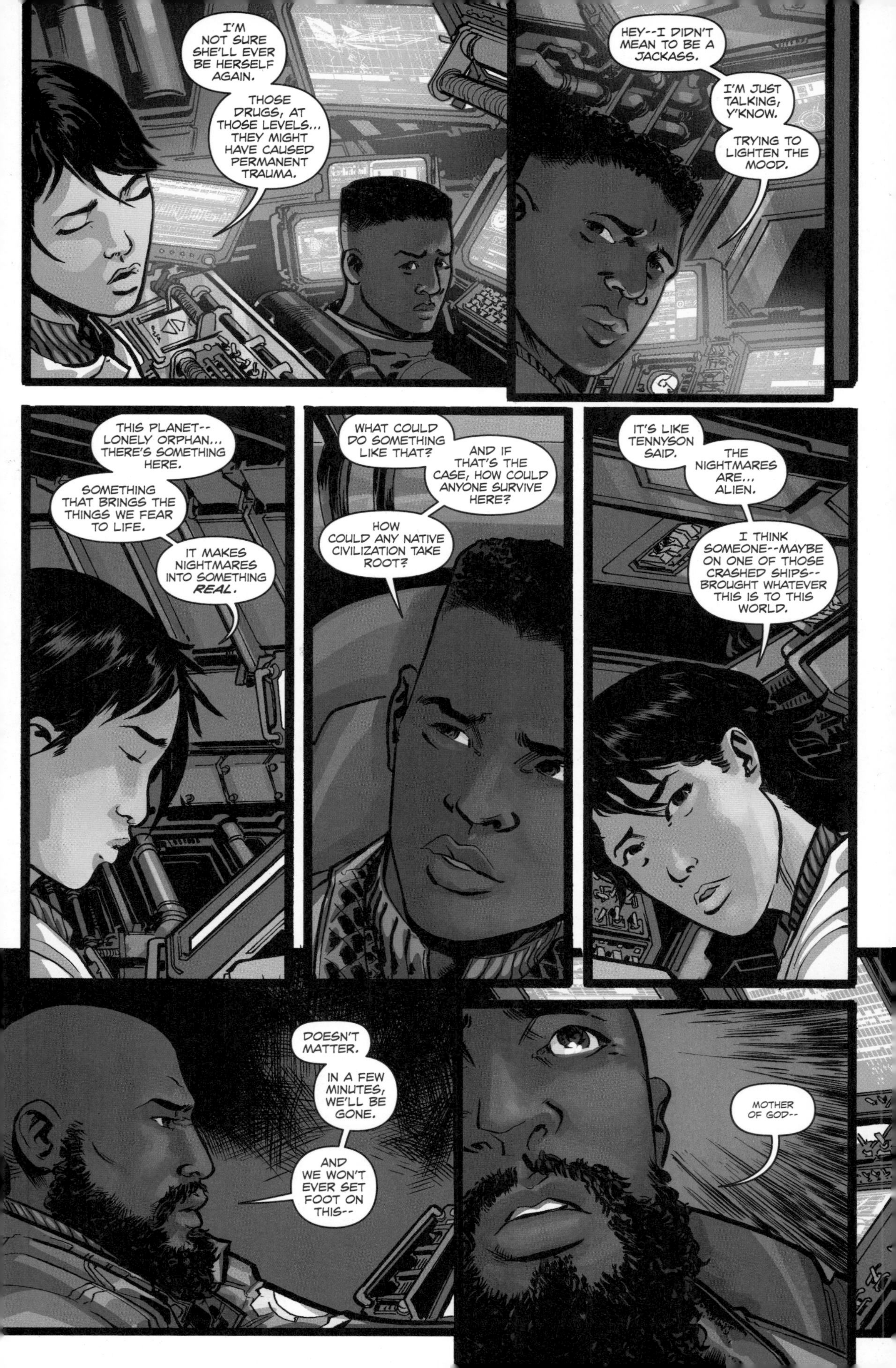
I'M NOT SURE SHE'LL EVER BE HERSELF AGAIN.
THOSE DRUGS, AT THOSE LEVELS... THEY MIGHT HAVE CAUSED PERMANENT TRAUMA.
HEY--I DIDN'T MEAN TO BE A JACKASS.
I'M JUST TALKING, Y'KNOW.
TRYING TO LIGHTEN THE MOOD.
THIS PLANET--LONELY ORPHAN... THERE'S SOMETHING HERE.
SOMETHING THAT BRINGS THE THINGS WE FEAR TO LIFE.
IT MAKES NIGHTMARES INTO SOMETHING *REAL*.
WHAT COULD DO SOMETHING LIKE THAT?
AND IF THAT'S THE CASE, HOW COULD ANYONE SURVIVE HERE?
HOW COULD ANY NATIVE CIVILIZATION TAKE ROOT?
IT'S LIKE TENNYSON SAID.
THE NIGHTMARES ARE... ALIEN.
I THINK SOMEONE--MAYBE ON ONE OF THOSE CRASHED SHIPS--BROUGHT WHATEVER THIS IS TO THIS WORLD.
DOESN'T MATTER.
IN A FEW MINUTES, WE'LL BE GONE.
AND WE WON'T EVER SET FOOT ON THIS--
MOTHER OF GOD--

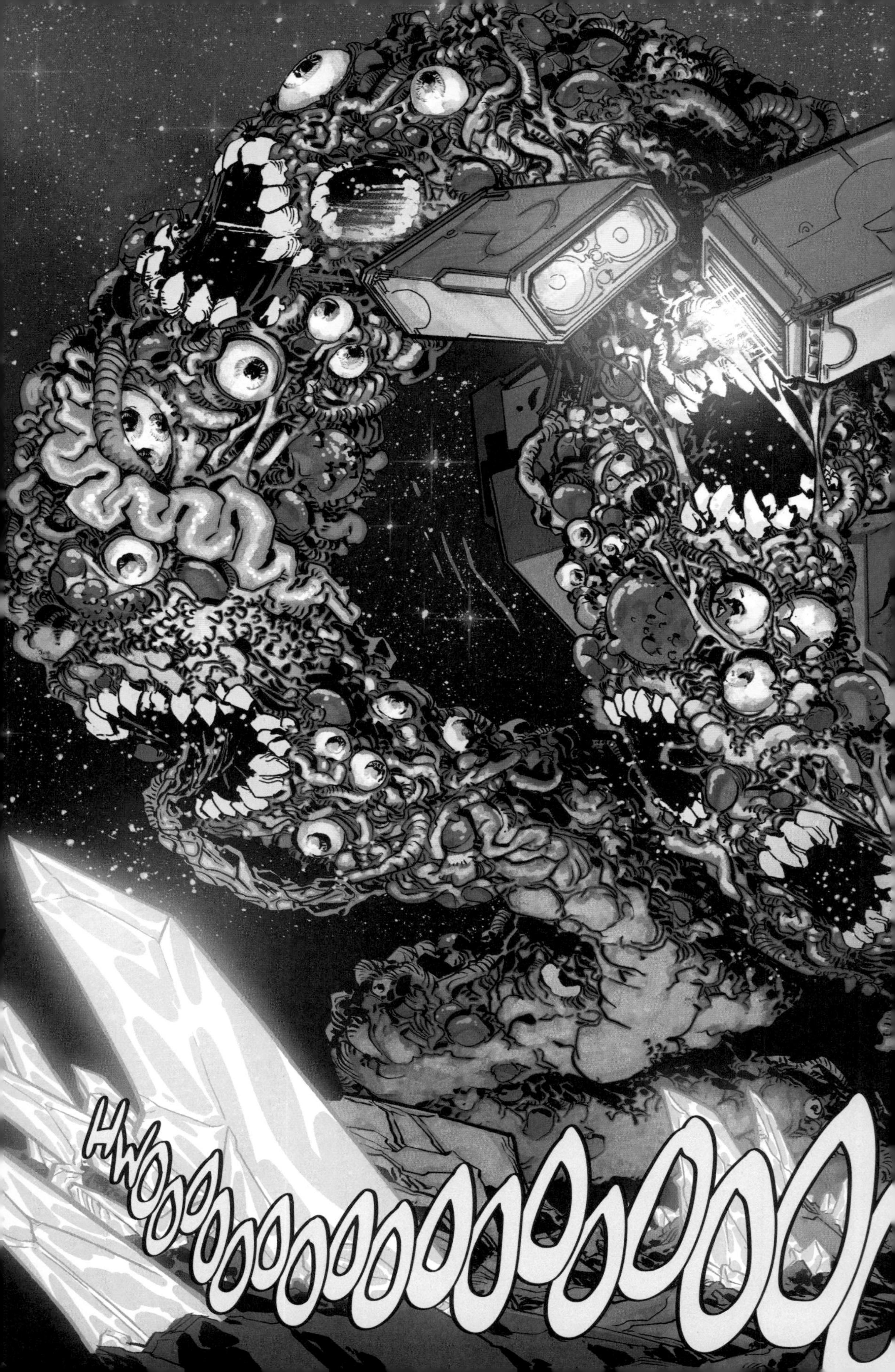
HWOOOOOOOOOOOOOOOOOOO

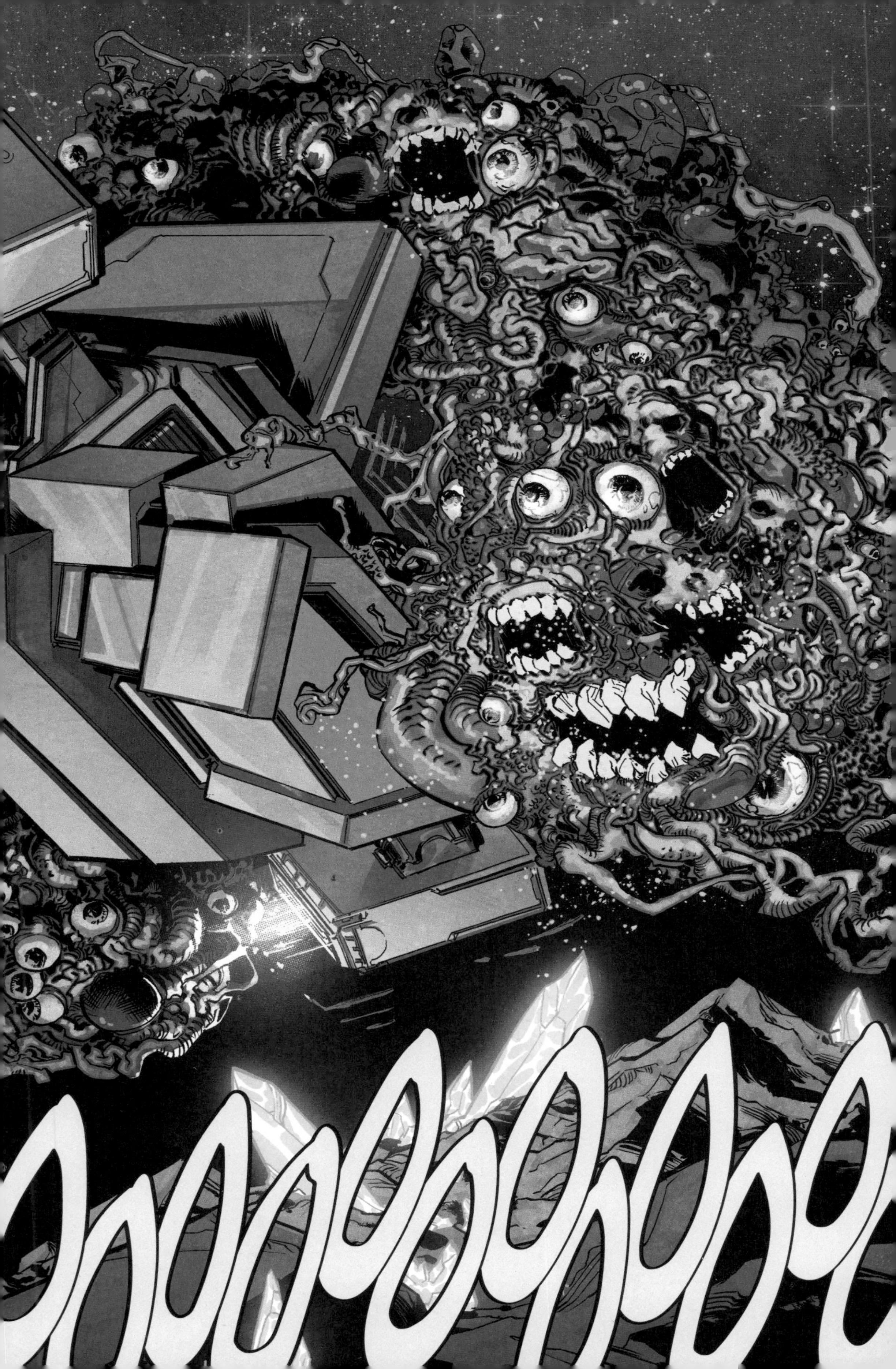

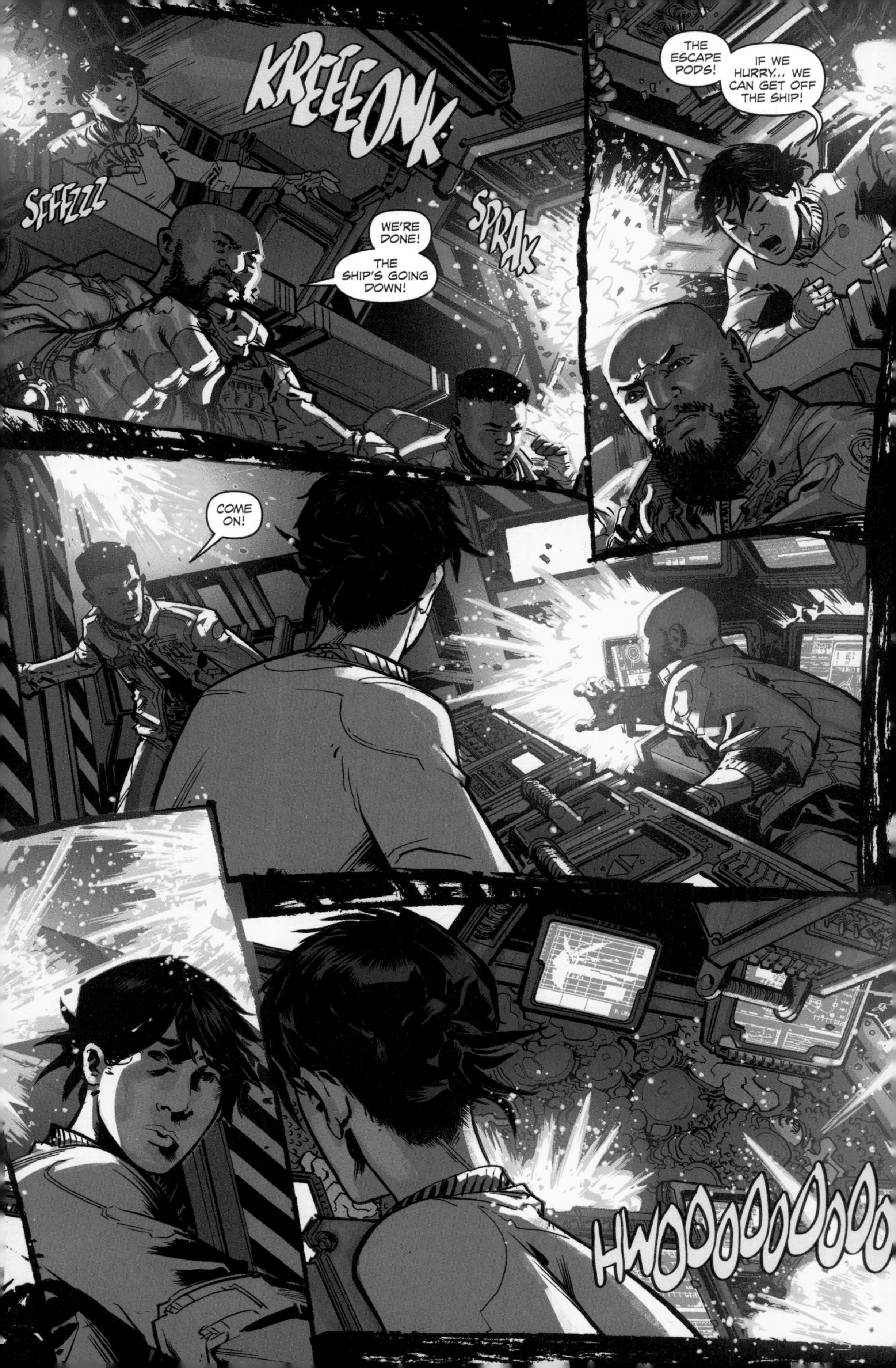
KREEEONK
SFFEZZZ
WE'RE DONE!
THE SHIP'S GOING DOWN!
SPRAK
THE ESCAPE PODS!
IF WE HURRY... WE CAN GET OFF THE SHIP!
COME ON!
HWOOOOOOOOO

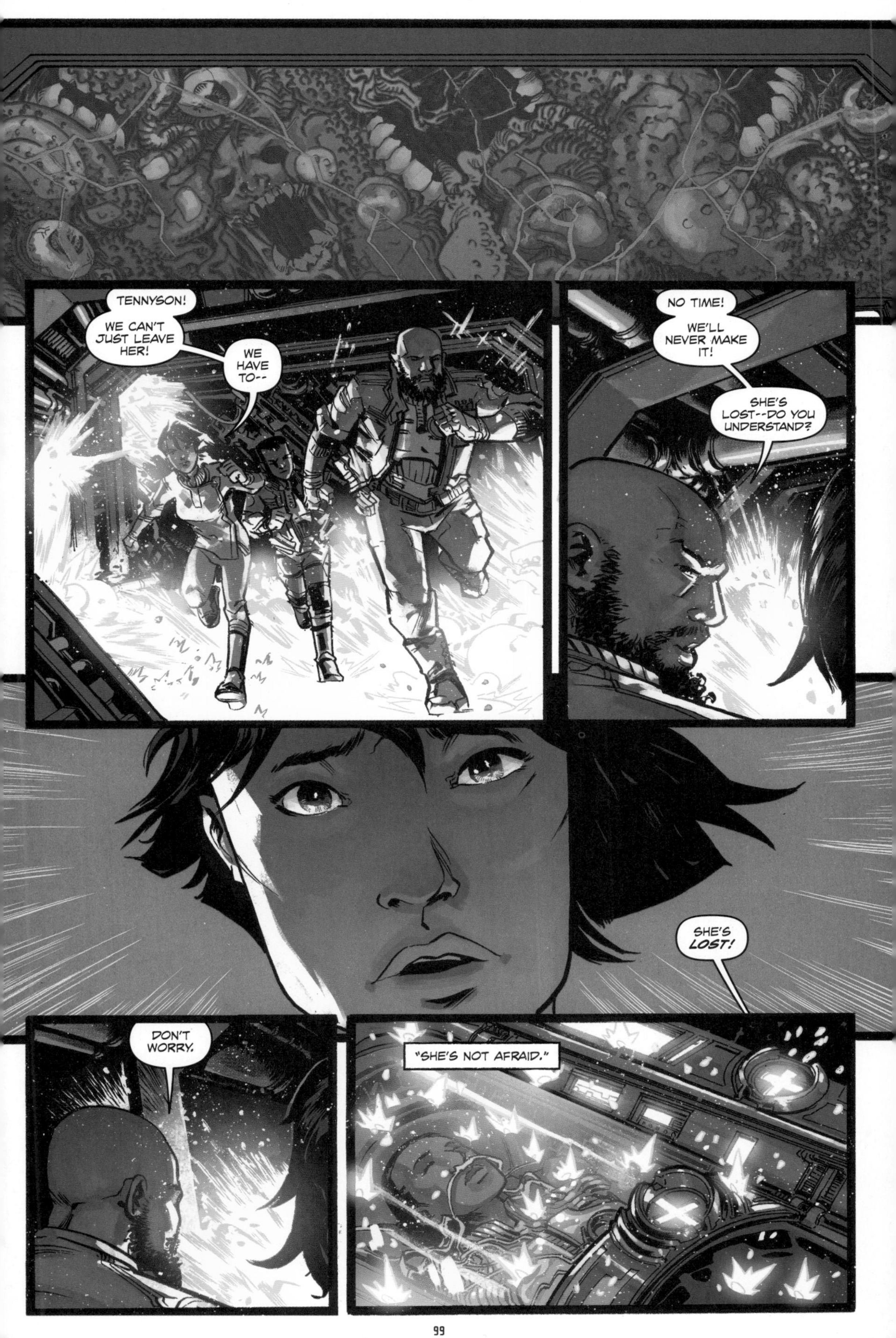
TENNYSON!
WE CAN'T JUST LEAVE HER!
WE HAVE TO--
NO TIME!
WE'LL NEVER MAKE IT!
SHE'S LOST--DO YOU UNDERSTAND?
SHE'S *LOST!*
DON'T WORRY.
"SHE'S NOT AFRAID."

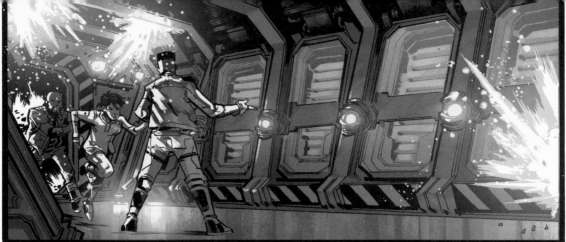

WE'RE NOT GONNA BE ABLE TO PROGRAM IN A DESTINATION.

BUT THESE PODS AREN'T DESIGNED TO GO FAR.

THERE ARE TRACKERS ON BOARD, SO ONCE YOU LAND, STAY CLOSE.

BLASTING OUT AT THIS ELEVATION...

...WILL THE PODS EVEN SURVIVE A LANDING?

KEITH--

KEITH!

ALEX!

THUNK

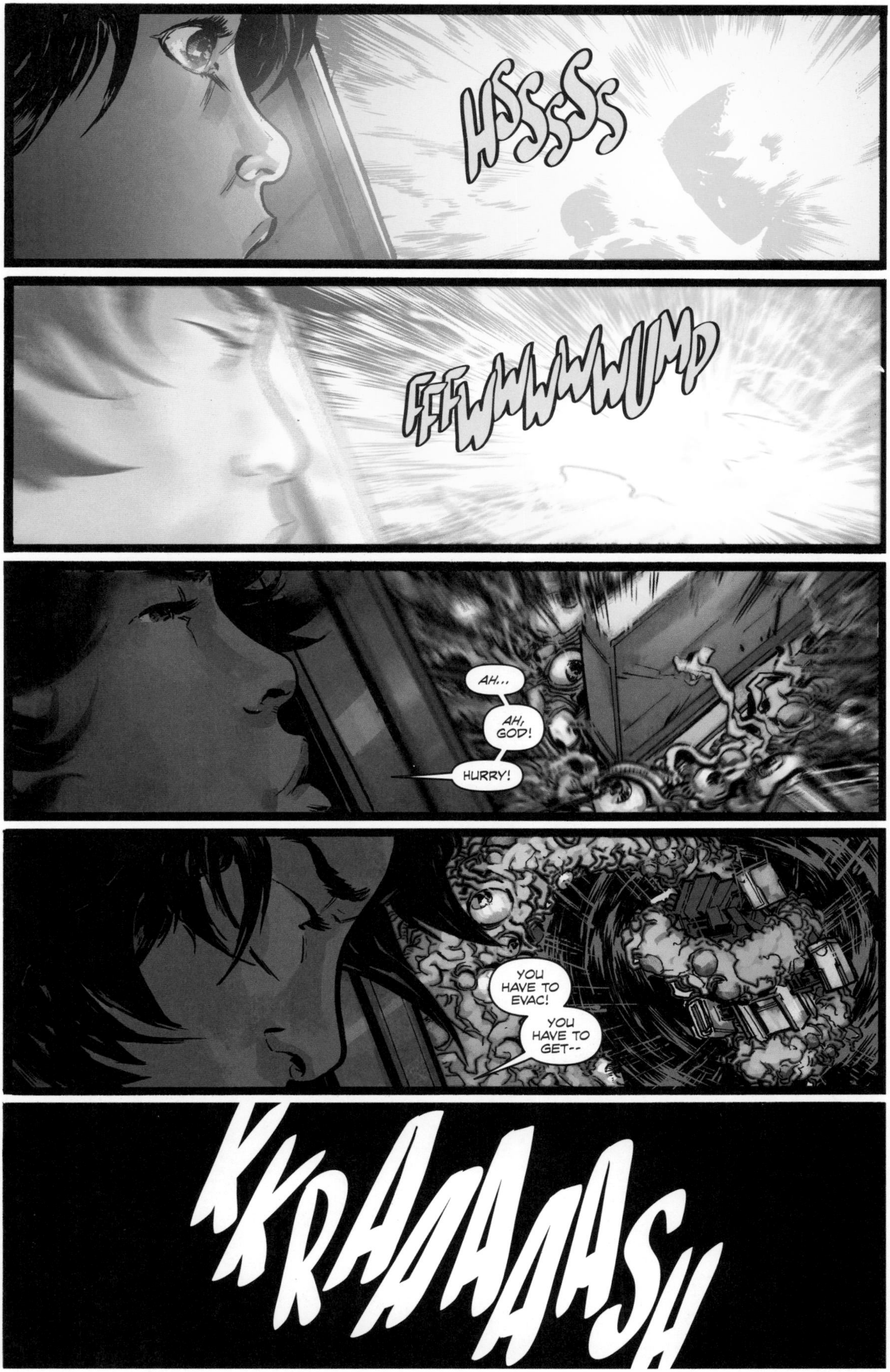
HSSSSS
FFWWWWWUMP
AH...
AH, GOD!
HURRY!
YOU HAVE TO EVAC!
YOU HAVE TO GET--
KRAAAASH

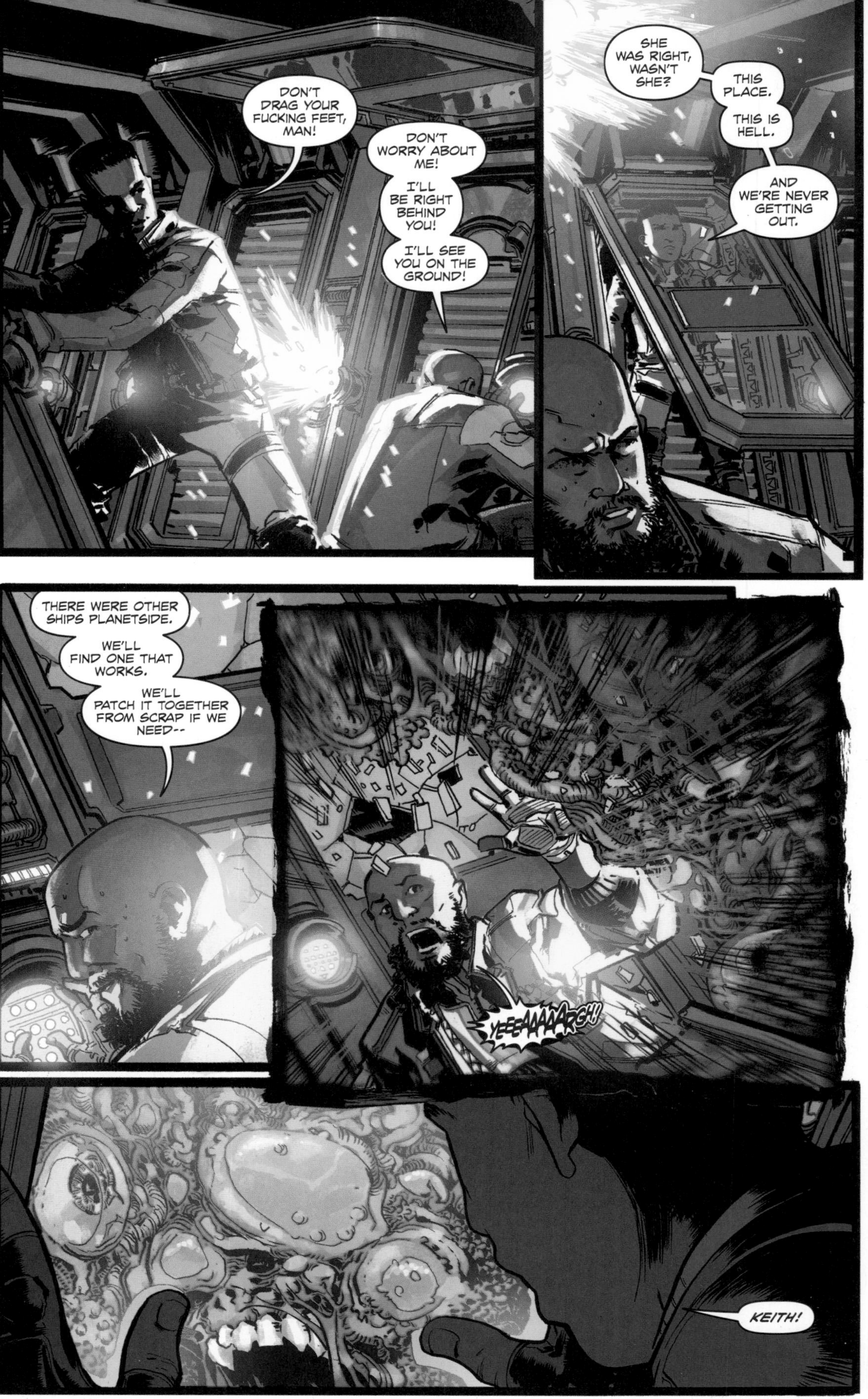

DON'T DRAG YOUR FUCKING FEET, MAN!
DON'T WORRY ABOUT ME!
I'LL BE RIGHT BEHIND YOU!
I'LL SEE YOU ON THE GROUND!
SHE WAS RIGHT, WASN'T SHE?
THIS PLACE.
THIS IS HELL.
AND WE'RE NEVER GETTING OUT.
THERE WERE OTHER SHIPS PLANETSIDE.
WE'LL FIND ONE THAT WORKS.
WE'LL PATCH IT TOGETHER FROM SCRAP IF WE NEED--
YEEEAAAAARGH!!
KEITH!

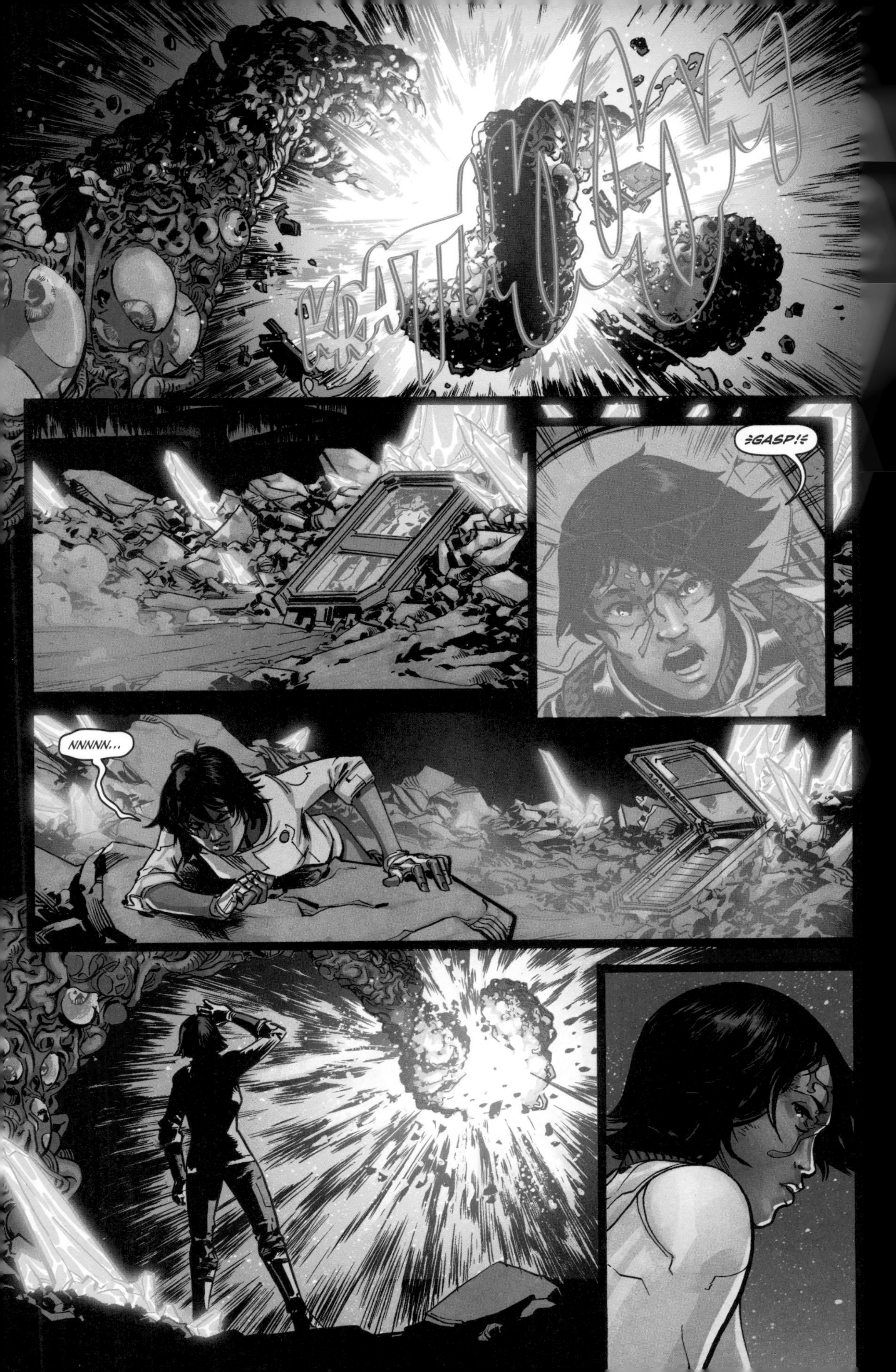
KRATHOOOM
GASP!
NNNNN...

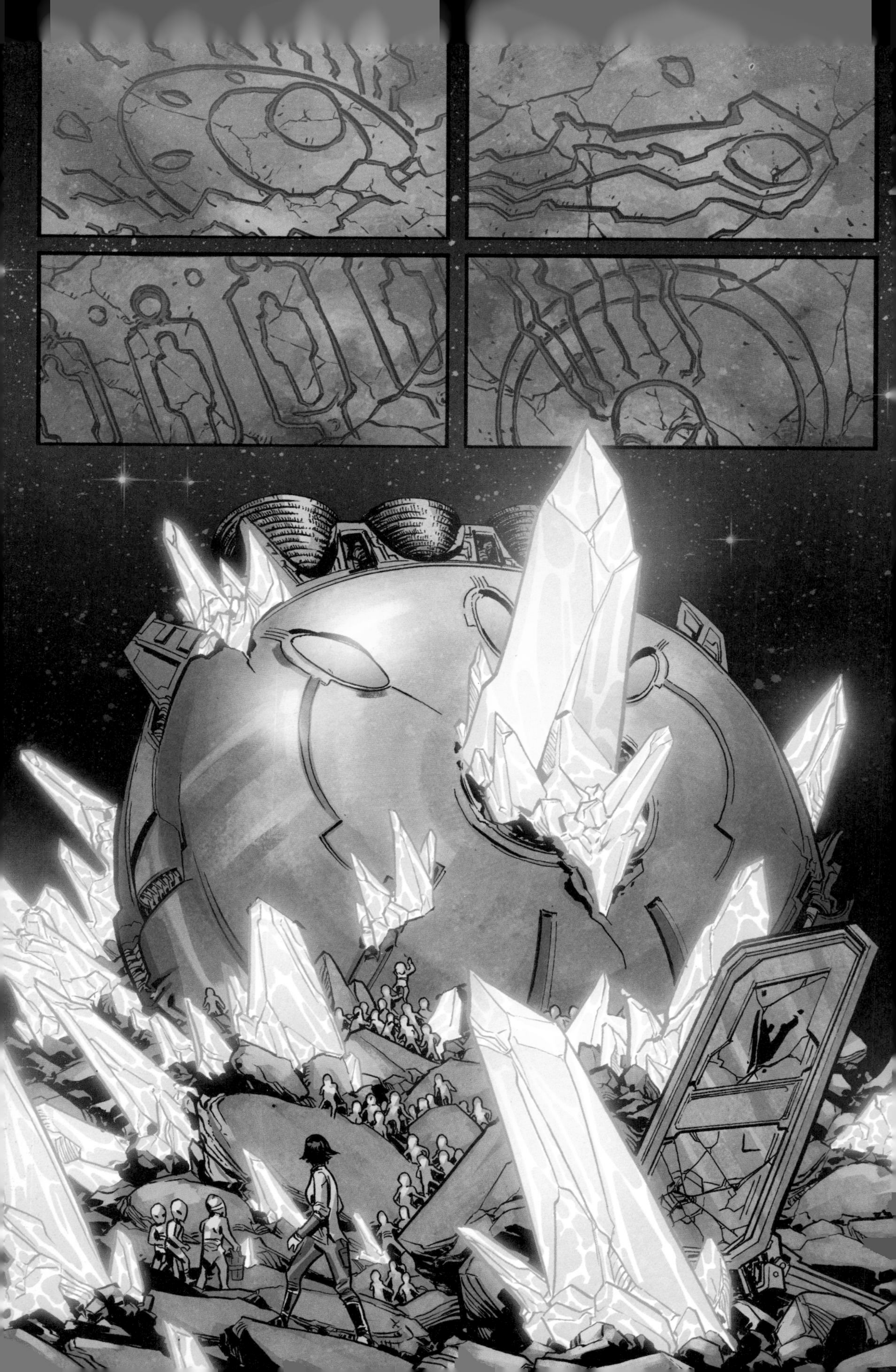

CHAPTER 05

THE ROGUE AWAKENS

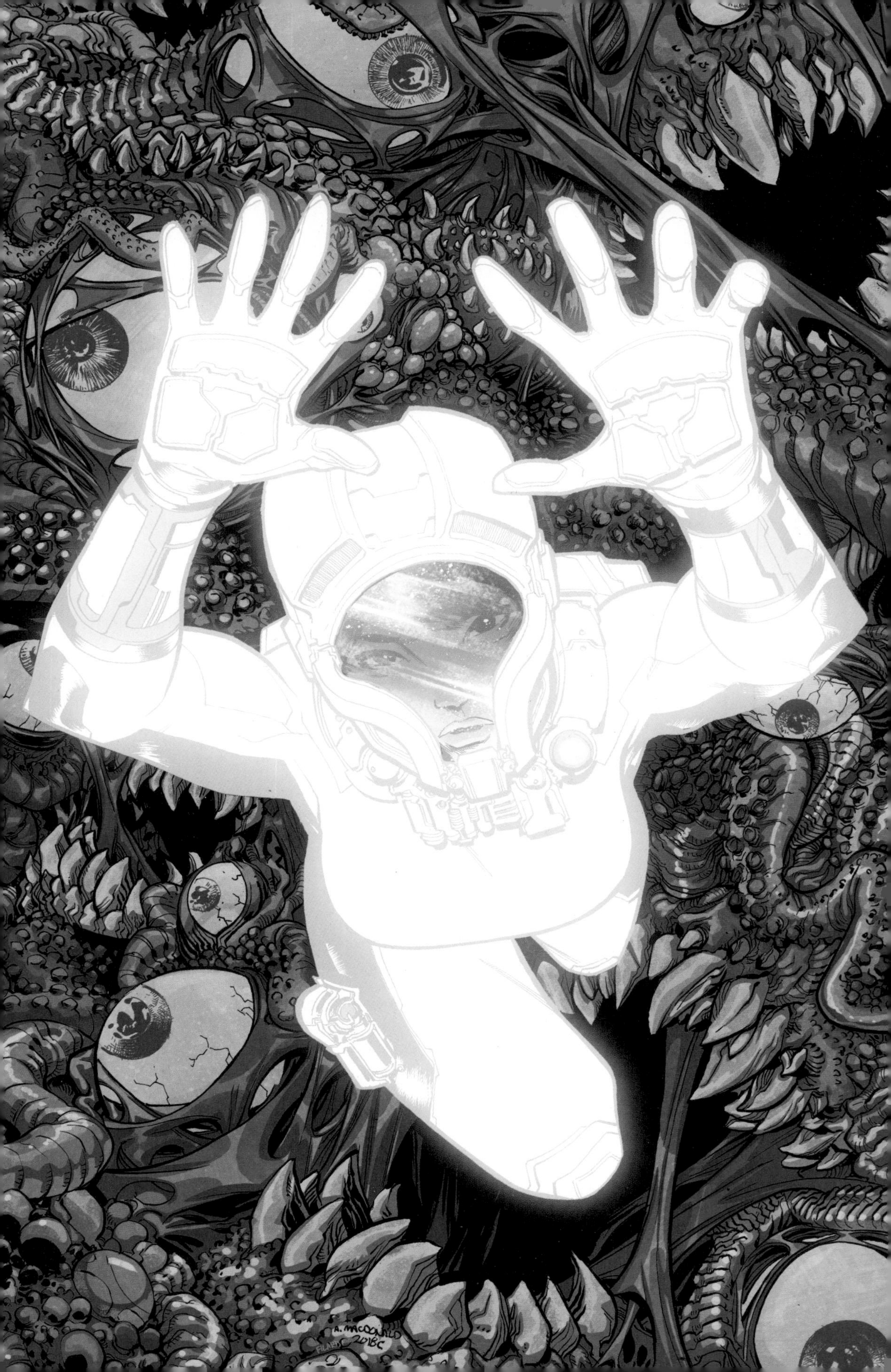

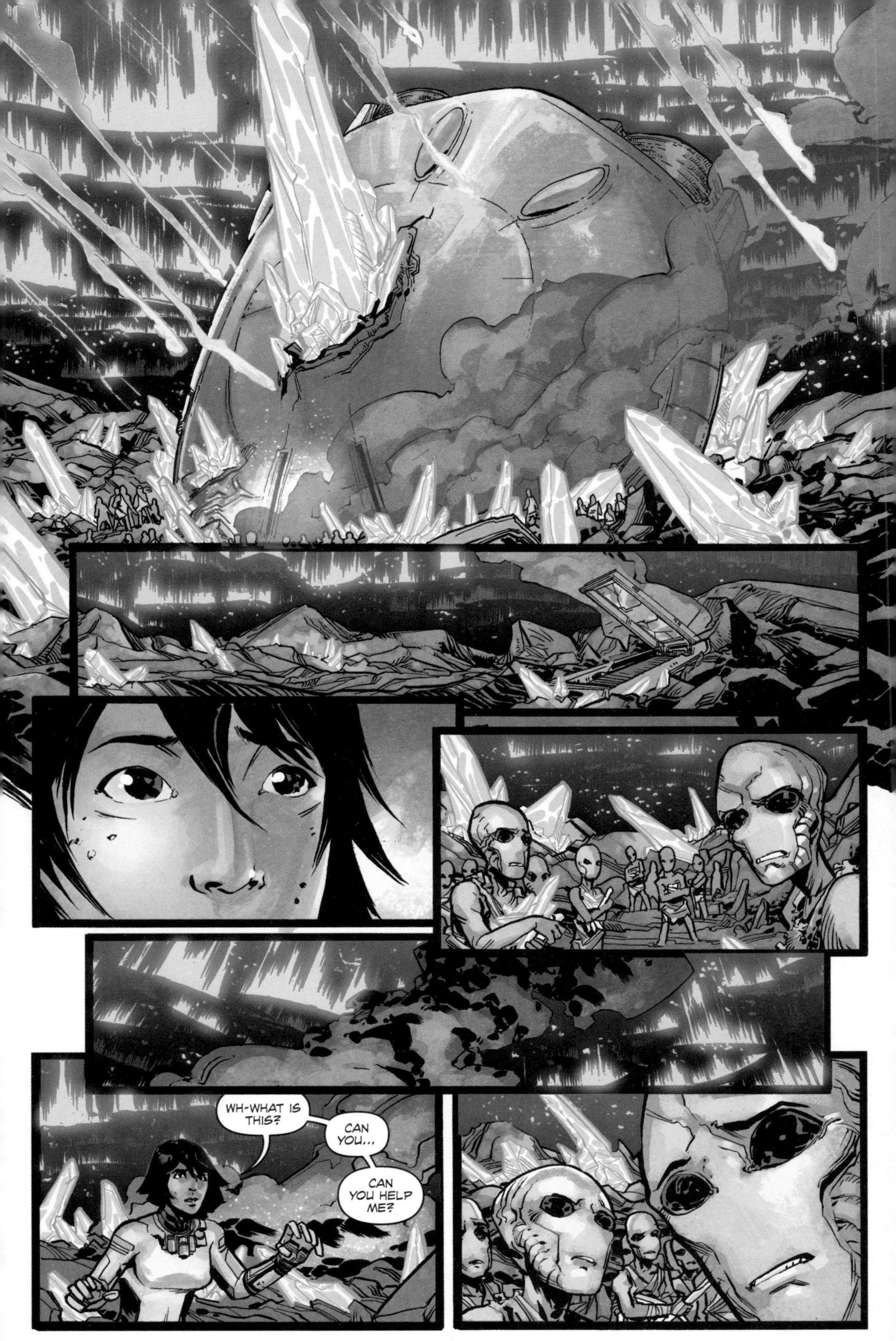
WH-WHAT IS THIS?
CAN YOU...
CAN YOU HELP ME?

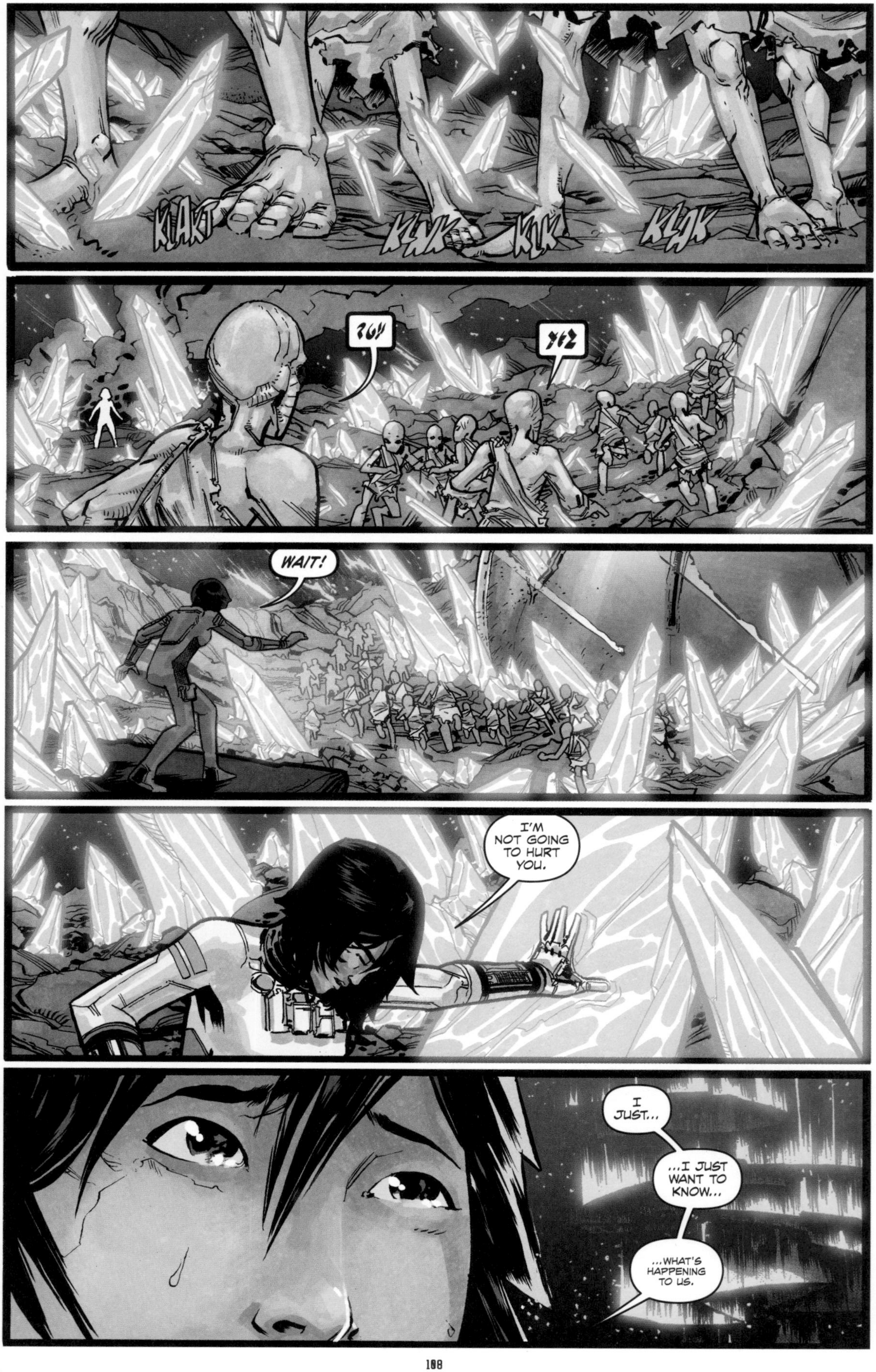
KLAKT
KLAK
KLK
KLAK
WAIT!
I'M NOT GOING TO HURT YOU.
I JUST...
...I JUST WANT TO KNOW...
...WHAT'S HAPPENING TO US.

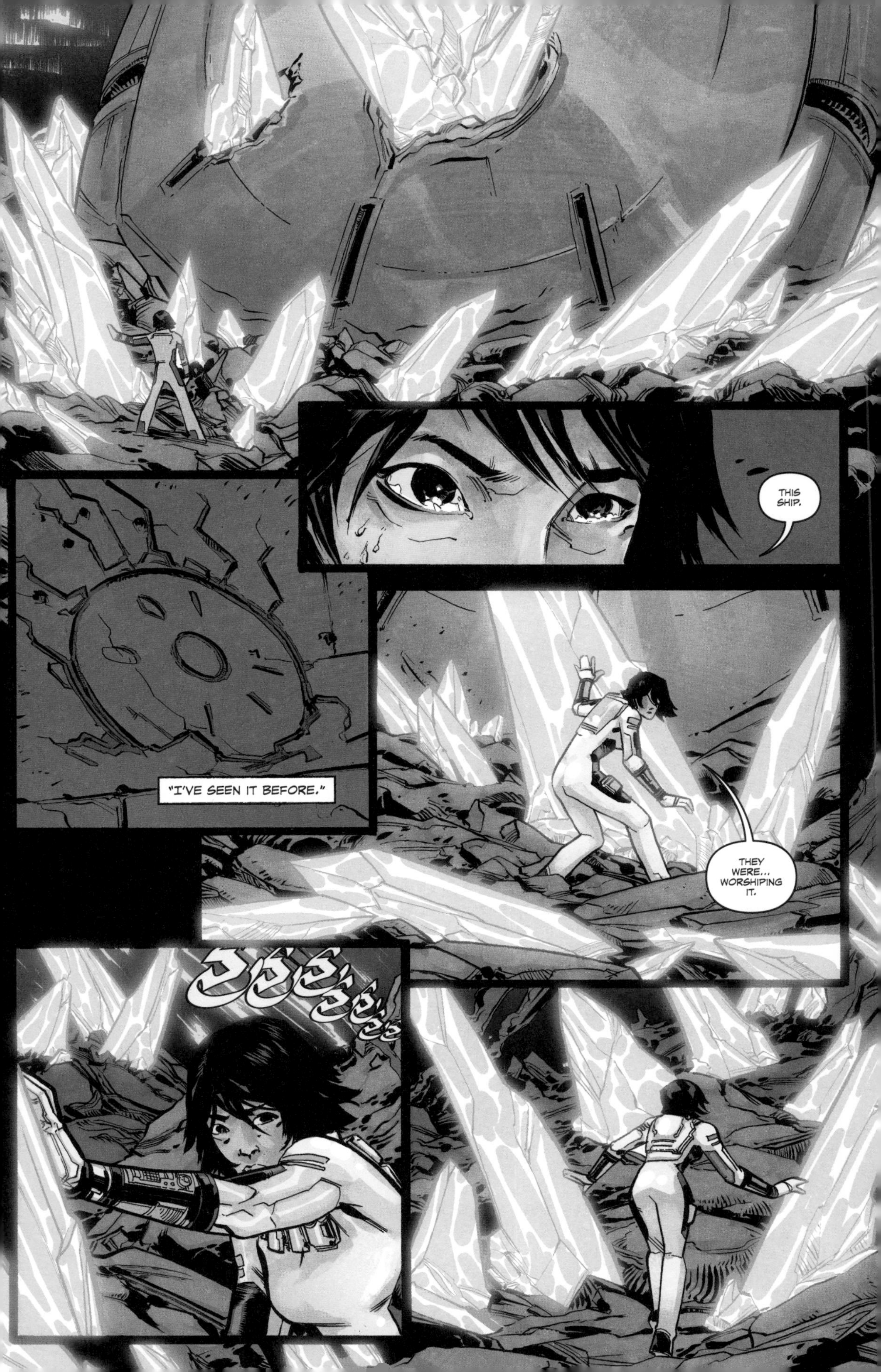
THIS SHIP.
"I'VE SEEN IT BEFORE."
THEY WERE... WORSHIPING IT.
SSSSSSS

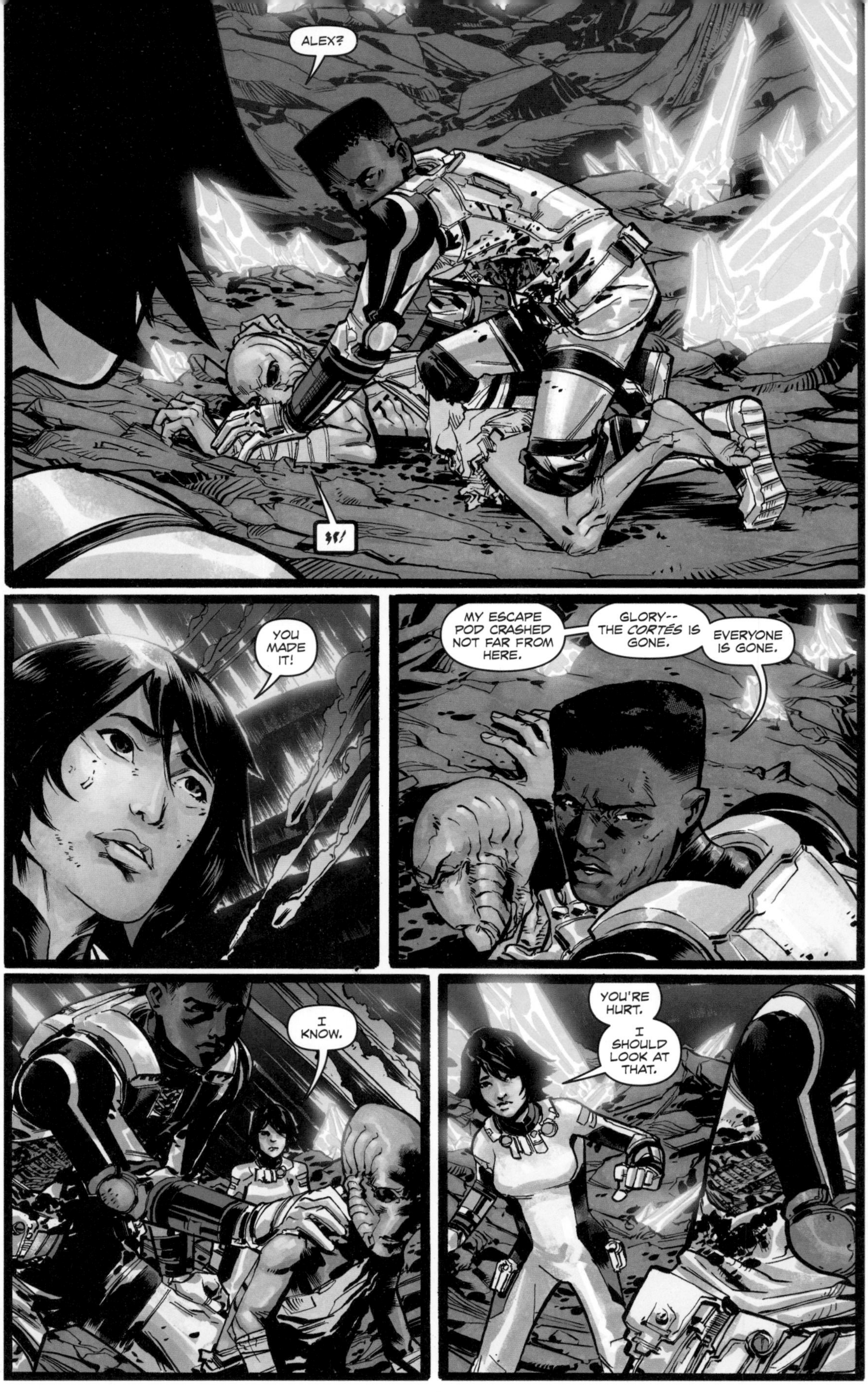
ALEX?
YOU MADE IT!
MY ESCAPE POD CRASHED NOT FAR FROM HERE.
GLORY-- THE *CORTÉS* IS GONE.
EVERYONE IS GONE.
I KNOW.
YOU'RE HURT.
I SHOULD LOOK AT THAT.

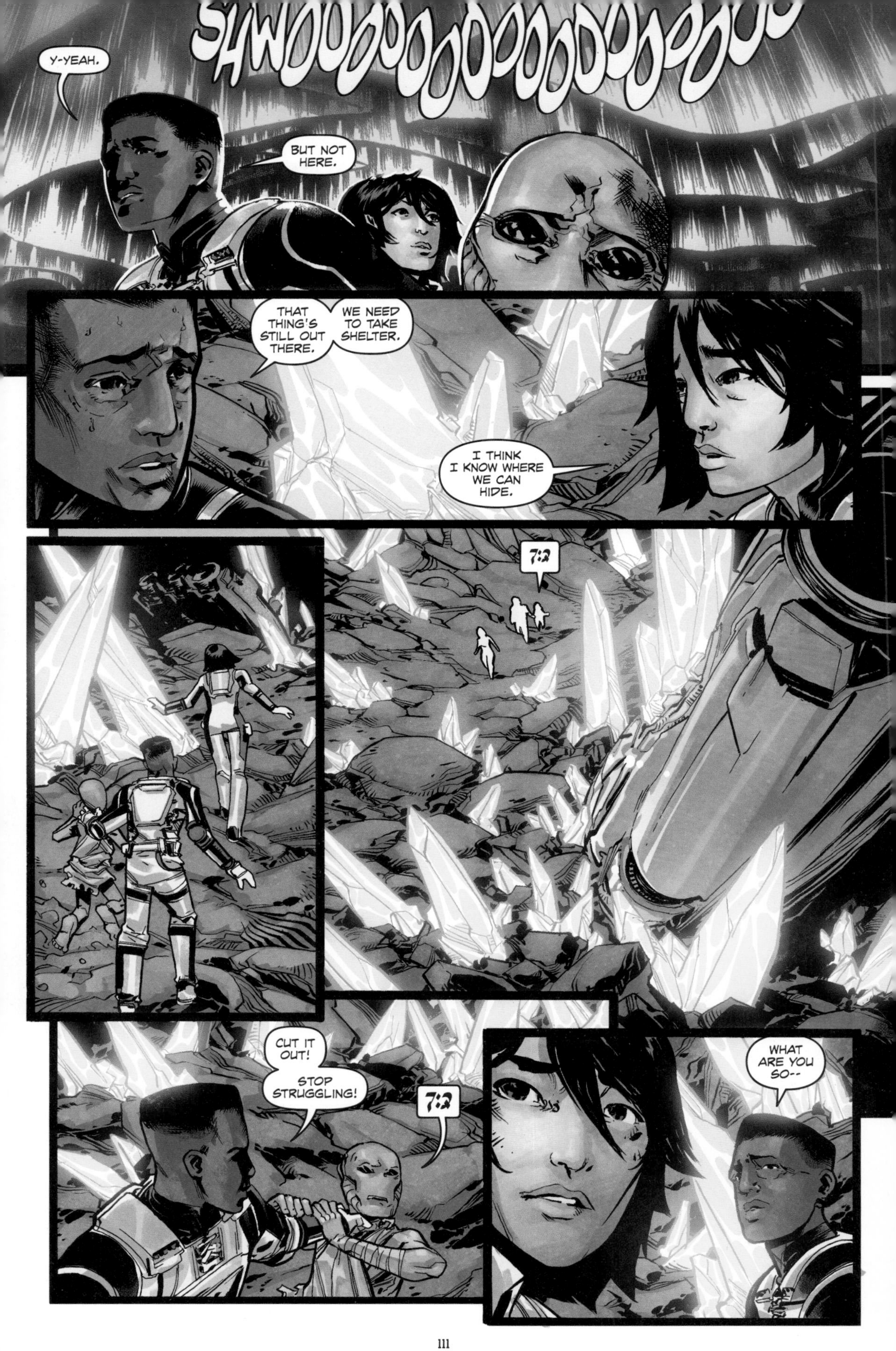
SHWOOOOOOOOOOOOOOOOO
Y-YEAH.
BUT NOT HERE.
THAT THING'S STILL OUT THERE.
WE NEED TO TAKE SHELTER.
I THINK I KNOW WHERE WE CAN HIDE.
7:2
CUT IT OUT!
STOP STRUGGLING!
7:2
WHAT ARE YOU SO--

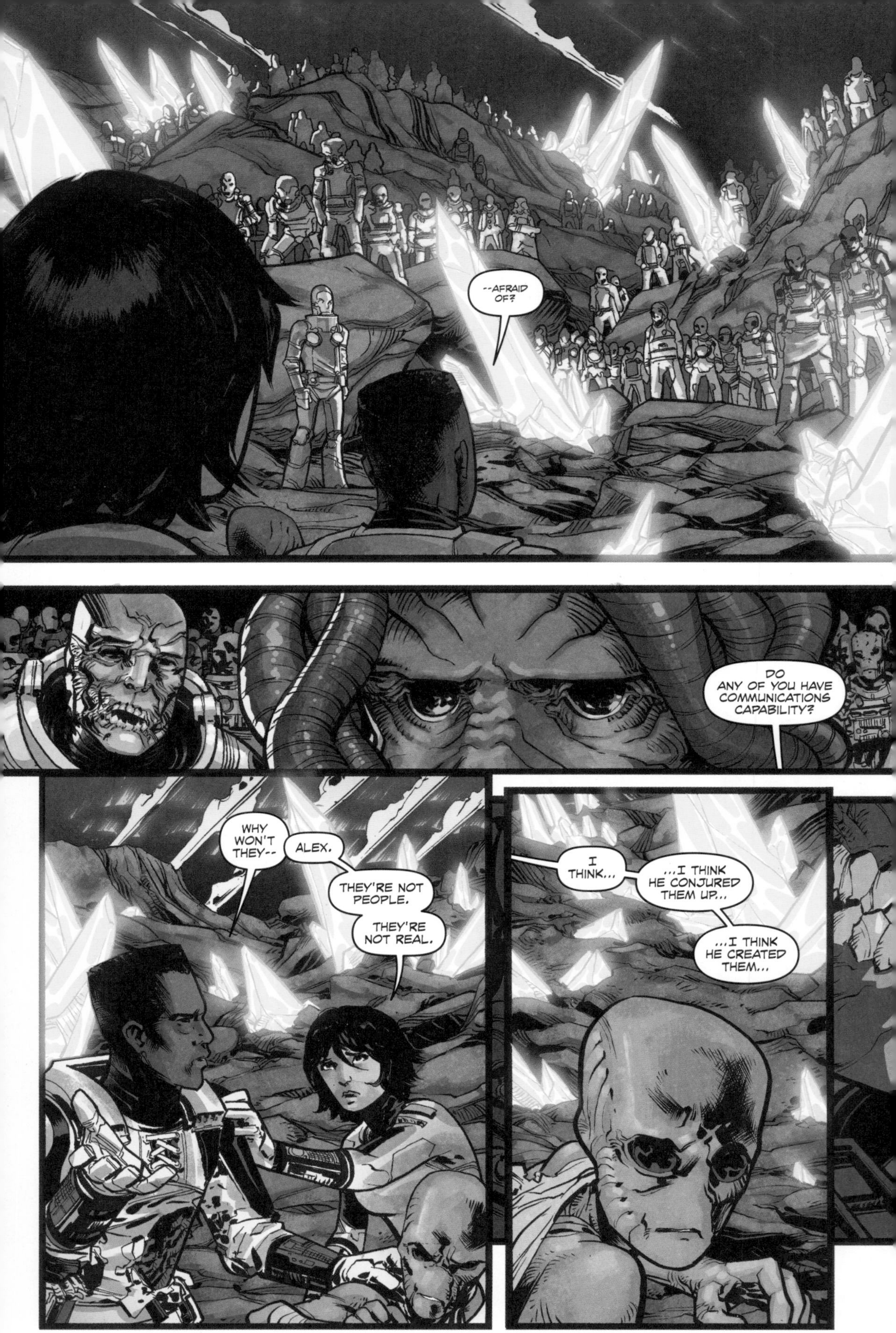
--AFRAID OF?
DO ANY OF YOU HAVE COMMUNICATIONS CAPABILITY?
WHY WON'T THEY--
ALEX.
THEY'RE NOT PEOPLE.
THEY'RE NOT REAL.
I THINK...
...I THINK HE CONJURED THEM UP...
...I THINK HE CREATED THEM...

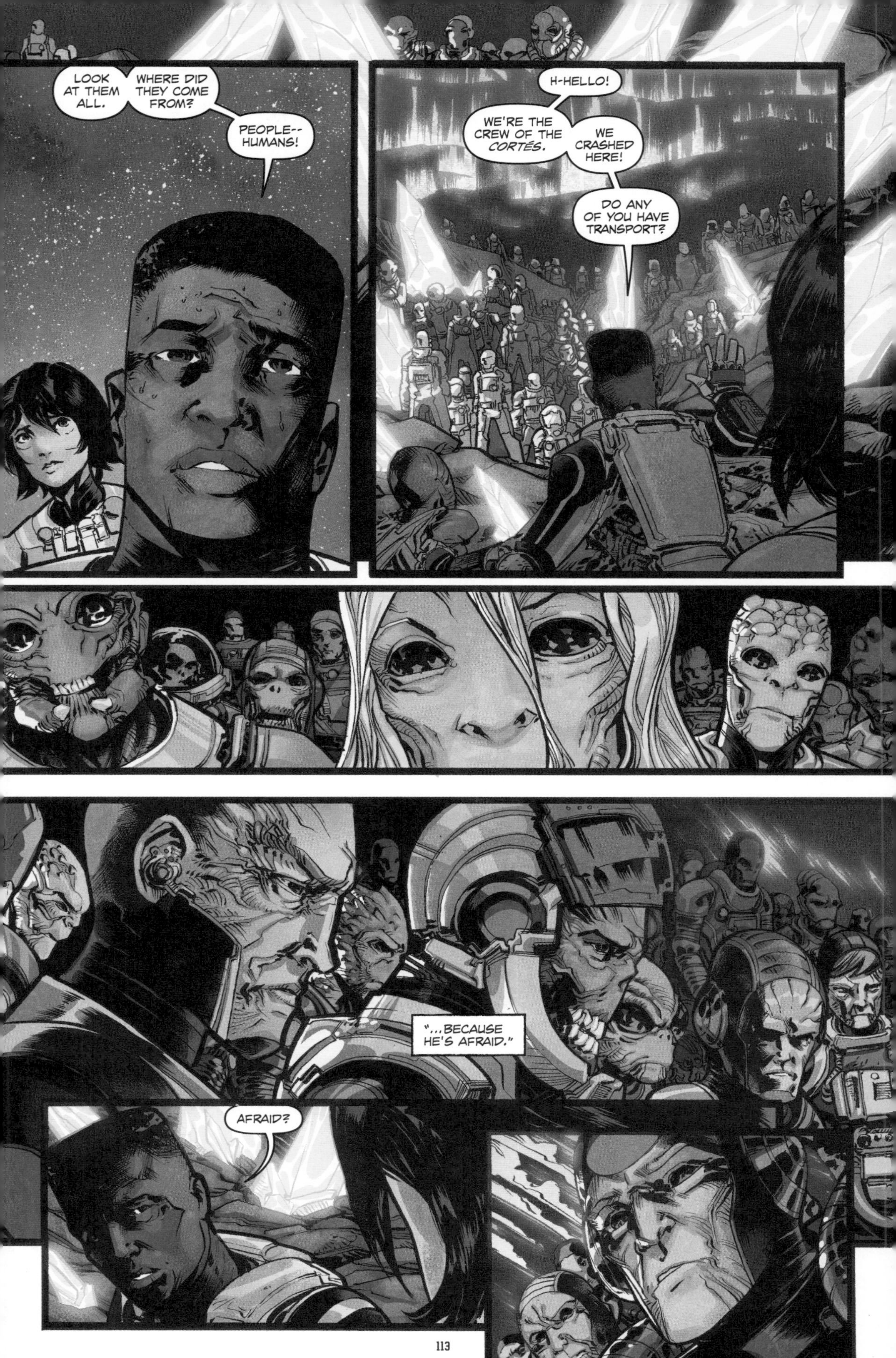
LOOK AT THEM ALL.
WHERE DID THEY COME FROM?
PEOPLE-- HUMANS!
H-HELLO!
WE'RE THE CREW OF THE CORTÉS.
WE CRASHED HERE!
DO ANY OF YOU HAVE TRANSPORT?
"...BECAUSE HE'S AFRAID."
AFRAID?

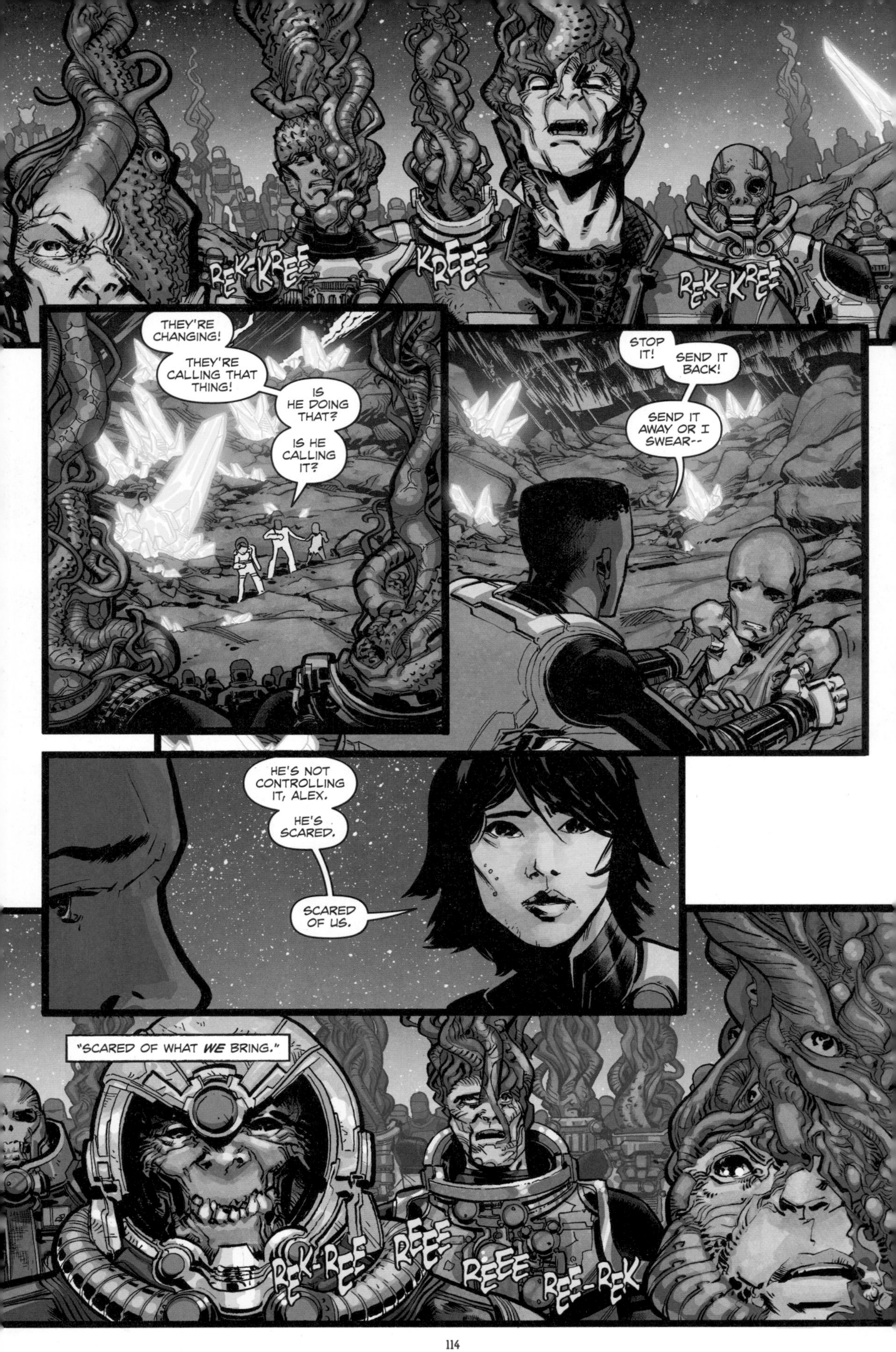
REK-KREE
KREEE
REK-KREE
THEY'RE CHANGING!
THEY'RE CALLING THAT THING!
IS HE DOING THAT?
IS HE CALLING IT?
STOP IT!
SEND IT BACK!
SEND IT AWAY OR I SWEAR--
HE'S NOT CONTROLLING IT, ALEX.
HE'S SCARED.
SCARED OF US.
"SCARED OF WHAT WE BRING."
REK-REE
REEE
REEE
REE-REK

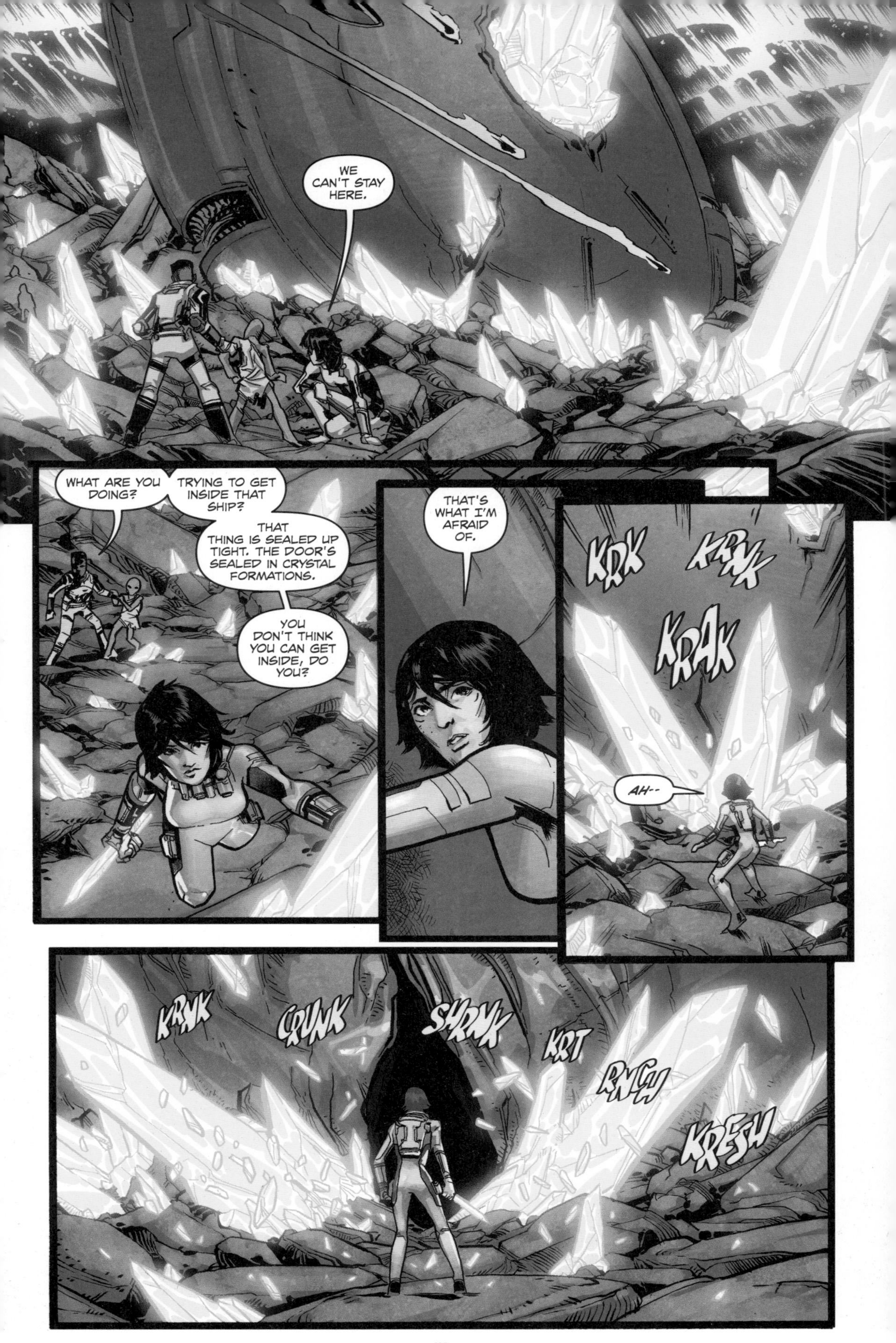
WE CAN'T STAY HERE.
WHAT ARE YOU DOING?
TRYING TO GET INSIDE THAT SHIP?
THAT THING IS SEALED UP TIGHT. THE DOOR'S SEALED IN CRYSTAL FORMATIONS.
YOU DON'T THINK YOU CAN GET INSIDE, DO YOU?
THAT'S WHAT I'M AFRAID OF.
KRK
KRNK
KRAK
AH--
KRNK
CRUNK
SHRNK
KRT
RNCH
KRESH

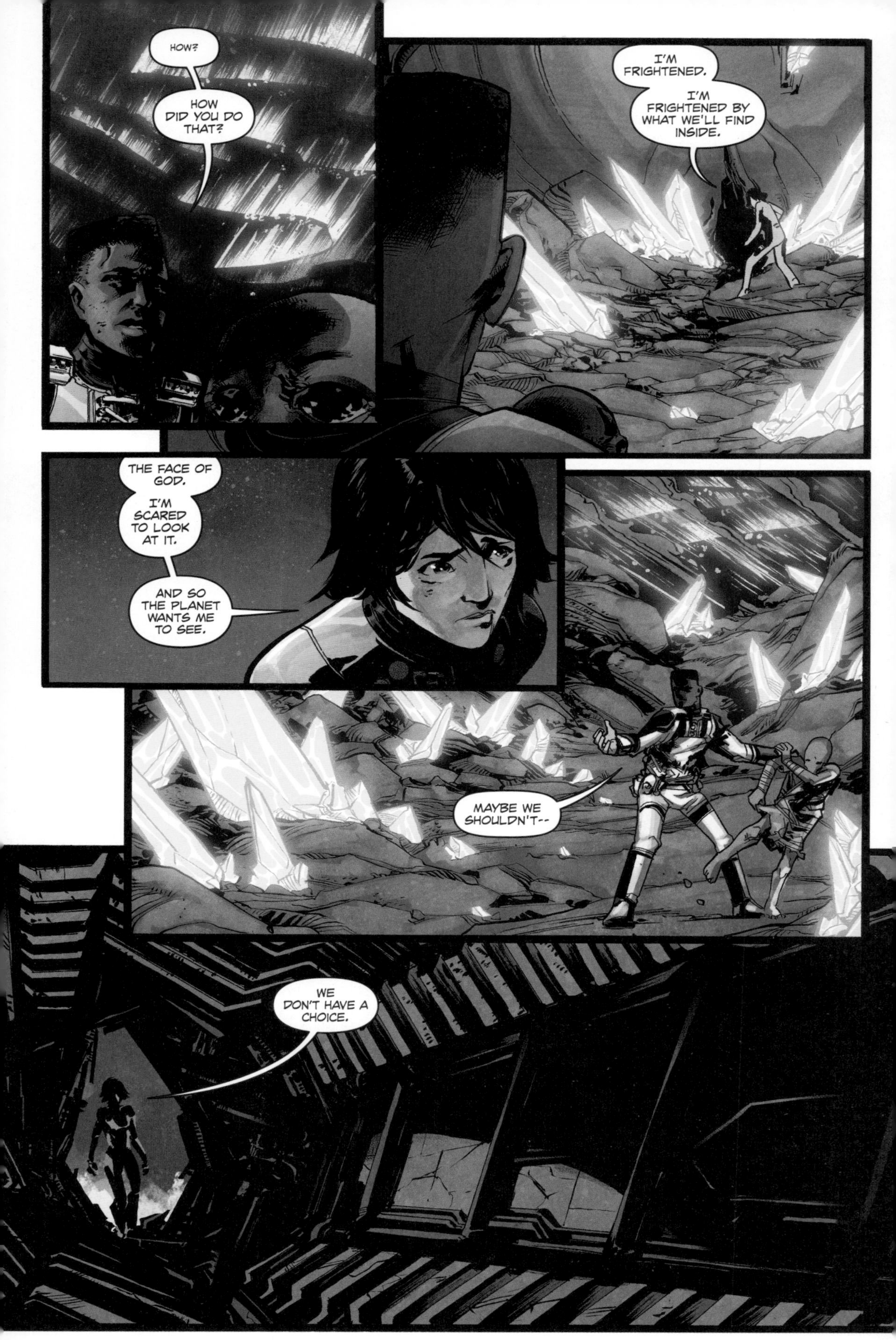
HOW?
HOW DID YOU DO THAT?
I'M FRIGHTENED.
I'M FRIGHTENED BY WHAT WE'LL FIND INSIDE.
THE FACE OF GOD.
I'M SCARED TO LOOK AT IT.
AND SO THE PLANET WANTS ME TO SEE.
MAYBE WE SHOULDN'T--
WE DON'T HAVE A CHOICE.

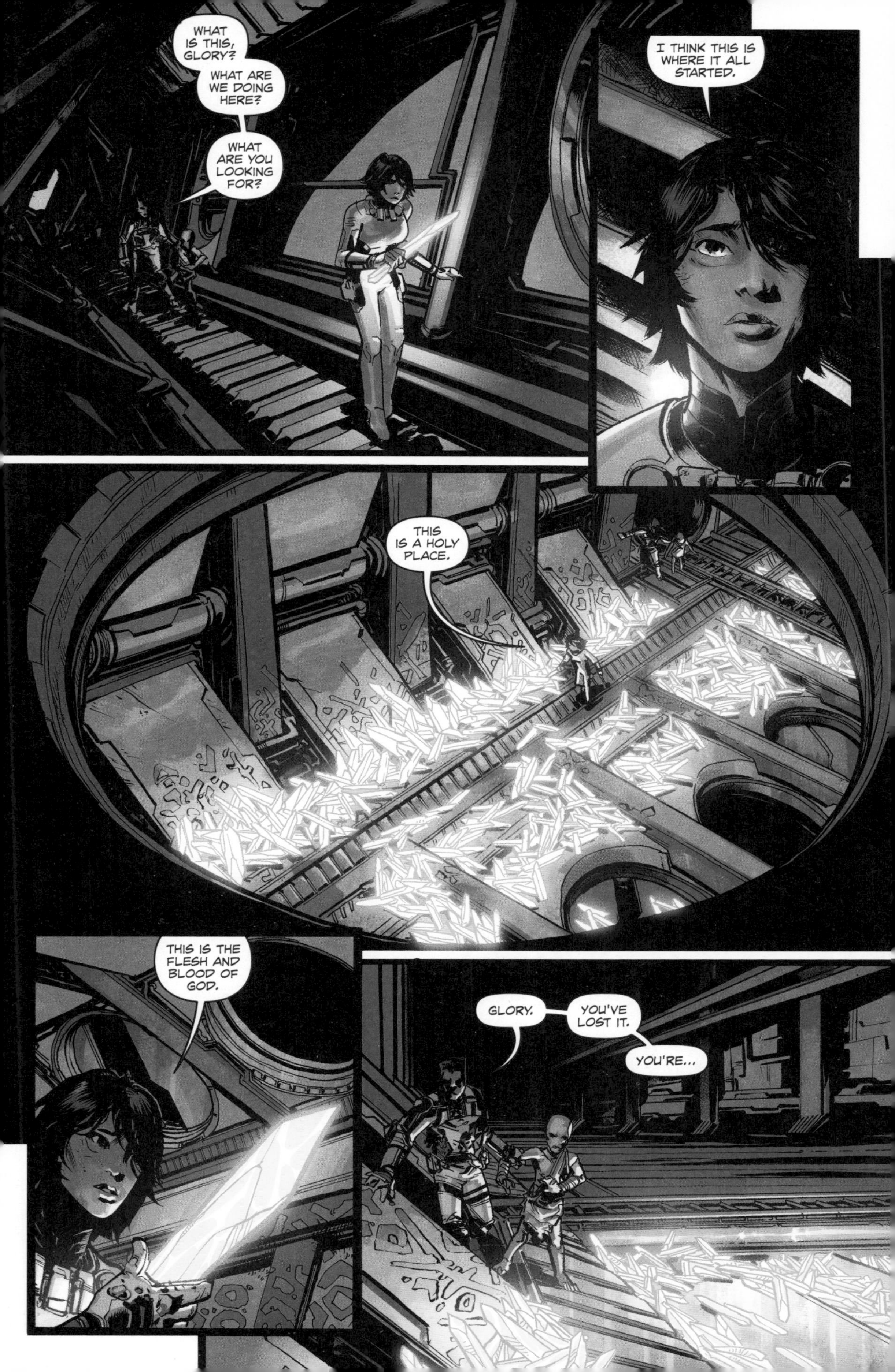
WHAT IS THIS, GLORY?
WHAT ARE WE DOING HERE?
WHAT ARE YOU LOOKING FOR?
I THINK THIS IS WHERE IT ALL STARTED.
THIS IS A HOLY PLACE.
THIS IS THE FLESH AND BLOOD OF GOD.
GLORY.
YOU'VE LOST IT.
YOU'RE...

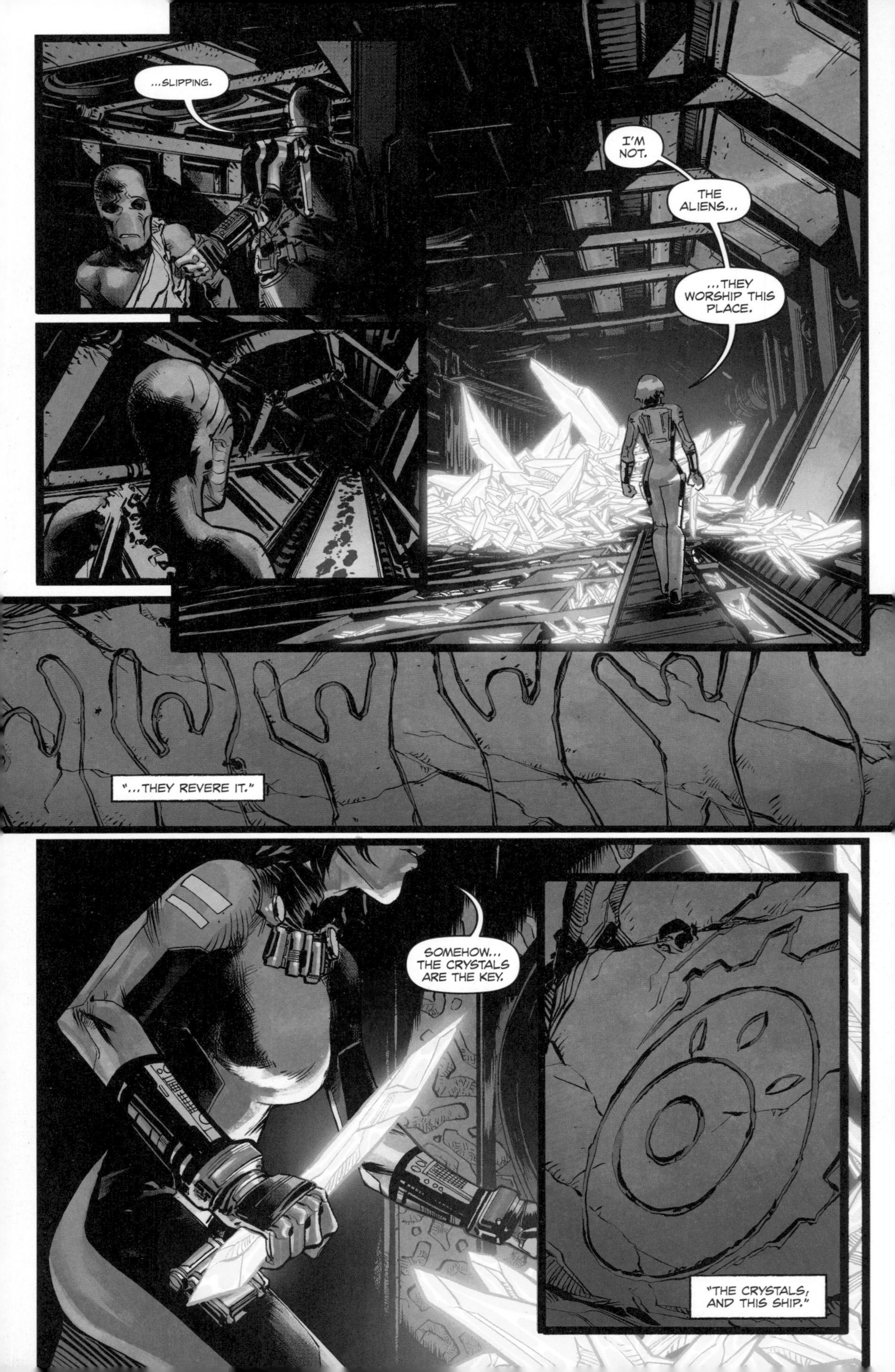
...SLIPPING.
I'M NOT.
THE ALIENS...
...THEY WORSHIP THIS PLACE.
"...THEY REVERE IT."
SOMEHOW... THE CRYSTALS ARE THE KEY.
"THE CRYSTALS, AND THIS SHIP."

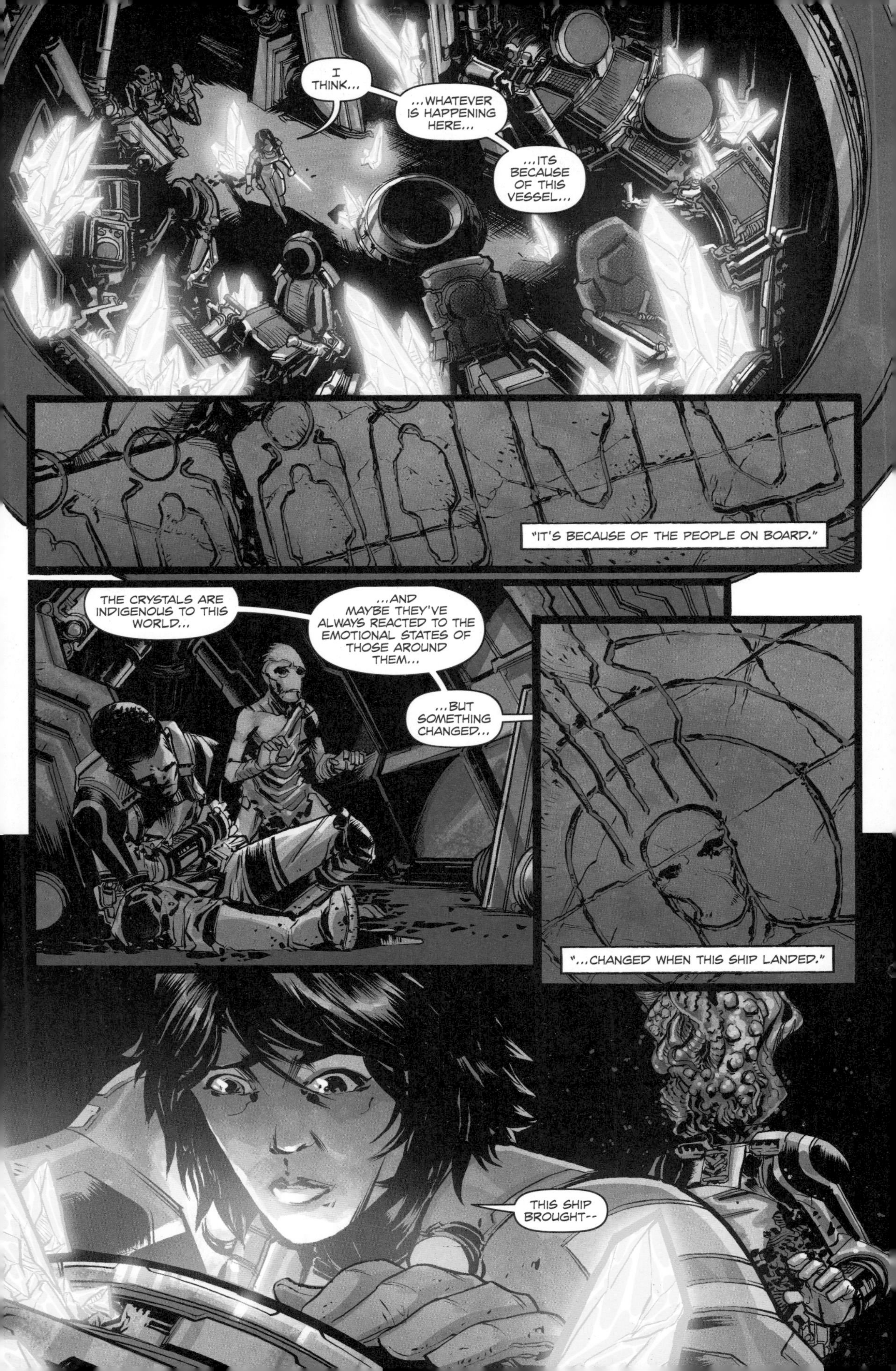
I THINK...
...WHATEVER IS HAPPENING HERE...
...ITS BECAUSE OF THIS VESSEL...
"IT'S BECAUSE OF THE PEOPLE ON BOARD."
THE CRYSTALS ARE INDIGENOUS TO THIS WORLD...
...AND MAYBE THEY'VE ALWAYS REACTED TO THE EMOTIONAL STATES OF THOSE AROUND THEM...
...BUT SOMETHING CHANGED...
"...CHANGED WHEN THIS SHIP LANDED."
THIS SHIP BROUGHT--

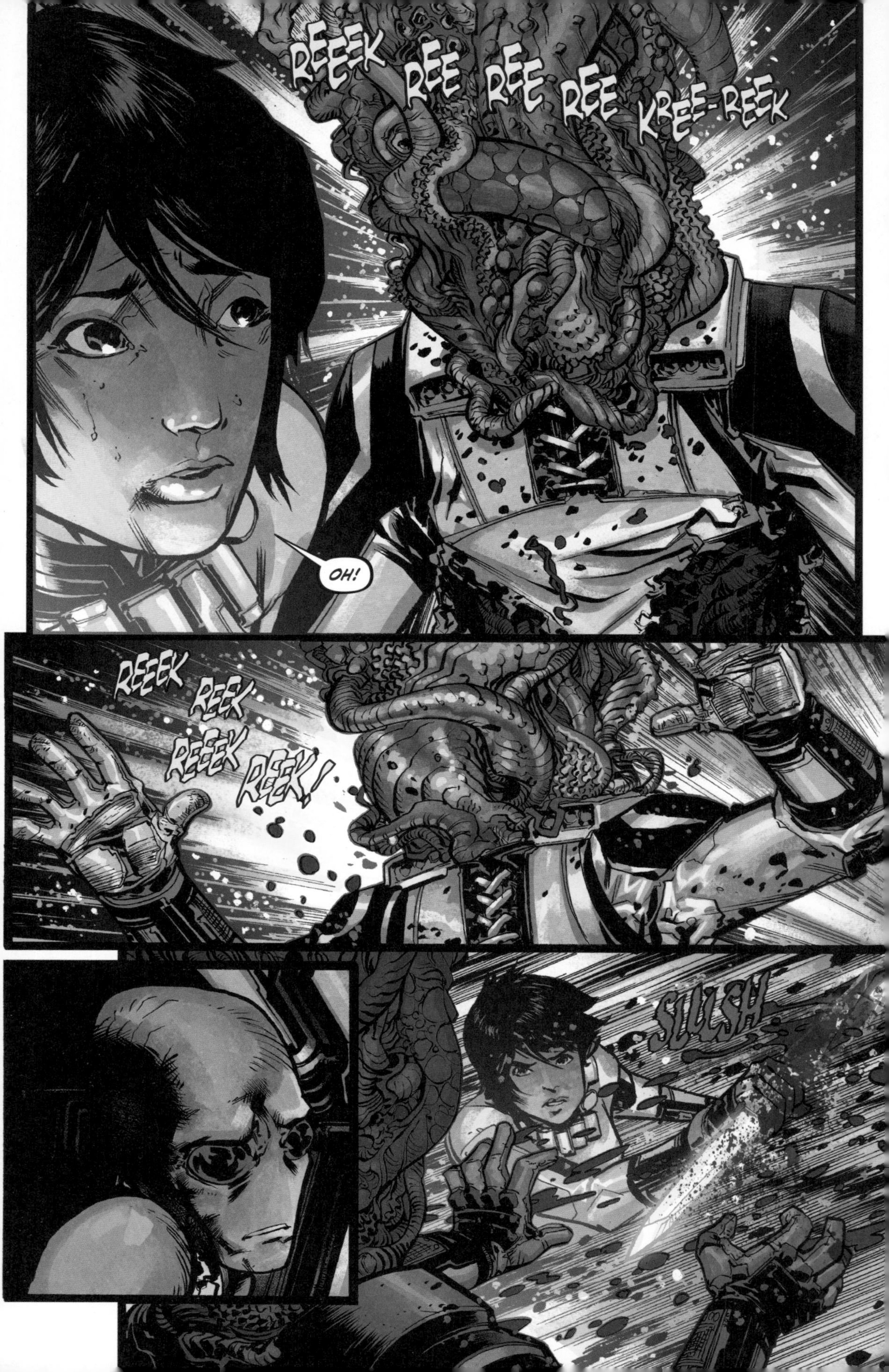
REEEK REE REE REE KREE-REEK
OH!
REEEK REEK REEEK REEK!
SLLLSH

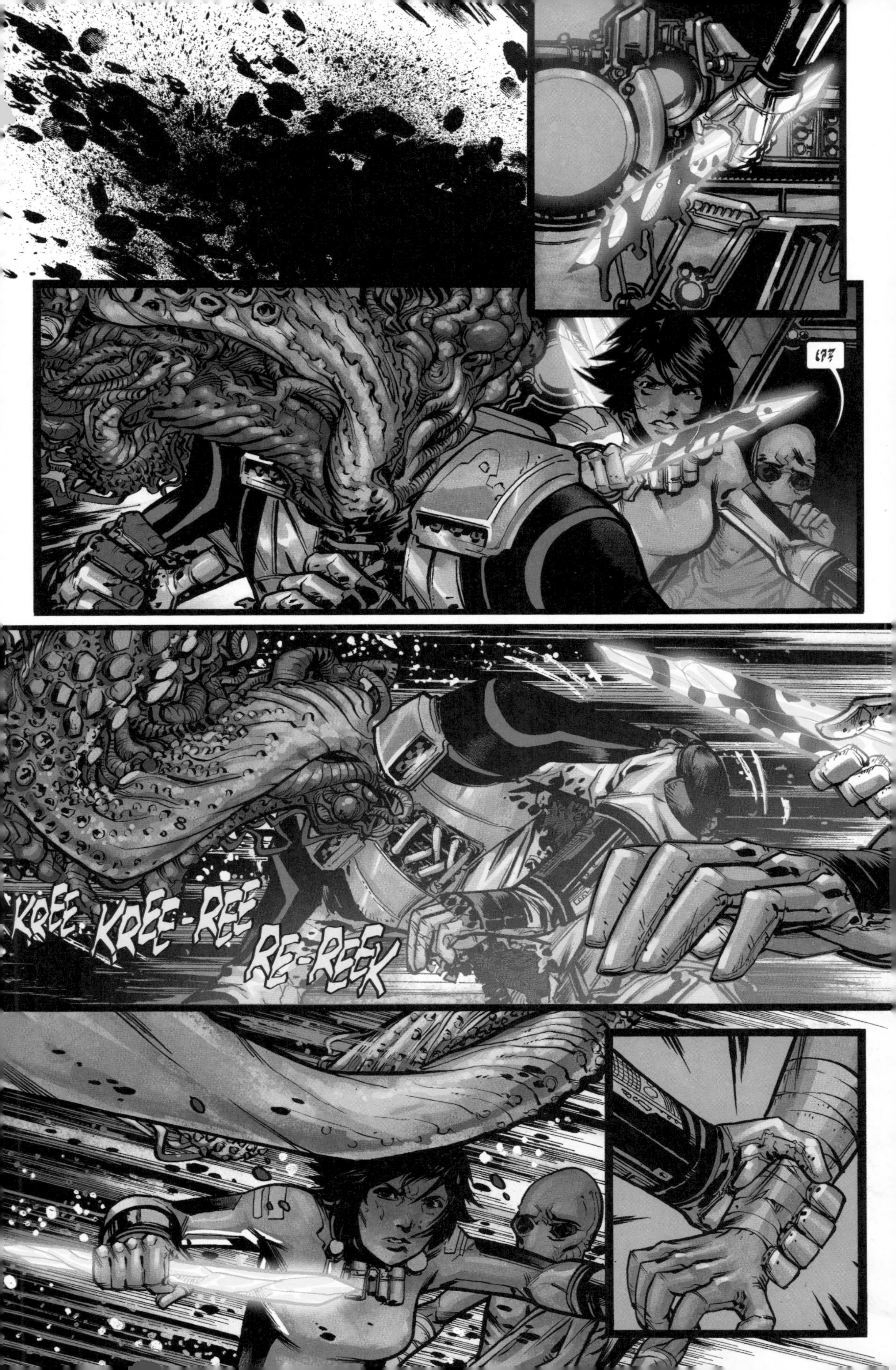
KREE KREE-REE
RE-REEK

COME ON!

REEE-REEE
REEE-REEE

ALEX--

ALEX...

...I'M...

...I'M SO SORRY...

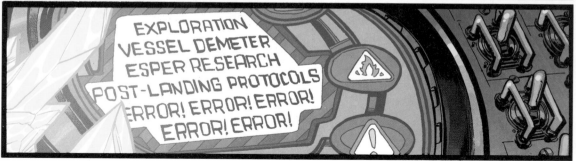

EXPLORATION VESSEL DEMETER ESPER RESEARCH POST-LANDING PROTOCOLS ERROR! ERROR! ERROR! ERROR! ERROR!

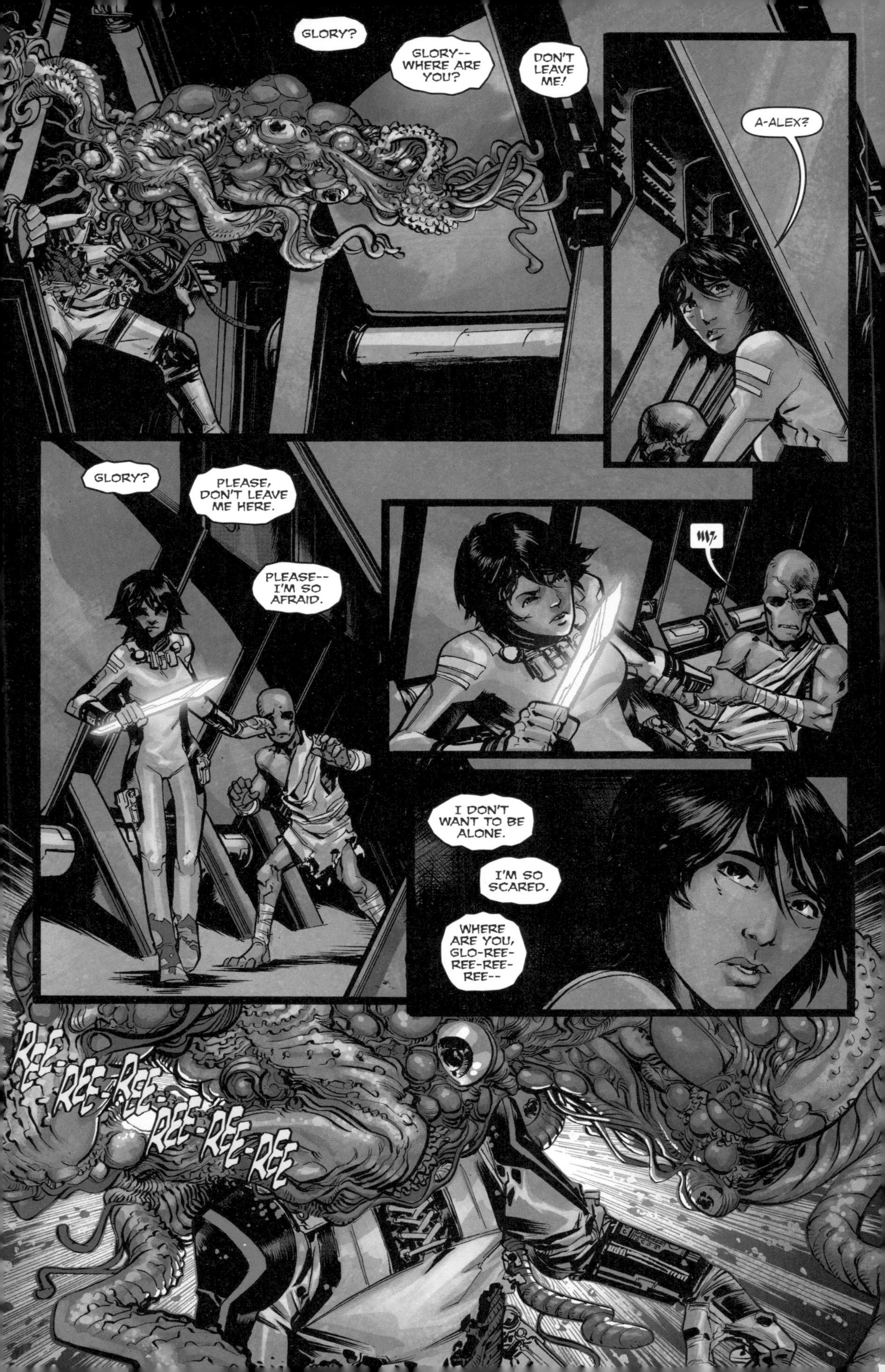
GLORY?
GLORY-- WHERE ARE YOU?
DON'T LEAVE ME!
A-ALEX?
GLORY?
PLEASE, DON'T LEAVE ME HERE.
PLEASE-- I'M SO AFRAID.
I DON'T WANT TO BE ALONE.
I'M SO SCARED.
WHERE ARE YOU, GLO-REE-REE-REE-REE--
REE-REE-REE-REE-REE-REE-REE

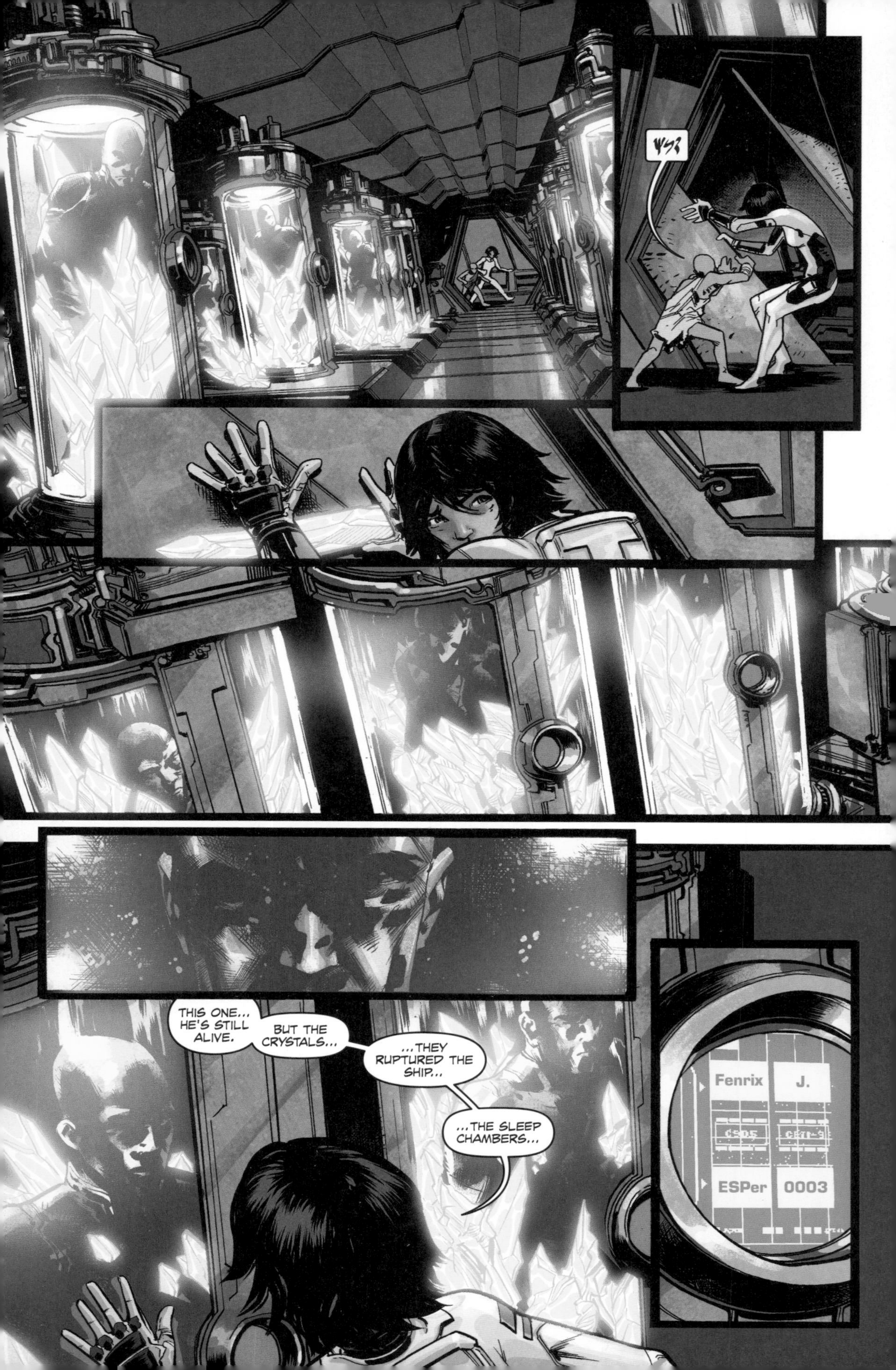
THIS ONE... HE'S STILL ALIVE.
BUT THE CRYSTALS...
...THEY RUPTURED THE SHIP...
...THE SLEEP CHAMBERS...
Fenrix
J.
ESPer
0003

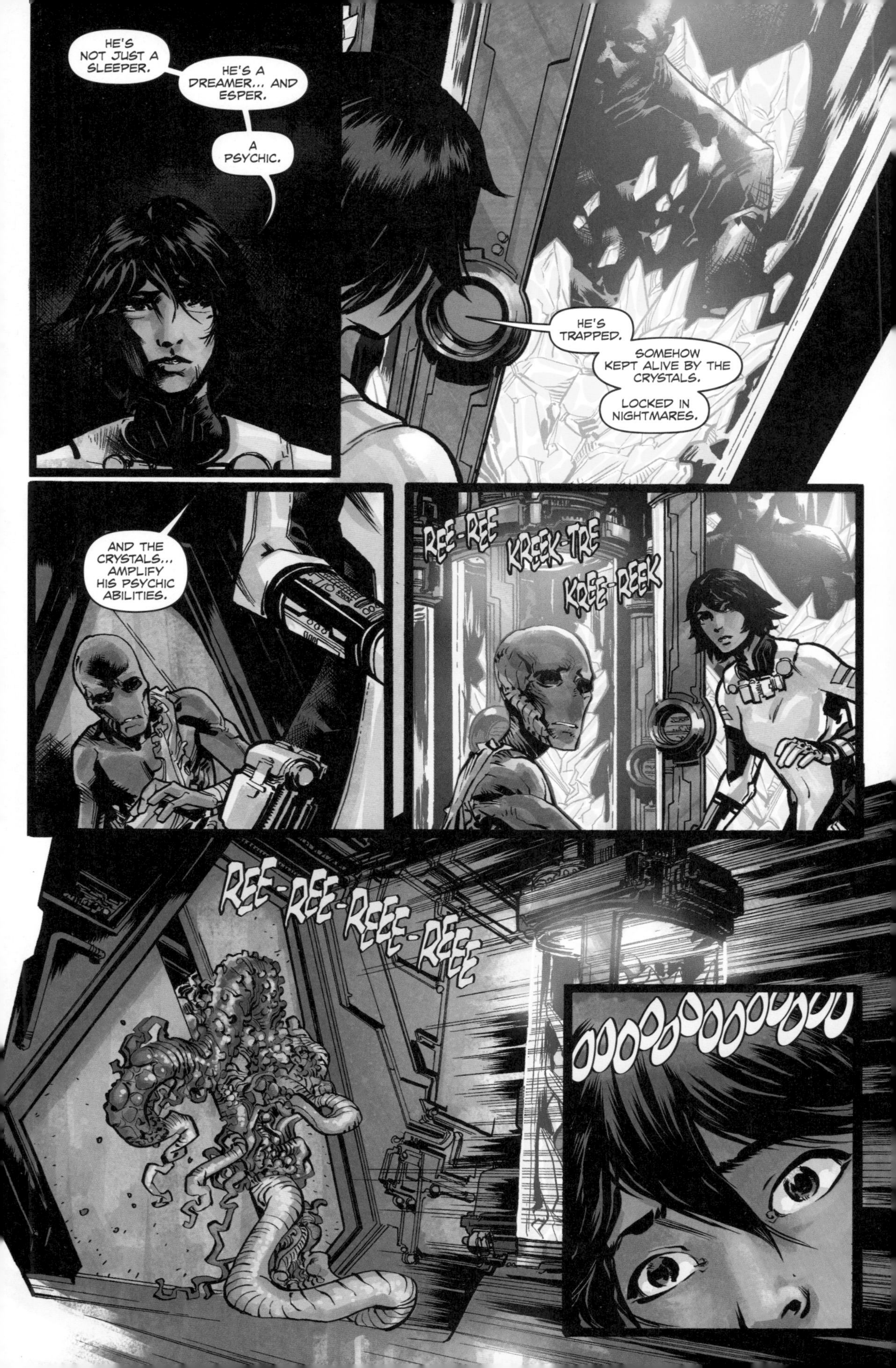
HE'S NOT JUST A SLEEPER.
HE'S A DREAMER... AND ESPER.
A PSYCHIC.
HE'S TRAPPED.
SOMEHOW KEPT ALIVE BY THE CRYSTALS.
LOCKED IN NIGHTMARES.
AND THE CRYSTALS... AMPLIFY HIS PSYCHIC ABILITIES.
REE-REE
KREEK-TRE
KREE-REEK
REE-REE-REEE-REEE
OOOOOOOOOOOOOO

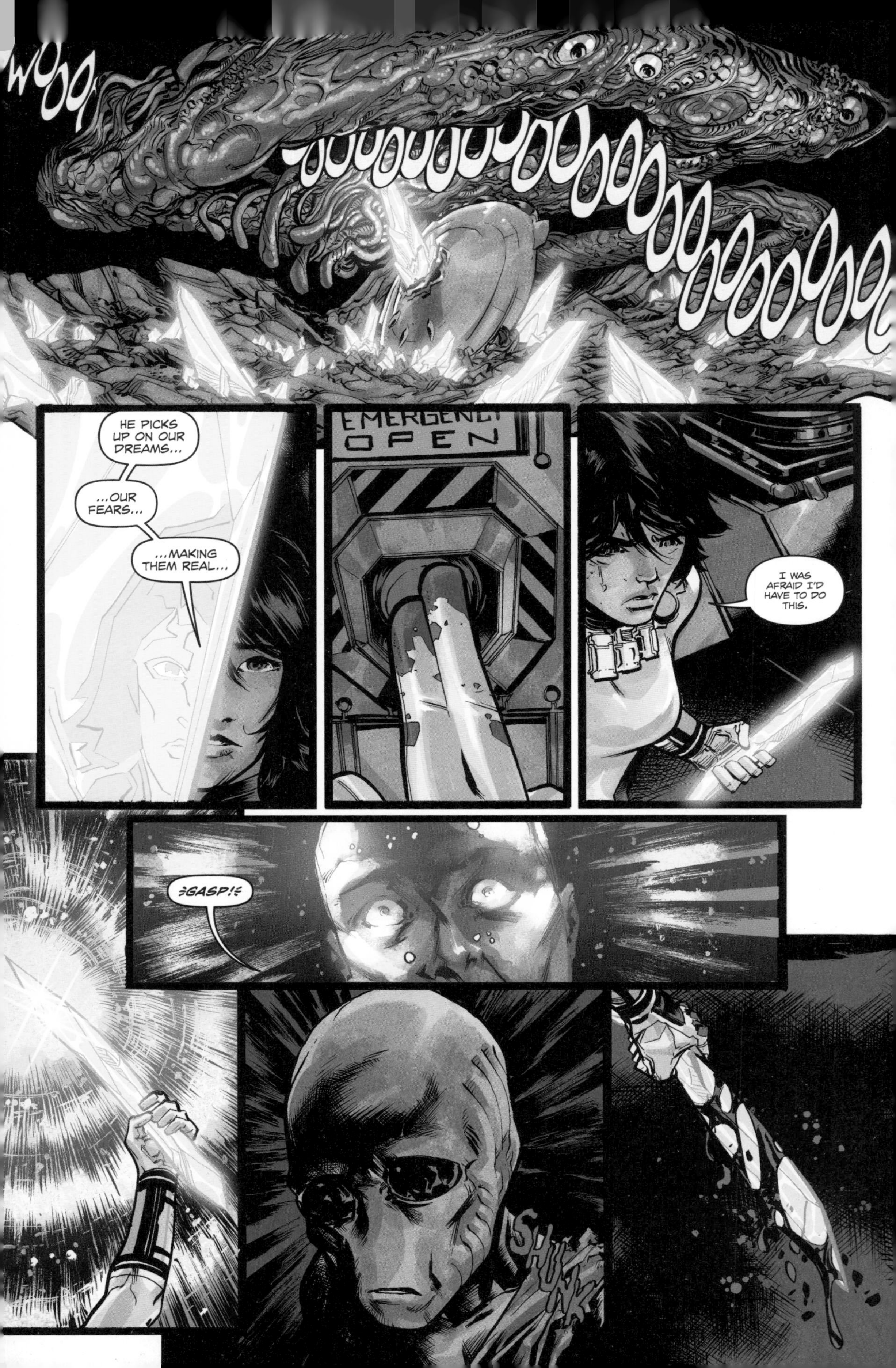
WOOOOOOOOOOOOOOOOOOOOOOOOOOOOO
HE PICKS UP ON OUR DREAMS...
...OUR FEARS...
...MAKING THEM REAL...
EMERGENC
OPEN
I WAS AFRAID I'D HAVE TO DO THIS.
GASP!
SHUNK

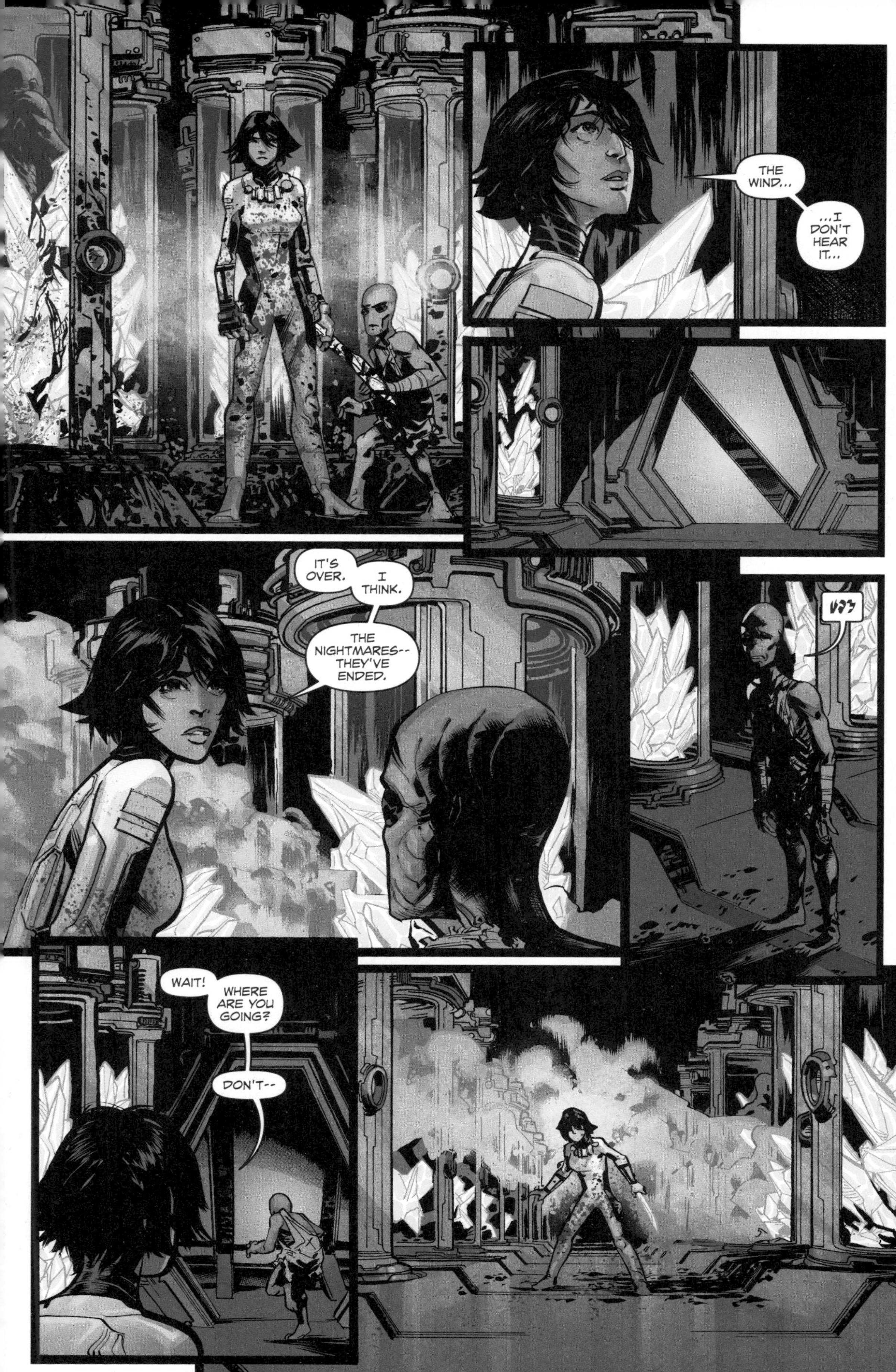
THE WIND...
...I DON'T HEAR IT...
IT'S OVER.
I THINK.
THE NIGHTMARES--THEY'VE ENDED.
WAIT!
WHERE ARE YOU GOING?
DON'T--

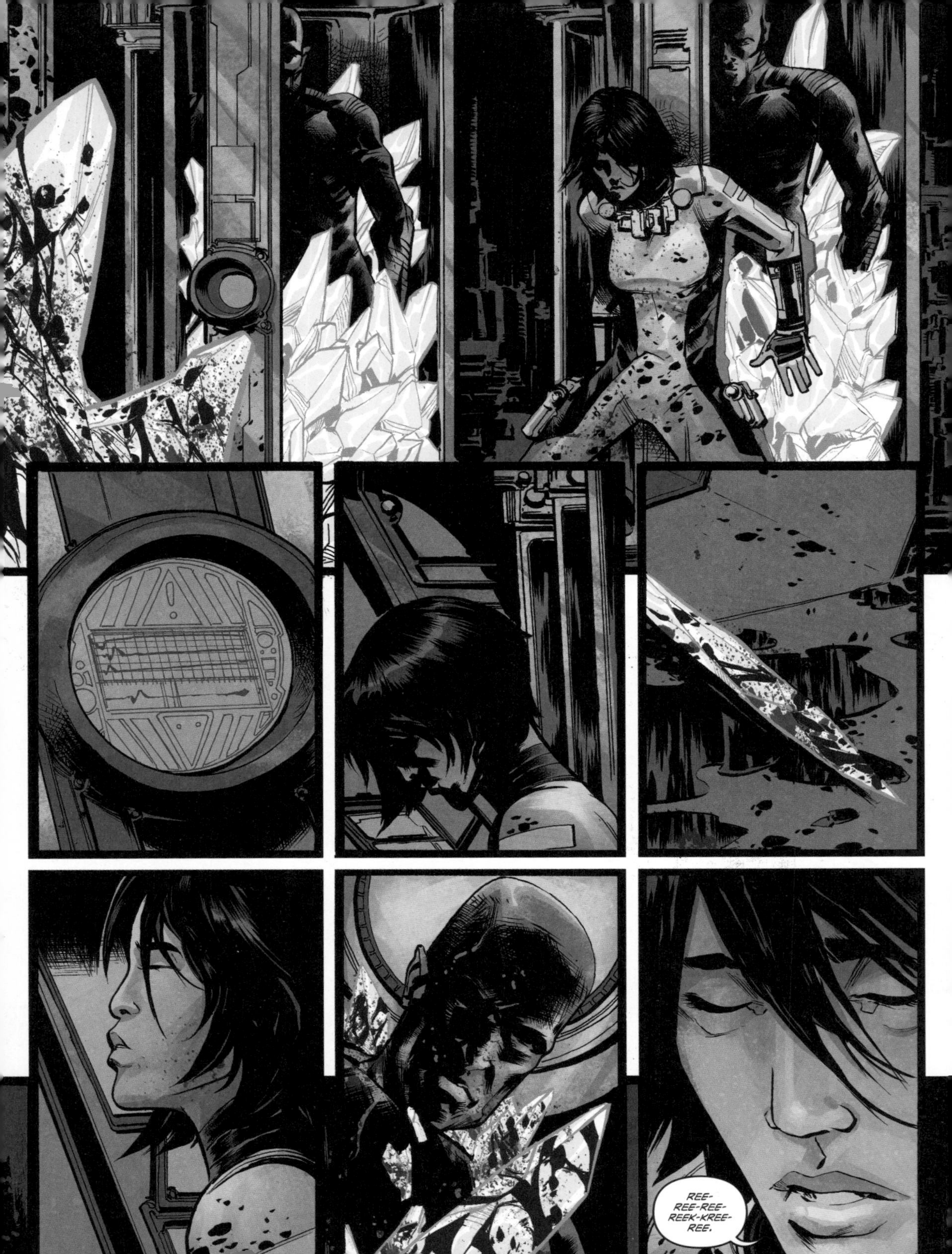
REE-REE-REE-REEK-KREE-REE.

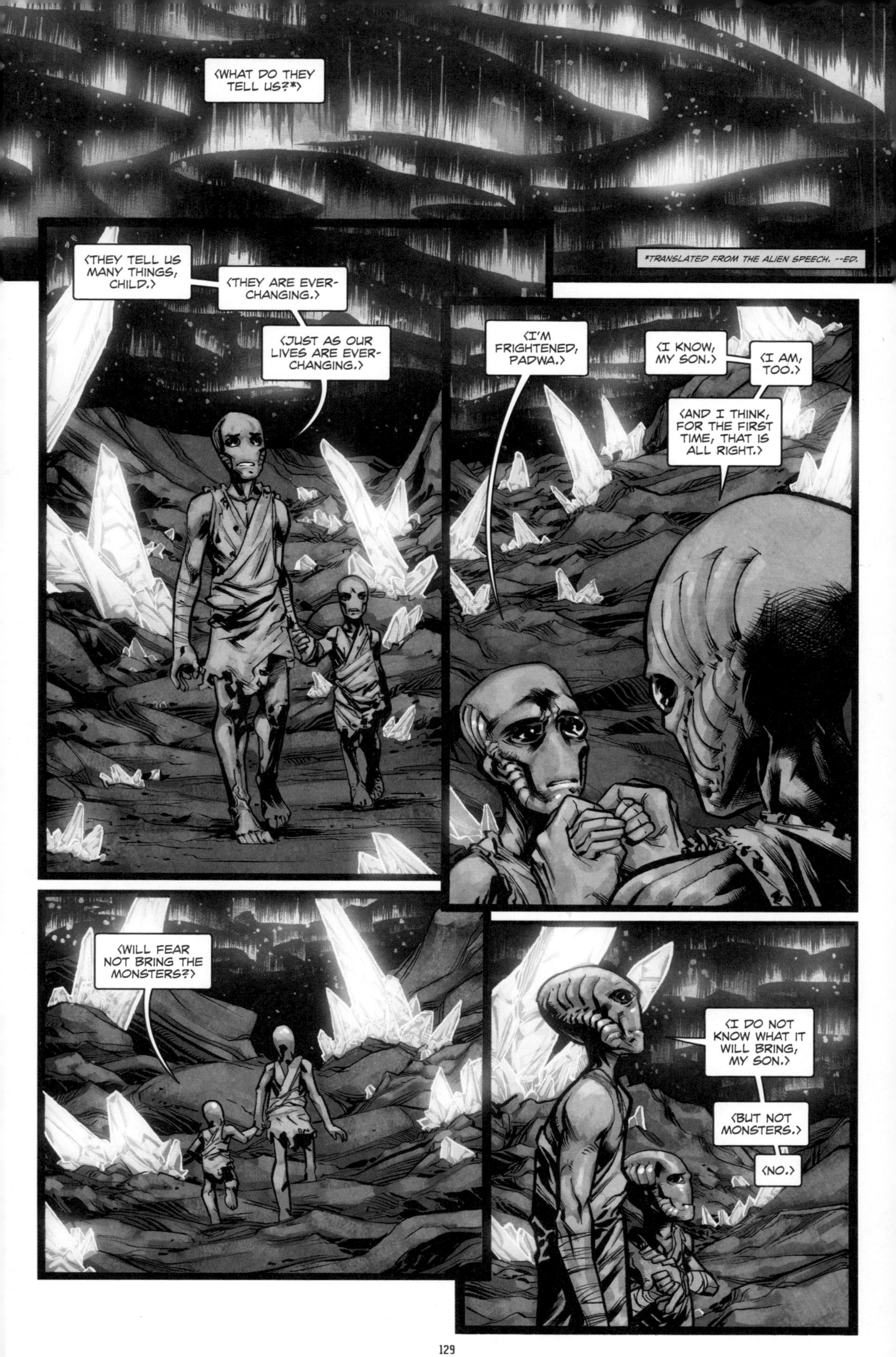
<WHAT DO THEY TELL US?*>
*TRANSLATED FROM THE ALIEN SPEECH. --ED.
<THEY TELL US MANY THINGS, CHILD.>
<THEY ARE EVER-CHANGING.>
<JUST AS OUR LIVES ARE EVER-CHANGING.>
<I'M FRIGHTENED, PADWA.>
<I KNOW, MY SON.>
<I AM, TOO.>
<AND I THINK, FOR THE FIRST TIME, THAT IS ALL RIGHT.>
<WILL FEAR NOT BRING THE MONSTERS?>
<I DO NOT KNOW WHAT IT WILL BRING, MY SON.>
<BUT NOT MONSTERS.>
<NO.>

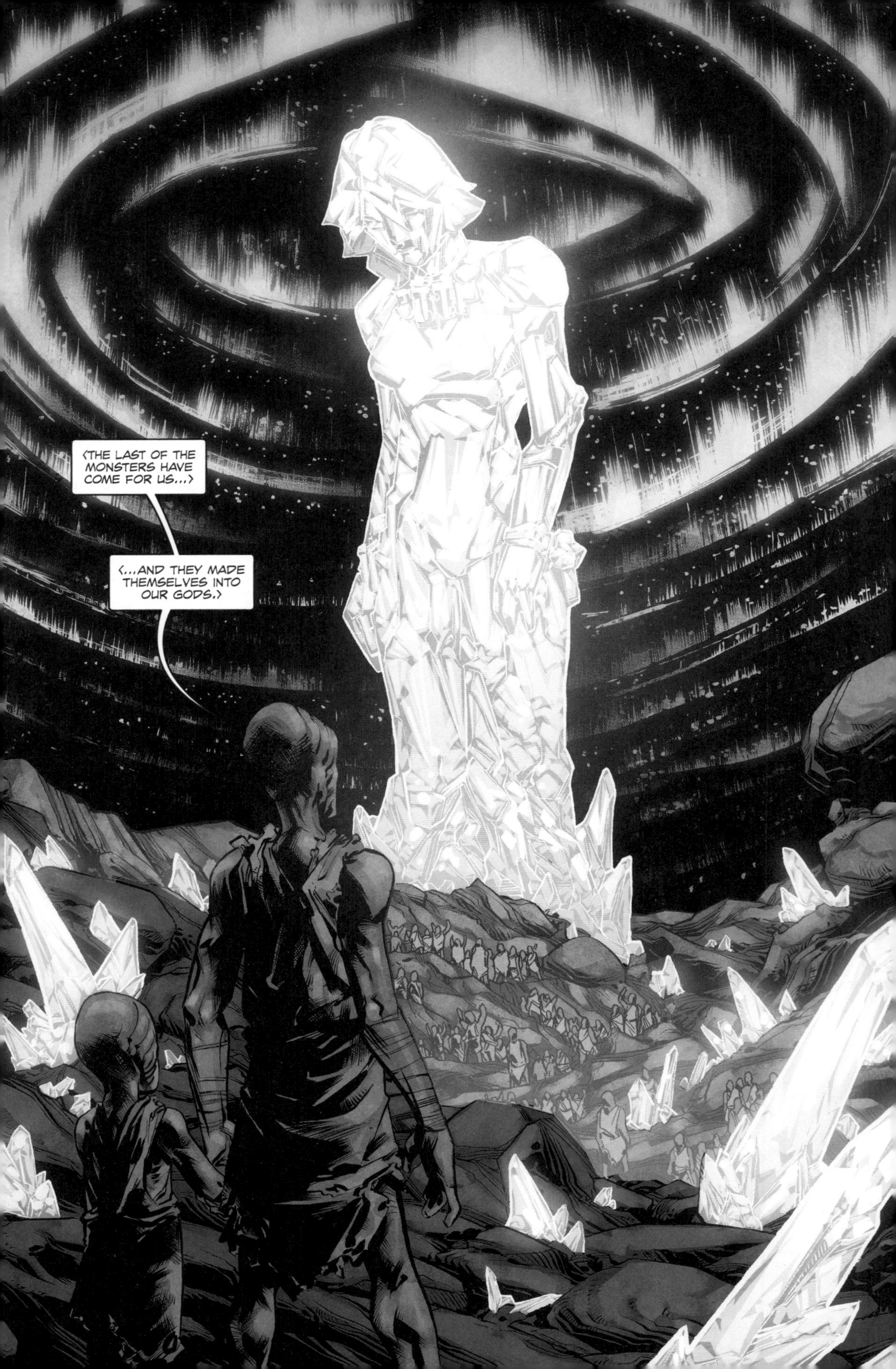
‹THE LAST OF THE MONSTERS HAVE COME FOR US...›
‹...AND THEY MADE THEMSELVES INTO OUR GODS.›